T0094199

SOFTWARE ENGINEERING
THE CURRENT PRACTICE

Chapman & Hall/CRC Innovations in Software Engineering and Software Development

Series Editor
Richard LeBlanc
Chair, Department of Computer Science and Software Engineering, Seattle University

AIMS AND SCOPE

This series covers all aspects of software engineering and software development. Books in the series will be innovative reference books, research monographs, and textbooks at the undergraduate and graduate level. Coverage will include traditional subject matter, cutting-edge research, and current industry practice, such as agile software development methods and service-oriented architectures. We also welcome proposals for books that capture the latest results on the domains and conditions in which practices are most effective.

PUBLISHED TITLES

Software Development: An Open Source Approach
Allen Tucker, Ralph Morelli, and Chamindra de Silva

Building Enterprise Systems with ODP: An Introduction to Open Distributed Processing
Peter F. Linington, Zoran Milosevic, Akira Tanaka, and Antonio Vallecillo

Software Engineering: The Current Practice
Václav Rajlich

CHAPMAN & HALL/CRC INNOVATIONS IN
SOFTWARE ENGINEERING AND SOFTWARE DEVELOPMENT

SOFTWARE ENGINEERING
THE CURRENT PRACTICE

VÁCLAV RAJLICH

CRC Press
Taylor & Francis Group
Boca Raton   London   New York

CRC Press is an imprint of the
Taylor & Francis Group an **informa** business

A CHAPMAN & HALL BOOK

The picture on the cover is by Tomas Rajlich (1940). This untitled painting was done in acrylic on hardboard and copyrighted in 1973 by Pictorights, Amsterdam, Netherlands. Reprinted with permission.

CRC Press
Taylor & Francis Group
6000 Broken Sound Parkway NW, Suite 300
Boca Raton, FL 33487-2742

© 2012 by Taylor & Francis Group, LLC
CRC Press is an imprint of Taylor & Francis Group, an Informa business

No claim to original U.S. Government works

Printed in the United States of America on acid-free paper
Version Date: 20111019

International Standard Book Number: 978-1-4398-4122-8 (Hardback)

Library of Congress Cataloging-in-Publication Data

Rajlich, Václav.
    Software engineering : the current practices / author, Václav Rajlich.
        p. cm. -- (Chapman & Hall/CRC innovations in software engineering and
        software development)
    Includes bibliographical references and index.
    ISBN 978-1-4398-4122-8 (hardcover : alk. paper)
    1. Software engineering. 2. Computer programming. I. Title.

QA76.758.R36 2012
005.1--dc23   2011039392

Visit the Taylor & Francis Web site at
http://www.taylorandfrancis.com

and the CRC Press Web site at
http://www.crcpress.com

To the colleagues who worked with me on software projects and
to the students who took my software engineering courses.

Contents

SECTION III SOFTWARE PROCESSES

Preface

This book introduces the fundamental notions of contemporary software engineering. From the large body of knowledge and experience that software engineering has accumulated, it selects a very small subset. The purpose is to introduce the software engineering field to students who want to learn basic software engineering skills and to help practitioners who want to refresh their knowledge and learn about the recent developments in the field.

The field of software engineering has accumulated a great deal of knowledge since the first appearance of software in the 1950s. There have also been two revolutions in the field, each substantially changing the views and the emphasis within the field. In the 1970s, the first revolution established software engineering as an academic discipline, and in the 2000s, the second revolution identified the broadly understood software evolution as the central software engineering process. This second revolution is still in progress, with holdouts and unfinished battles. This book unashamedly subscribes to the results of both revolutions and emphasizes the software evolution; the remnant of the formerly formidable waterfall model is relegated to a single chapter in the latter part of the book (Chapter 14) under the title of "Initial Development."

In order to explain the style of the book, let me share a little bit of my background. In my studies, I majored in mechanical engineering and mathematics. I studied from the well-organized textbooks that are common in these two classic fields. After my schooling was finished, I changed direction and embarked on a career in software engineering. It has been an exciting and rewarding adventure. However, I have to admit that I am still nostalgic for the well-organized textbooks in the fields of mechanical engineering and mathematics. They served as an inspiration for this book, and I am trying to emulate their purposefulness, brevity, and gradual increase in the complexity of the topics covered.

Software engineering processes are the core of this book; they cannot be taught without references to the software technologies that support them. However, the technologies are changing at a different pace, and they respond to the imperatives of the marketplace. This book uses very few proven technologies as a context for explanation of the software engineering processes.

Finally, I have to confess that as a hot-headed young software manager of the 1970s, I convinced and coerced my best team into a then-novel and highly hyped waterfall software development process. Doing that, I created what was later called a "death march project." The programmers spent most of their time in endless· requirements elicitation; there was always one more very important requirement to be added to the list, a classic demonstration of the infamous "requirements creep." After the schedule slipped, the programmers were trying to meet impossible implementation deadlines and spent nights in sleeping bags on the floor of the lab; they did not have time to go home to take a decent rest or a shower. This book is a partial and belated atonement for that unfortunate experience.

***

This book addresses both the professionals and the students of software engineering.

Use of this Book by Professionals

Programmers and software managers can use this book to acquire a unified view of the contemporary practice of software engineering. This book will give them an overview of how various recent developments fit together and fit into the contemporary software engineering mosaic. The knowledge gained from this book may allow them to evaluate and improve the software engineering processes they are employing in their projects.

Use of this Book by Students and Instructors

Prerequisites

The prerequisite of the course is the knowledge of object-oriented programming accompanied by a moderate programming maturity and experience. A typical computer science student usually achieves that maturity after passing satisfactorily the second programming course, often called "Data Structures." Some of the prerequisite material is briefly surveyed in sections 3.1, 3.2, 4.1, and 4.2, but the sole purpose of these sections is to unify the terminology for the rest of the book and to define the absolute minimum that is necessary for understanding the rest of the book. These four brief sections cannot substitute for prerequisite courses that cover these topics in greater depth. Our experience shows that the students who do not have this background cannot do well in this software engineering course.

If the prerequisite courses did not cover some of these topics in sufficient depth, for example, missing the advanced use of object-oriented technology or more complete coverage of UML (Unified Modeling Language), the instructors should carefully balance the "remedial" work against the core message of this course. There is a real danger that the whole course could turn into a remedial instruction in the software technologies, and the whole software engineering point can be missed.

Lectures

The topics can be covered roughly at a pace of two chapters per week in a three-credit course. In a well-prepared class, sections 3.1, 3.2, 4.1, and 4.2 can be skipped entirely, or covered very quickly. On the other hand, Chapters 10, 13, and 14 usually take a full week or more. At this pace, the textbook presents about 11–12 weeks of material and leaves ample time for midterms, reviews, projects, or presentation of additional material that delves more deeply into the topics listed at the end of the chapters as the "Further Reading and Topics."

The order of the presentations should follow the graph of dependencies among the chapters and project phases; project phases are explained in the next section.

$$17 \qquad 18$$
$$\uparrow \qquad \uparrow$$
$$1{\to}2{\to}3{\to}4{\to}5{\to}6{\to} \quad 7{\to}8{\to}9{\to}10{\to} \quad 11{\to}12{\to} \quad 13{\to}14{\to}15{\to}16$$
$$\downarrow \qquad\qquad\qquad \downarrow$$

Project	Project
phase 1	phase 2

The standard order (traversal) of the chapters roughly follows the order of the chapters in the book, with the exception of Chapters 17 and 18, which contain examples; Chapter 17 can be presented immediately after Chapter 10, and Chapter 18 immediately after Chapter 12. The resulting order is:

$1 \to 2 \to 3 \to 4 \to 5 \to 6 \to$ "Project phase 1" $\to 7 \to 8 \to 9 \to 10 \to$ "Project phase 2" $\to 17 \to 11 \to 12 \to 18 \to 13 \to 14 \to 15 \to 16$

If there is pressure to speed up the lectures in the beginning so that the students can start on the projects earlier, the following may be the alternative "fast start":

$3 \to 4 \to 5 \to 6 \to$ "Project phase 1" $\to 7 \to 8 \to 9 \to 10 \to$ "Project phase 2" $\to 17 \to 11 \to 1 \to 2 \to 12 \to 18 \to 13 \to 14 \to 15 \to 16$.

This sequence allows getting through Chapter 6 by the second week and through Chapter 10 by the fifth week. The pace of the lectures then can slow down, and Chapters 1, 2, and the rest of the book can be presented at a more leisurely pace.

Projects

In traditional software engineering projects, the students develop small, low-quality programs from scratch; in contrast, the industry programmers typically evolve much larger and already-existing systems that contain many features and a high code quality. Traditional software engineering projects organize students into an unstructured team, and the whole team often receives the same grade; such an organization promotes abuse of the system in which a few motivated students carry the workload on behalf of the less-motivated students, who contribute little to the success of the project.

The projects proposed here avoid both problems: They give the students an experience with software of the size and quality comparable to that of industrial software. While students still work in teams, they have individual assignments and individual visibility, as is the case in the industry.

The projects run in parallel with lectures, and they complement the learning experience by giving the students the opportunity to practice the new knowledge. In terms of the processes explained in the book, the students work in the role of developers in a classroom-tailored directed iterative process (DIP) of Chapter 13; the instructor supplies all other roles of the process.

Project Selection

The following are the criteria when selecting the projects:

Technology of the projects: The best projects use only the technology that students are already familiar with. If the projects use any unfamiliar technology, it should be possible to avoid problems by the appropriate selection of the assigned software changes. Our preferred projects use pure Java or pure C++ with some localized graphical user interface technologies that can be avoided.

Size of the projects: In order to give students a realistic experience of software change, the projects should not be too small, which make the concept location trivial. They also should not be so large that handling the code and the recompilation becomes an issue. The best project sizes range between 50 and 500 kLOC (thousand lines of code).

Domain of the project: The best domains are the ones that the students are already familiar with, or that are easy to learn. There is not enough time in the semester to delve into complicated or unfamiliar domains. Based on this criterion, the best domains are various drawing, editing, and file managing programs that are grasped by the students immediately.

We select our projects from open sources because of their availability and predictable quality, but industry projects or local academic projects—if they are chosen carefully and follow the project selection criteria—also could serve as valuable

Table 1   Projects Used in the Class

Project	Size	Years When Used
NotePad++	333 kLOC	2009–2010
A Note	20 kLOC	2008
JEdit	316 kLOC	2006, 2008
WinMerge	63 kLOC	2002–2005, 2007, 2010

classroom projects. Examples of the project selections from the SourceForge.net open-source website are presented in Table 1.

Project Phase 0

This is an introductory phase where the students become familiar with the software environment (Visual Studio, Eclipse), version control system (Subversion, CVS), and message board (Blackboard, Wiki). They receive individual accounts, decide what hardware resources they are going to use for their version-control client (their own laptop or a university lab computer), form the teams, and become familiar with the software projects provided by the instructor. This typically takes 2 weeks at the beginning of the semester.

Project Phase 1

This phase consists of the first primitive change in the system. Each student does an individual concept location and a minimal code modification. The purpose of the modification is just to prove that a correct location was found; typically, the modification does not have any impact on any other modules. Examples of the first change requests are: Display the name of the student in the "about" window; allow the user to enter a numeric value for the zoom rate; print a word count for the selected text; and so forth. Chapters 3–6 are the prerequisite for Phase 1.

Project Phase 2

This phase consists of a sequence of software changes of increasing complexity and increasing code conflicts among the team members that force them to collaborate in conflict resolution.

The change requests can be taken from the official backlog of the selected projects; however, sometimes these change requests have to be clarified and described in more detail. Change requests can be decomposed into several related tasks and distributed among the team members, giving them a cooperative experience. At the end of the project phase, the best solutions can be committed to the official open-source project repository. For these changes, Chapters 3–10 are a prerequisite.

Other Processes and Roles

As mentioned previously, these projects emphasize the role of developers in a classroom-tailored version of DIP software evolution. In our opinion, this is the best gateway into the world of software engineering suitable for a one-semester course. If a more complete project experience with other software engineering roles in other software engineering processes is desired, it should be taught in follow-up courses. In these courses, the students can learn and experience additional roles, such as testers or project managers; they can learn additional evolutionary processes, such as the agile process or experience initial development or late life-span processes.

Acknowledgments

The book is based on experience from a course taught repeatedly for several years at Wayne State University. Farshad Fotouhi is credited with providing the resources for the course and other support. Other venues where earlier versions of this course were taught are the University of Sanio (through invitation by Aniello Cimitile and Gerardo Canfora), the University of Klagenfurt (through invitation by Roland Mittermeier), and the University of Regensburg (through invitation by Franz Lehner). While working on these courses and later on the book, I was partially supported by grants CCF-0438970 and CCF-0820133 from National Science Foundation and grant 1 R01 HG003491-01A1 from National Institutes of Health.

Several graduate students contributed to the development of the course: Maksym Petrenko, Denys Poshyvanyk, Joseph Buchta, Radu Vanciu, Chris Dorman, Neal Febbraro, and Prashant Gosavi. The writing process was assisted by Radu Vanciu and Chris Dorman.

Valuable comments on the manuscript were provided by Giuliano Antoniol, Edward F. Gehringer, Jonathan I. Maletic, Keith Gallagher, Laurie Williams, Tibor Gyimóthy, Árpád Beszédes, Michael English, and Romain Robbes. The editors, Alan Apt and Randi Cohen, deserve thanks for their friendly and patient guidance and help.

I want to thank my wife, Ivana, for her continual support, which made this book possible. I also want to dedicate this book to my sons and my daughters-in-law: Vasik, Iweta, Paul, Cindy, John, Rebekah, and Luke. Finally, I want to acknowledge my grandchildren Jacob, Joey, Hannah, Hope, Henry, Ivanka, Vencie, and Vasiczek. You have been a joy!

Detroit
April 24, 2011

Author

Václav Rajlich is professor and former chair of computer science at Wayne State University. Before that, he taught at the University of Michigan and worked at the Research Institute for Mathematical Machines in Prague, Czech Republic. He received a PhD in mathematics from Case Western Reserve University and has been practicing and teaching software engineering since 1975.

His research centers on software evolution and comprehension. He has published approximately 90 refereed papers in journals and conferences, was a keynote speaker at five conferences, has graduated 12 PhDs, and has supervised approximately 40 MS student theses. He is a member of the editorial board of the *Journal of Software Maintenance and Evolution*. He is also the founder and permanent steering committee member of the IEEE International Conference on Program Comprehension (ICPC) and was a program chair, general chair, and steering committee chair of the IEEE International Conference on Software Maintenance (ICSM).

INTRODUCTION 1

Contents

Four introductory chapters present the basic notions and prerequisites. They are the properties of software, and, in particular, the essential difficulties of software that have shaped the history of software engineering. This is followed by an account of the history of software engineering, with the emphasis on the two paradigm shifts: from ad hoc paradigm to waterfall, and then from waterfall to iterative paradigm. The next chapter contains the models of software life span, consisting of stages through which software passes, followed by a brief survey of technologies that are used in this book to explain the software engineering principles. The last chapter of this part surveys software models that are frequently used in the software engineering tasks.

Chapter 1

History of Software Engineering

Objectives

In this chapter, you will learn about the software accomplishments. You will also learn about software properties and, in particular, about the contrast between accidental and essential properties. Among them, the essential difficulties of software are the biggest challenge for software engineers, and they shape the nature of the software engineering profession. After you have read this chapter, you will know:

- The essential difficulties of software
- Three software engineering paradigms and their history
- The origins of software and ad hoc techniques of software creation
- The reasons why software engineering became an established discipline
- The waterfall model of software life span and its limits
- Software evolution and its role in software life span

***

Software is everywhere. While buying bread, driving a car, riding the bus, or washing clothes, you may be interacting with software running somewhere on a computer or on a computer chip. Software has penetrated the most unlikely venues; even cars now run tens of millions of lines of code that control everything from windshield wipers to engine ignition (Charette, 2009).

Software has changed the way we interact with each other; the Internet is changing the way we communicate, shop, and even relate to one another (Leiner et al., 2009), and sociologists are still trying to sort out the full impact of this unprecedented change.

Software has also changed the way we view ourselves. Chess playing has always been considered a pinnacle of human intelligence, but that perception was drastically adjusted when a computer (and software) defeated the reigning human world chess champion (Hsu, 2002). The software that runs nowadays on a standard PC is more powerful than any human chess player.

People who accomplished these feats and bring the software to the computers or the computer chips near you are called software engineers; sometimes they are also called programmers. They participate in these challenging projects and possess skills and tools that allow them to develop and evolve software so that it can continue to serve you in the ever-changing world. This book is an introductory exposition of their trade.

Software is a product, but it is very different from other products and other things in the world. It has certain properties that make it different; properties of this kind are called *essential properties*. The other properties that software may or may not have are called *accidental properties*. The next section deals with essential properties first, and then with accidental properties.

1.1 Software Properties

Software is sometimes called a *program;* software that is interacting with a human user is often called an *application*. Software controls computers or computer chips, implements algorithms, processes data, and so forth. These properties are essential because only software has these properties.

Among the essential properties, certain properties make the work of software engineers challenging, and therefore, they are especially worthy of our attention. They have been called *essential difficulties* of software. They are complexity, invisibility, changeability, conformity, and discontinuity. Fred Brooks (1987) introduced the first four of these.

1.1.1 Complexity

Software is complex, and software applications often contain millions of lines of code. Software ranks among the most complex systems ever created by mankind, including large cities, country governments, large armies, large corporations, and so forth. When dealing with this complexity, the programmers are equipped with a very small short-term memory (Miller, 1956); hence, they have to employ various strategies to handle this complexity. There are several well-known strategies that deal with complexity, and they have been adopted by software engineers.

One of the strategies that has been proposed and used in software engineering is the creation of simplified *models* that ignore various details. Without these details, the models are simpler and easier to understand than the original, and that helps when dealing with the complexity. Software models are explored in chapter 4. The quality of the model depends on whether the distinction between important and unimportant was done correctly; if a model ignores important things, it is an incorrect model that hinders rather than helps understanding.

Another strategy is based on *decomposition* of large software into smaller parts. This decomposition helps software engineers to orient themselves in the software. The same strategy is used when dealing with complex organizations like universities; they are divided into colleges and departments that help orientation within these organizations.

Another approach is the *as-needed* approach, where people concentrate only on the part of the software that they need to understand to do the required task, and ignore all the rest. Tourists who visit a large city like Prague instinctively adopt this approach. They learn how to reach their hotel and how to get to the historical sites they want to see, and pay no attention to the rest of the city and all its complexity.

Abstraction is an approach where a complex or messy object is recognized as belonging to a certain category in which all things have the same properties. Understanding this category helps in understanding the original object. For example, when dealing with Fido, it helps to understand that he belongs to the category of dogs, which all share certain behaviors, require certain types of food, and so forth.

Despite the successful use of these strategies by software engineers, software complexity is still a problem, and much of the software engineer's effort is spent in coping with it.

1.1.2 Invisibility

Software is invisible, and neither sight nor the other senses can be employed when trying to comprehend it. Our comprehension is closely tied to our senses, and it is much easier for us to comprehend what we can sense. For example, we can easily comprehend small things that we can see in their entirety, or things that we can hear or touch. Abstract concepts like mathematical formulas or abstract philosophical accounts are much harder to understand. Software belongs to the category of abstract things, and that demands that software engineers deal with it like mathematicians and philosophers do.

Some software tools visualize certain aspects of software; for example, a display of a graph that depicts software components and their relation allows programmers to use their vision when they deal with some properties of software. Other tools employ sonification, which allows programmers to hear certain aspects of their software. These tools lessen the impact of invisibility, but they offer only a very limited solution, and there is still a long way to go before these tools will fully employ human senses in the understanding of software.

1.1.3 Changeability

Software is easy to change: It is not necessary to tear down massive walls, to drill, or do anything of that magnitude; all that is needed is to sit at the keyboard and make a couple of key strokes. It is this ease of change that allows software engineers to modify software quickly in response to changing needs, and this is the foundation for the iterative processes that this book emphasizes.

However, the ease of changeability has its dark side, as it can act as an encouragement to introduce ill-prepared or hasty changes that will be regretted later. Although software is easy to change, it is much harder to change it *correctly*, to produce the desired outcome, and to have the new code fit with the old. This is particularly true for programs that have accumulated a large amount of work that each change must respect. As the programs grow more complex, the correct changes become increasingly difficult. Another aspect of the dark side of changeability is the fact that rapid changes make the knowledge of old software obsolete, and they require a continuous effort just to keep up.

1.1.4 Conformity

Software is always a part of a larger system that consists of the hardware, the users that interact with it, other stakeholders or customers affected by it, other interacting software like operating systems, and so forth. Software integrates all these parts into one system, and it is the glue that holds this system together as a whole. This larger system that software interconnects is called a *domain*. For example, if the application is related to banking, the software domain consists of the banking customers, clerks, accounts, transactions, and all relevant banking rules. If the application deals with taxes, it must contain complete and accurate tax rules, and so forth.

Software must communicate with disparate components that constitute the domain. Consequently, there is no clear boundary between software and the domain, and the properties of the domain seep into software; software has to *conform* to its domain. As a result of conformity, the changes anywhere in the domain force software to change also. For example, a change in banking law or a court decision that changes tax rules results in immediate changes in software.

Conformity adds to the complexity of the work with software. The *domain knowledge* is an essential tool in the software engineer's tool chest; without it, the software engineer would be unable to implement the proposed system.

1.1.5 Discontinuity

Software is discontinuous, while people easily understand only continuous semilinear systems. An example of such a semilinear system is the shower with two knobs: one for hot water, the other one for cold water. If the shower is too cold, then the knob for hot water has to be turned up or the knob for cold water must be turned down, or both; the small motion of the knobs will cause small change in the shower temperature. The semilinear nature of the shower system makes it easy to use.

Discontinuous systems have counterintuitive properties; a small change of the input can cause an unexpected and huge change of the output. An example of the large discontinuity is the use of passwords: If the user wants to use an application and uses a correct password, the application will open and all its functionality will be available to the user. On the other hand, mistyping a single letter of the password will keep the application closed and none of its functionality will be available; the difference of the input is small, but the difference of the outcome is huge. The same is true for changes in the system; in some situations, the repercussions of what appears to be a very small change can be huge.

1.1.6 Some Accidental Properties

While essential properties of software are always present, accidental properties differ from one application to another and are dependent on the time and place where these applications have been developed.

Software technology is one such accidental property. The software technology includes programming languages, their compilers, editors, libraries, frameworks, and so forth. There are many programming languages currently used, and many other languages that were employed in the past but are no longer used. The same is true about various software tools that are or were used in software development.

Software engineers of different schools may use different *processes* to develop software. These processes depend on a particular time and place, and therefore, they also belong to the category of accidental properties.

Another accidental software property is the *role* that software plays in the life of the organization that uses it. *Mission-critical* software is the software that permits the organization to fulfill its role. For example, the software that calculates insurance premiums is mission critical for insurance companies; if that software is unavailable or down, the company is unable to function. *Noncritical* software enhances the functioning of the organization but it is not critical; unavailability of such software may be an inconvenience, but it does not stop the organization from functioning. The same software can be mission critical for some organizations and noncritical for others.

Software engineering deals with software and all its properties, both essential and accidental. It offers solutions to the problems that some of these properties cause. The problems caused by essential properties are particularly important for the software engineering discipline to solve, because these properties and their accompanying problems are going to be present in all software—past, present, and future—while accidental properties come and go. Essential properties are the main driving force in the history of software engineering.

1.2 Origins of Software

In the context of the ubiquity of software in today's world, it can come as a surprise how new software technology is. The newness of software can be illustrated by a bit of historical trivia: The term *software* appeared in print for the first time only in 1958 in an article written by the statistician John Wilder Tukey, as reported by Leonhardt (2000). Before that, software was so rare that there was no need for a special word. In a short time after 1958, the term *software* became widespread, and software became pervasive. Contemporary economy and our way of life depend on software, and without software, most of our economy and a large part of our daily routine would grind to a halt.

When the first software applications appeared in the 1950s, they were written by teams of electrical engineers, mathematicians, and people of similar backgrounds. At that time, software managers believed that no special knowledge or special sets of skills were necessary for writing software. The programmers of that time used ad hoc techniques and likened software production to an art. Using their artlike techniques, they implemented software applications that included compilers, operating systems, early business applications, and so forth.

To describe what happened next, we have to visit the philosophy of science and the development of scientific and technical disciplines. Thomas Kuhn coined the word *paradigm* that, according to him, is a "coherent tradition of scientific research" (Kuhn, 1996). In the case of software engineering and other engineering disciplines, paradigm means a "coherent tradition of engineering research and practice." In both cases, it includes theory, applications, instrumentation, terminology, research agenda, norms, curricula, culture of the field, and so forth. It also involves investments in tools, textbooks, training, careers, and funding.

A naïve view of the development of scientific and technical discipline assumes that a discipline steadily and continuously accumulates knowledge, within the framework of the same paradigm. However, this naïve view is incorrect: The study of the history of the scientific and technical disciplines shows that they pass from time to time through serious upheavals or revolutions, where the old paradigm is abandoned and a new paradigm is adopted. The revolution is triggered by an *anomaly*. According to Thomas Kuhn, "Anomaly is an important fact that directly contradicts the old paradigm." When that happens, the scientific or technical community faces a choice: to change the paradigm, or to disregard the anomaly. Because changing paradigm means abandoning a large part of the accumulated knowledge and devaluing past investment in the discipline, the anomaly must be compelling; otherwise, the community will simply ignore it. Even if the anomaly is compelling, the paradigm shift is usually accompanied by acrimony and strife, where people who invested heavily into the old paradigm try to defend it as long as they can to protect their investment.

History of Phlogiston

A historical example of the paradigm shift is the introduction of the notion of oxygen in the 1770s, often considered to be the beginning of modern chemistry. Before that, chemists used a notion of phlogiston that was supposed to be a substance that escapes from the burning material during a fire, and it was probably inspired by the smoke that escapes from burning wood. The anomaly arose when new and more accurate scales became available and chemists burned other substances than wood; it turned out that the ashes of some burned substances weighed more than the original material, and the theory of phlogiston was unable to explain this fact. The explanation was found in the notion of oxygen, which does exactly the opposite of what it was supposed that phlogiston did: It joins the material during the fire. This new explanation and transition from phlogiston to oxygen triggered a massive crisis in the discipline of chemistry that required an overhaul of all knowledge accumulated up to that point; hence, it was a genuine revolution, a paradigm shift. There were some people who never accepted oxygen as an explanation and persisted in the use of phlogiston to the very end.

Without understanding paradigm shifts, it is impossible to understand the history of software engineering and some of the controversies that are still raging today in the software engineering community. The first paradigm shift was the birth of the software engineering discipline in the 1970s.

1.3 Birth of Software Engineering

The ad hoc, artlike techniques used to create the earliest software functioned relatively well until about the mid 1960s. The anomaly that caused the paradigm shift at that time was software complexity, one of the essential difficulties of software. With the success of the early software, an appetite for larger and more complex software began to grow, and in the 1960s, software requirements outgrew the capabilities of the ad hoc approach. For the implementation of new software, it was no longer possible to rely on a handful of ingenious programmers recruited from other fields. Software development at that time required a fundamentally different approach. The situation is well described by Brooks (1982).

Fred Brooks was a manager of a software project that was developing a new operating system, OS/360, for the IBM Corporation. IBM was a leader in the computer field and decided to develop a new series of computers. The OS/360 operating system was expected to utilize resources of these computers more effectively than what was customary at the time and to take over some computer operations that were previously done by human computer operators. However, the operating system turned out to be large and complex, and its implementation taxed the limits of the participating programmers, project managers, and the resources of the IBM Corporation.

Some experience drawn from that large software project was surprising and very counterintuitive. An example is the famous observation that adding new people to a large software project that is already underway will slow it down rather than speed it up. It was discovered later that the reason for this paradox is that the new people first have to learn everything that was already accomplished by the project; otherwise they would be unable to contribute. The experienced people have to teach them all this knowledge and help them to catch up. The teaching process is a new additional task for them, so they have to redirect some of their energy from the software implementation toward teaching the latecomers, and this slows the project's progress.

The increased complexity of the software was an anomaly that led to the paradigm shift of the 1970s. The community developed awareness that software requires people with special training, and that dealing with the software complexity requires specialized skills. This awareness gave birth to the new discipline of software engineering. The beginning of software engineering is usually associated with the years 1968 and 1969, when the first international conferences on software engineering met and attempted to define the new field. This attempt to define the field generated controversies. The controversies were so acrimonious that the original organizers gave up, and there were no software engineering conferences between 1969 and 1974. Only in 1974 did a completely new group of people start a new software engineering conference that defined the new discipline of software engineering.

The need for a new discipline became recognized, and software engineering grew from then on. Today, there are teachers, employers, and software managers, and they all agree that for work on large software projects, a special set of skills and specialized training is required. Software engineering as a discipline is now firmly established and has its own curricula, textbooks, conferences, and so forth.

1.3.1 Waterfall

After the paradigm shift of the 1970s, the new discipline of software engineering explored the *software life span models* that describe the stages through which software passes during its useful life. The life span models are important for software engineers because different processes take place in each stage. To study these processes, the first step is to find out what the stages are.

The new software engineering community quickly reached a broad consensus about the software life span model that is called the *software waterfall*. A schema of the software waterfall is given in Figure 1.1. In the first stage of the waterfall model, software *requirements* are elicited from the future users; these requirements describe the software functionality from the point of view of future users. Software requirements may also cover nonfunctional properties like expected speed, reliability, and so forth. Based on the requirements, designers of software complete the *design*, which consists of the software modules, their interactions, and the algorithms and data structures that the software is going to use. The *implementation* follows the design and consists of writing the actual code and verification that it is doing what it is expected to do. Once the implementation is done, software is transferred to the users, and if any problems appear later, they are taken care of during the *maintenance* phase.

The name "waterfall" originates from the one-directional flow of information, from requirements to design to implementation to maintenance. No information

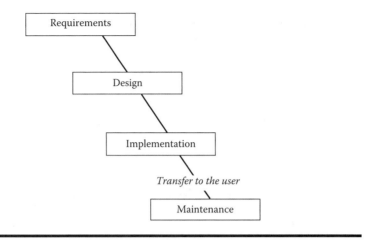

Figure 1.1   Waterfall model of software lifespan.

flows backwards, similar to a natural waterfall, where water flows in only one direction and no water flows backwards. The waterfall model exercised enormous influence on both the research and practice of the software engineering community for many years. For example, the U.S. Department of Defense required all contractors to follow the waterfall model and defined it in Department of Defense Standard 2167A. This standard basically follows Figure 1.1, but it contains more details and exact definitions of what is to be delivered for requirements, design, and so forth. Many other software customers followed suit and required their software vendors to follow the waterfall as defined in DOD-Std-2167A or similar documents.

The waterfall model promised the following: If requirements and design are done up-front and if they are done well, the implementation that follows them will avoid many unnecessary and expensive late changes that are the result of requirements omissions and misunderstandings. Late changes are much more expensive than early changes; hence, the reasoning was that the waterfall approach lowers software costs.

The waterfall model is accepted in other engineering fields, and it is not surprising that it was also accepted by software engineers, perhaps based on the experience from these other fields. An example of a field where the waterfall approach is widely and successfully used is house construction.

When Ann and Michael Novak want to build a house, they hire an architect who will ask them what is the price range; how do they want the house to be built; how many people are going to live in the house; how many visitors are they planning; do they want to have an office, entertain large parties, maintain a wine cellar, play ping pong with the children; and so forth. These are the requirements that the architect collects. Based on these, the architect produces the blueprint that contains the layout of the house, all utilities, and materials to be used.

Using the blueprints, the construction crew builds the house and, when done, it transfers the house to the Novaks. If any problems with plumbing or other house details appear after the transfer, the maintenance crew fixes them; the waterfall works perfectly in this setting. Not surprisingly, software engineers assumed it would work similarly well for building complex software applications. Historians still argue how the consensus behind the waterfall was reached, but there is no doubt that it dominated the thinking of the software engineering community for many years.

1.4 Third Paradigm: Iterative Approach

While the waterfall model works well in home construction, in the context of software engineering it is plagued by the problem of the *volatility of requirements*, which is a direct result of software conformity, one of the essential difficulties of software. As explained in section 1.1.4, software conformity requires that software reflect the properties of its application domain. If there is any change anywhere in the domain, that change is likely to trigger a corresponding change in the software. For example, consider a software application that calculates insurance premiums: Any changes in laws governing insurance, all relevant court decisions, changing demographics of the insured population, and everything else that has an impact on the calculation of premiums must be immediately reflected in the software.

Different domains have different levels of volatility. Table 1.1 is from Jones (1996) and shows how swiftly requirements can change. According to this table, "Commercial software" has a staggering monthly 3.5% of requirements change, which translates to approximately half of the requirements change in a year! Also, about 30% of the requirements for Microsoft projects change during an average project (Cusumano & Selby, 1997).

Table 1.1 Monthly Requirements Change

Software Type	Monthly Rate of Requirements Change
Contract or outsource software	1.0%
Information systems	1.5%
Systems software	2.0%
Military software	2.0%
Commercial software	3.5%

Note: From "Strategies for Managing Requirements Creep," by C. Jones, 1996, *IEEE Computer, 29*(6), pp. 92–94. Copyright 1996 by IEEE. Reprinted with permission.

The volatility of the requirements is an anomaly that cannot be accommodated by the waterfall; if the requirements keep changing at these high rates, the design that is based on them must keep changing also, and all advantages of the waterfall disappear. It is like building a family home for mad customers who keep changing their mind; no blueprint lasts, walls that have been recently built have to be torn down and have to be erected in a different place. Unfortunately, this is the way of life in most software projects.

The volatility plays exactly the same role as the previously discussed anomaly of burning substances in early chemistry. In its consequences, it means an overhaul of most of the software engineering knowledge and practice. Instead of concentrating all attention on the techniques of a perfect up-front design, software engineers must pay attention to the techniques that allow them to keep up with the volatile requirements. Instead of concentrating on how to avoid software changes, they have to concentrate on how to live with them and how to make them less expensive and more manageable. Because of requirements volatility, the late software changes are going to happen no matter what, and software engineers have to find out how to deal with them.

Besides the volatility of requirements, there are other sources of volatility that plague software projects. There is the volatility of the technology that is used in the project: New computer hardware is used; a new version of the operating system or compiler is released; or a new version of a library becomes available. These changes also mean changes in the project plan, sometimes substantial.

There is also the volatility of knowledge; software engineers learn as they progress with the projects. They learn new things about the domain, about the algorithms and techniques to be used, about the technology. On the other hand, experienced project members leave the project, and their knowledge is lost to the project team. This knowledge volatility also requires adjustment of the plans.

The waterfall bears an uncomfortable resemblance to the rigid five-year plans of the late and ossified Soviet Union. The Soviet planners tried to stop time and freeze the economic plan for five years, but life went on and quickly made those plans obsolete. Software engineers should not emulate old Soviets; they need to react swiftly to changing circumstances and plan as small successful companies do. They must find a compromise between long-term plans and a quick reaction to the constantly changing circumstances in which they operate.

Iterative and evolutionary software development is the software engineers' response to the volatility. Requirements constantly change, but software engineers cannot operate in complete chaos and cannot constantly change the marching orders. They have to plan. However, they have to accept the fact that their plans are temporary and will have to be revised when they get out of date. Instead of planning the whole life span, they plan for a limited amount of time, called iteration.

During iteration, the programmers take the current version of the requirements and prepare a plan for a limited time; then they work on the basis of that plan. After a certain time, they revisit the requirements, see how much they have changed in the meantime, and update the plan. Iterative software development is a process that consists of such repeated iterations.

Software engineering is not the only human activity that needs to strike the balance between plan and flexibility. We have already mentioned the type of planning that occurs in small companies, where a balance between the long-term plan and changing outside circumstances must be found. Another example is college education. College studies also cannot be fully planned in all detail in advance; they must be divided into iterations that are called semesters. The students create semester plans and register for the appropriate courses. After the semester is over and the results—the grades—are in, students prepare the plan for the next semester. If students experience unexpected problems and setbacks, or if some courses were cancelled or new courses were introduced, they may take a different path than the path that they originally planned. This system is based on long academic experience, and it combines a very specific plan for each semester with the flexibility to adjust long-term direction.

The iterative approach to software engineering is based on a similar idea. This approach is also called an *evolutionary approach*, because it is capable of responding to the changing external circumstances, and that is a characteristic of an evolution.

1.4.1 Software Engineering Paradigms Today

In this chapter, we explained three basic paradigms of software engineering—ad hoc, waterfall, and iterative—and explained the revolutions that introduced them. During the revolutions, there have been huge and sometimes acrimonious debates among the adherents of competing paradigms. After all the ink has dried and all the arguments have been made, all three paradigms still coexist in the software engineering practice.

The iterative paradigm is the mainstream of today's industrial practice, which could not ignore the fact of requirements volatility and had to find a way to cope with it, no matter what was being said in various debates, books, and papers. It embraced the iterative paradigm as the only workable solution. In particular, information systems and web applications experience large volatility, and the success of these systems depends on how well and how fast they respond to this volatility. This book reflects the prevalence of the iterative paradigm in the practice, and therefore, most of the discussion is devoted to the techniques and tools that support it.

The waterfall paradigm still exists, but it has been relegated to the status of a small player; according to a recent survey, approximately 18% of managers and software engineers use the waterfall approach (SoftServe, 2009). We speculate that the waterfall is still useful in situations where there is no volatility, for example, in especially stable domains of some small embedded systems where software controls a specific mechanical device and that device is not changing. At the same time, the small size of the program guarantees that the volatility of the knowledge also does not play any role. An example of this is a washing machine that has several different washing cycles, and the washing cycles are controlled by software. As long as the washing machine is used, the hardware and the washing cycles are the same, and therefore, there is no volatility of the requirements. The control program is small, and therefore, there is no volatility of knowledge either. The waterfall paradigm works in this situation as intended, and it is the most likely life-span model to be used. The waterfall is also used in small throwaway projects, which are discarded when requirements change.

The ad hoc techniques were predominant at the very beginning of software engineering and they never truly disappeared; they are still used today, mostly by solitary programmers who see themselves more as artists than engineers and who do not see any need for constraints that the disciplined engineering approach imposes on the other two paradigms. However, there are serious limits to what can be accomplished in this way; it would be reckless to try a large software project today using ad hoc techniques. The ad hoc paradigm still can be found in the areas of computer art or small computer games, where creativity is the highest value and software quality is of a lesser value.

Summary

Software is a product that has been in existence since the 1950s. Software engineering is a discipline that deals with developing and evolving this product. In their work, software engineers face essential difficulties of complexity, invisibility, changeability, conformity, and discontinuity of software. In their history, they have worked with three different paradigms: First was the ad hoc paradigm, then the waterfall paradigm, and recently the iterative paradigm. The latter is the prevailing paradigm of today; it is based on iterations, which are based on specific time periods where programmers work according to an iteration plan. The iterations end with an evaluation of the project progress and preparation of the plan for the next iteration. The other two paradigms (ad hoc, waterfall) are used today in special circumstances only.

Further Reading and Topics

The origin of the waterfall paradigm, which played such an important role in the history of software engineering, is shrouded in mystery. Some authors trace the beginning of waterfall to a paper by Royce (1970) but that is, strictly speaking, a historical mistake. Royce criticized the waterfall as something that already existed and was widely used in software projects, but had serious shortcomings. Royce proposed various improvements, but his paper cannot be presented as an origin of the waterfall method. It would be an interesting task for historians to trace how the waterfall approach started in software engineering, and how and why it became so prevalent for so long. The inability of software managers to adequately plan water-fall software projects and the social consequences of that failure are described by Yourdon (1999).

The history of the second software engineering revolution that introduced the iterative and evolutionary paradigm is discussed in a historical survey (Larman & Basili, 2003) that is a very useful resource for anyone who is interested in this particular story. The iterative paradigm was known and practiced sporadically from the very beginning of software engineering; it was already being used successfully in Project Mercury in the 1960s (Randell & Zurcher, 1968). Several high-visibility software projects successfully used iterative evolutionary development in the 1970s, among them space shuttle software that was developed from 1977 to 1980 in 17 iterations (Madden & Rone, 1984). The first systematic expositions of the iterative and evolutionary paradigm were also published in the 1970s (Basili & Turner, 1975; Gilb, 1977). However, all these efforts faced a high level of skepticism on the part of the mainstream software engineering community, until the data on requirements volatility proved beyond a doubt the superiority of the iterative evolutionary paradigm in the late 1990s (Jones, 1996; Cusumano & Selby, 1997).

Some authors use the word *paradigm* for what we call in this book *technology*. For example, they talk about an "object-oriented paradigm," while this book talks about an "object-oriented technology." In this book, the word *paradigm* retains its original meaning as used by Thomas Kuhn (1996), as a "coherent tradition of scientific (engineering) research and practice." We make this distinction because each paradigm may be supported by many technologies, and a change in paradigms does not necessitate a change in technologies. As in the example citing the history of early chemistry, the technology responsible for the paradigm shift from phlogiston to oxygen was an increase in the accuracy of scales. Scales were introduced under the old paradigm and continued to be used under the new paradigm, and the paradigm shift did not impact the use of this particular technology. The same thing is happening with software technologies like programming languages. They can be used in the context of different paradigms, and a change in the paradigm does not mean that old programming languages must be replaced by new ones. Although technologies and paradigms interact, it is a complex interaction, and they both have an independent history.

A history of software engineering that is characterized by two revolutions was published by Rajlich (2006).

Exercises

    1.1   What are the essential difficulties of software?

    1.2   Approximately when did the first software product appear?

    1.3   What was the background of the first software developers?

    1.4   Why was the discipline of software engineering established?

    1.5   Explain the stages of the waterfall and the rationale for its adoption.

1.6   Why does the waterfall work for construction and for manufacturing but not for software engineering?

1.7   How long did the waterfall dominate the discipline of software engineering?

1.8   How high is the approximate yearly volatility in the requirements of commercial software?

1.9   When implementing a control program for a dishwasher that has fewer than 10 different washing cycles, what paradigm would you use? Why?

1.10 When implementing a website with 10 different pages for a medium-size business, what paradigm would you use? Why?

References

Basili, V. R., & Turner, A. J. (1975). Iterative enhancement: A practical technique for software development. *IEEE Transactions on Software Engineering, 4,* 390–396.

Brooks, F. P. (1982). *The mythical man-month.* Reading, MA: Addison-Wesley.

———. (1987). No silver bullet: Essence and accidents of software engineering. *IEEE Computer, 20*(4), 34–42.

Charette, R. N. (2009). This car runs on code. *IEEE Spectrum.* Retrieved June 16, 2011, from http://spectrum.ieee.org/green-tech/advanced-cars/this-car-runs-on-code

Cusumano, M. A., & Selby, R. W. (1997). *Microsoft secrets.* New York, NY: HarperCollins.

Gilb, T. (1977). *Software metrics.* Cambridge, MA: Winthrop.

Hsu, F. H. (2002). *Behind Deep Blue: Building the computer that defeated the world chess champion.* Princeton, NJ: Princeton University Press.

Jones, C. (1996). Strategies for managing requirements creep. *IEEE Computer, 29*(6), 92–94.

Kuhn, T. S. (1996). *The structure of scientific revolutions* (3rd ed.). Chicago, IL: University of Chicago Press.

Larman, C., & Basili, V. R. (2003). Iterative and incremental development: A brief history. *IEEE Computer, 36*(6), 47–56.

Leiner, B. M., Cerf, V. G., Clark, D. D., Kahn, R. E., Kleinrock, L., Lynch, D. C., et al. (2009). A brief history of the Internet. *ACM SIGCOMM Computer Communication Review, 39*(5), 22–31.

Leonhardt, D. (2000). John Tukey, 85, statistician; coined the word "software." *New York Times,* July 28.

Madden, W. A., & Rone, K. Y. (1984). Design, development, integration: Space shuttle primary flight software system. *Communications of the ACM, 27,* 914–925.

Miller, G. A. (1956). The magical number seven, plus or minus two: Some limits on our capacity for processing information. *Psychological Review, 63*(8), 1–97.

Rajlich, V. (2006). Changing the paradigm of software engineering. *Communications of ACM, 49,* 67–70.

Randell, B., & Zurcher, F. W. (1968). Iterative multi-level modeling: A methodology for computer system design. In *Proceedings of IFIP* (pp. 867–871). Washington, DC: IEEE Computer Society Press.

Royce, W. W. (1970). Managing the development of large software systems. In *Proceedings of IEEE WESCON* (pp. 328–339). Washington, DC: IEEE Computer Society Press.

SoftServe. (2009). *Survey finds majority of senior software business leaders see rise in development budgets*. Retrieved June 16, 2011, from http://www.softserveinc.com/news/survey-senior-software-business-leaders-rise-development-budgets/

Yourdon, E. E. (1999). *Death march: The complete software developer's guide to surviving "mission impossible" projects*. Upper Saddle River, NJ: Prentice Hall.

Chapter 2

Software Life
Span Models

Objectives

This chapter explains the staged model of software life span. After you have read this chapter, you will know:

- The staged model of software life span
- The initial development stage and its role
- The software evolution stage
- The end-of-evolution stage
- Servicing, phaseout, and closedown of software
- The versioned model of staged life span
- Other life span models, including prototyping model, V-Model, and spiral model

***

The software life span consists of several distinct stages. In each stage, software needs a different kind of software engineering work, and the life span models offer a bird's-eye summary of the whole software engineering discipline.

In the previous chapter, we discussed the waterfall model, which had an enormous influence on the discipline of software engineering, although it did not deal with requirements volatility and did not fit well with the practical experience of most software projects. This chapter explains another model, called the staged model, that reflects the iterative paradigm and fits better with the actual experience of software engineers. The "Further Reading and Topics" section lists several additional models.

2.1 Staged Model

Figure 2.1 presents the staged model of software life span. It consists of several stages that differ substantially from each other.

2.1.1 Initial Development

Initial development is the first stage that produces the first version of the software. During the initial development, the developers start from scratch. While implementing the first version, they make several fundamental decisions. They select the programming languages, libraries, software tools, and other technologies that the project uses. These technologies will accompany software through the rest of the life span and will support all work in the future stages.

Another fundamental choice during the initial development is the system architecture, which consists of the modules of the system and their interactions. These modules and their interactions also accompany software throughout its life span, and they either facilitate or hinder the inevitable changes that occur in later stages. The fundamental choices of the initial development set the course for the whole software life span. The reversal of these initial decisions later is very expensive, and often it is practically impossible. Chapter 14 contains more information on initial development.

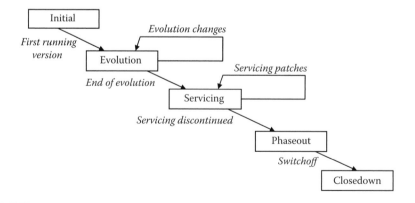

Figure 2.1   Staged model of software life span.

The resulting first version may have incomplete functionality and may not be ready for release to the users. If that happens, software developers postpone the first release and add the missing functionality during the next stage, the evolution.

2.1.2 Evolution

In software evolution, programmers add new capabilities and functionalities, and correct previous mistakes and misunderstandings. *Software changes* are the basic building blocks of software evolution, and each change introduces a new functionality or some other new property into software. Software evolution is an iterative process that consists of repeated software changes.

Software evolution requires highly skilled software engineers. They have to understand both the software domain and the current state of the software; without this knowledge, they could not evolve the software. The software they evolve usually grows in both complexity and size, because this additional functionality requires it. It also grows in value because the new functionality better satisfies the customer needs.

The customers receive the results of software evolution in form of *software releases* that differ from each other in the extent of their functionality. The managers decide when to release, taking into account various conflicting criteria, for example, timeliness of the release ("time to market"), and completeness of the desired software functionality.

Software engineers spend most of their time in software evolution, therefore, it is the most important topic of this book. Chapters 5–11 describe the phases of software change that form the foundation of software evolution; chapter 12 describes processes of software evolution as practiced by a solo programmer; and chapter 13 describes processes of software evolution as practiced by programming teams.

2.1.3 Final Stages of Software Life Span

Software stops evolving and enters the final stages of its life span for several different reasons. One is that software achieves *stability*, where there are no longer any large evolutionary changes requested, although infrequent minor corrections still may occur. Stability occurs in domains that do not have volatility, for example, *embedded software* that controls a mechanical device. The only volatility in this context is the volatility of the stakeholder knowledge, and once that problem is resolved, no further evolution is necessary.

Other domains never achieve such stability, and the volatility and the evolution can go on indefinitely. However, for business reasons, the managers sometimes decide to stop the expensive evolution, transfer software into servicing, and limit changes to a bare minimum.

The software evolution may also end involuntarily, when the complexity of the code gets out of hand or when the software team loses the skills necessary for evolution. In this situation, the programmers often resort to quick and superficial changes that confuse and complicate software structure even further. The resulting confused and complicated software code is called *decayed code*, and it makes further evolution harder and harder, eventually becoming impossible.

During software servicing, the programmers no longer make major changes to the software, but they still make small repairs that keep the software usable. Software in the servicing stage has been called legacy software, aging software, or software in maintenance. Once software is in the servicing stage, it is very difficult and expensive to reverse the situation and return it back into the evolution stage. *Reengineering* is a process that reverses code decay and returns software to the stage of evolution, but it is an expensive and risky process. Hence, there is a large asymmetry between the code decay that can happen unnoticed and the reengineering effort that tries to reverse it.

When software is not worthy of any further repairs, it enters the *phaseout* stage. Help may still be available to assist the remaining users who are still using the system, but change requests are no longer accepted, and the users must work around any remaining defects.

Sometime later, the managers completely withdraw the system from production, and this is called *closedown*. The data indicate that the average life span of large and successful software is somewhere between 10 and 20 years.

Chapter 15 describes the final stages of software life span in more detail.

2.2 Variants of Staged Model

Figure 2.1 contains the basic staged model of software life span. However, some software projects do not pass through all stages, but skip some of them. For example, *unsuccessful projects* terminate prematurely; some terminate even during initial development, and they never enter evolution and the following stages. Other projects terminate after several iterations of evolution, but they never enter the servicing stage.

Pure evolutionary projects start as an extension of an existing software and evolve it into a new and different one; these projects skip the initial development stage and start directly with evolution. *Small and short-lived projects* may skip software evolution and go directly into servicing and consequent stages, because there is no need to add new functionality through evolution.

Versioned projects deal with a large customer base. Some users receive new versions as soon as they become available, but other users choose to retain their older versions. The older versions no longer evolve, because it would be very complicated and wasteful to evolve several versions in parallel. However, these old versions are

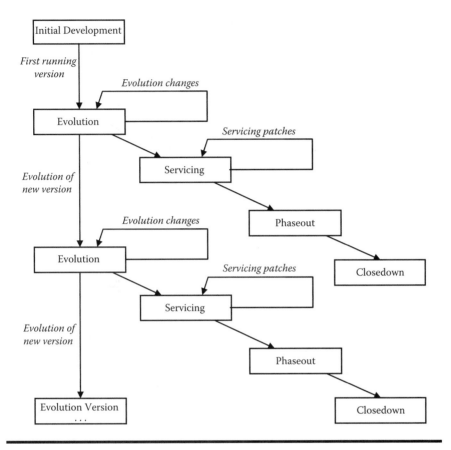

Figure 2.2   Versioned model of software life span.

still serviced for some time. When bugs surface and need a fix, servicing patches are distributed to the users of older versions. These servicing patches fix the bugs, but they very rarely implement a substantial new functionality. If the users want this substantial new functionality, they have to buy the new version. The corresponding variant of the staged life span is in Figure 2.2.

Mozilla Firefox Releases

An example of software with a large customer base is the Mozilla Firefox web browser (Mozilla, 2011). The versions released in 2008 and 2009 are in Table 2.1 Each row represents a new release of the browser with security updates, bugs fixed, and other new features; the three columns on the right emphasize the updates of versions 2, 3, and 3.5. Versions 2 and 3 were serviced in parallel until 12/18/2008, as highlighted in Table 2.1; on that date, version 2 moved into phaseout stage. On 4/24/2009, version 3.5 was introduced, while version 3 was still being serviced.

Table 2.1   Mozilla Firefox Releases

Date	Version #	2	3	3.5
2/7/2008	2.0.0.12/	x		
2/13/2008	3.0b3/		x	
3/11/2008	3.0b4/		x	
3/25/2008	2.0.0.13/	x		
4/9/2008	3.0b5/		x	
4/15/2008	2.0.0.14/	x		
5/15/2008	3.0rc1/		x	
6/4/2008	3.0rc2/		x	
6/11/2008	3.0rc3/		x	
6/19/2008	3.0/		x	
6/23/2008	2.0.0.15/	x		
7/11/2008	2.0.0.16/	x		
7/16/2008	3.0.1/		x	
9/17/2008	2.0.0.17/	x		
9/22/2008	3.0.2/		x	
10/7/2008	3.0.3/		x	
11/11/2008	2.0.0.18/	x		
11/11/2008	3.0.4/		x	
12/15/2008	2.0.0.19/	x		
12/15/2008	3.0.5/		x	
12/18/2008	2.0.0.20/	x		
2/2/2009	3.0.6/		x	
3/3/2009	3.0.7/		x	
3/27/2009	3.0.8/		x	
4/9/2009	3.0.9/		x	

(continued)

Table 2.1   Mozilla Firefox Releases (continued)

Date	Version #	2	3	3.5
4/24/2009	3.5b4/			x
4/27/2009	3.0.10/		x	
6/7/2009	3.5b99/			x
6/10/2009	3.0.11/		x	
6/16/2009	3.5rc1/			x
6/17/2009	3.5rc2/			x
6/24/2009	3.5rc3/			x
7/1/2009	3.5/			x
7/17/2009	3.5.1/			x
7/20/2009	3.0.12/		x	
7/30/2009	3.5.2/			x
7/31/2009	3.0.13/		x	
8/24/2009	3.5.3/			x
9/8/2009	3.0.14/		x	
10/19/2009	3.5.4/			x
10/26/2009	3.0.15/		x	

Summary

Life span models offer a simplified and comprehensive view of the entire software engineering discipline. The models differ from each other and fit more or less accurately with the actual software life span. The staged model consists of the stages of initial development that produces the first version of software, followed by a stage of evolution, where additional functionality is added. Software evolution stops by code stabilization, management decision, or by code decay, and the stage after that is called servicing, where only minor deficiencies are fixed. The next stage is phaseout, where even this limited servicing is discontinued, although some users may continue to use the software. Finally, closedown terminates the software life span.

Further Reading and Topics

Life span models are often called *life cycle* in the literature, although paradoxically there is no cycle in the life cycle. Perhaps an unspoken assumption is that when a life span of one program ends, another program will emerge and replace it. This assumption is, of course, very often untrue because many programs run their course and nothing replaces them. For example, when a software company goes out of business and all its products are withdrawn from the market, then there is no cycle; the same is true for projects that terminate prematurely during initial development. The term *life cycle* also understates the fact that it is a model, and each model is a simplification of the reality and may or may not correspond to what the reality truly is. Nevertheless, the word *life cycle* became prevalent, and an overwhelming number of authors nowadays call life span models a life cycle. Every reader of the relevant literature should be aware of this fact.

Belady and Lehman (1976) have documented the existence of software evolution of a large software system. Later, Sneed (1989) classified software systems into three categories. *Throwaway systems* typically have a lifetime of less than two years and are neither evolved nor serviced. Then there are *static systems* that work in special stable domains, and their rate of change is less than 10% in a year. The rest are *evolutionary systems* that undergo substantial changes and last many years.

Using Sneed's model, Lehner (1991) surveyed the life span of 13 business systems from Upper Austria. He found that some systems belong to the category of static systems with a very short evolution after the initial development and dramatically decreasing servicing work, while other systems consume substantial effort over many years. Lehner confirmed a clear distinction between what he called "growth" and "saturation" that corresponds to the stages of evolution and servicing, respectively. Thus, he refuted earlier opinions that the evolution and growth of software continues indefinitely and empirically confirmed the difference between evolution and servicing. These empirical observations later led to the staged model presented in this chapter (Rajlich & Bennett, 2000; Bennett & Rajlich, 2000).

Code decay is an important fact of software management, and there is a need for early warning that such decay is taking place so that the managers can take a timely remedial action (Eick, Graves, Karr, Marron, & Mockus, 2001). One of the indicators of code decay is the prevalence of replicated code, the so-called clones (Burd & Munro, 1997). Besides problems in the code, there could be other deeper reasons for code decay, such as use of obsolete technologies, or obsolete programming techniques, or obsolete ways and views of how to implement the software. This aspect of code decay was investigated by Rajlich, Wilde, Buckellew, and Page (2001). The code decay makes software more and more expensive to evolve or service, and it leads to the phaseout and closedown that ends the software life span. Data from Japan indicate the average life span of large software systems in various domains to be about 12 years (Tamai & Torimitsu, 1992).

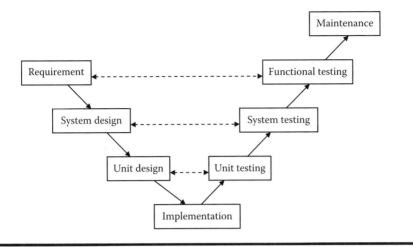

Figure 2.3   V-model of software life span.

The literature contains many additional models of software life span. Chapter 1 introduced the waterfall model, which has several variants that improve some of its aspects. The V-model is a variant of the waterfall model that is particularly popular in Germany and places a large emphasis on testing (Bröhl & Dröschel, 1993). It has two branches in the shape of the letter *V*: The left branch follows the waterfall from requirements through design and implementation; the design is divided into two steps: system design and unit design. When the implementation is complete, the testing retraces this process backwards: First, the unit tests verify the unit design; then system tests verify the system design; and functional tests verify the requirements. When testing is complete, the system is delivered to users and maintained as in the original waterfall (see Figure 2.3).

Another popular variant of the waterfall model is the *prototyping model* (Naumann & Jenkins, 1982), which addresses the issue of requirements elicitation. Often it is difficult to elicit from the future users what they really want. When the users see the first version of software, they often say, "But we wanted something different!" A software prototype is a fast and tentative implementation whose sole purpose is to verify the requirements and present them to the user as a provisional first version. After that, the prototype is thrown away and the real implementation starts. A picture of the prototyping life span is in Figure 2.4.

The prototyping model offers a partial answer to the problem of requirements volatility. It takes into account all volatility that occurred during requirements elicitation and prototyping, but unfortunately, volatility continues and the prototyping does not deal with this late volatility.

The *spiral model* emphasizes the risky nature of software projects (Boehm, 1988). Each phase of the spiral model is preceded by a risk analysis, and a strategy is devised to mitigate the most serious risks. For example, if during the requirements

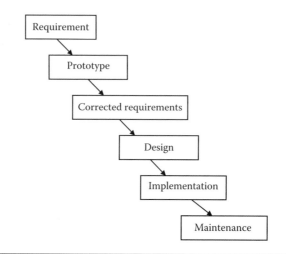

Figure 2.4 Prototyping model of software life span.

phase the most serious risk is the misunderstanding with the customers, a strategy is devised to lessen that risk, for example, by a fast production of the user interface prototype that can be presented to the user. If during design the most serious risk is the possibility of the slow response time from the system, then a strategy is devised to lessen that particular risk, for example, by speedy implementation of the algorithms that affect the response time. Spiral life cycle focuses the attention of software developers on the most risky part of their job, and the purpose is to increase the likelihood of the project's success.

Exercises

2.1 What are the five stages of the staged model of software life span?

2.2 What important software properties does the initial development establish? Why are they important?

2.3 How is software evolution different from servicing?

2.4 How can code decay if it is not physical?

2.5 How long on average does large software last?

2.6 In what situation is it better to skip initial development and start software by evolution of an already existing software?

2.7 What are the issues that have to be addressed during software closedown?

2.8 Why is the term *life cycle* misleading? Which term is more commonly used: *life span model* or *life cycle*?

2.9 In what situation can the V-model of the software life span be used?

2.10 What are the advantages and disadvantages of the prototyping model?

References

Belady, L. A., & Lehman, M. M. (1976). A model of large program development. *IBM Systems Journal, 15*, 225–252.

Bennett, K. H., & Rajlich, V. T. (2000). Software maintenance and evolution: A roadmap. In *Proceedings of Conference on the Future of Software Engineering* (pp. 73–87). New York, NY: ACM.

Boehm, B. W. (1988). A spiral model of software development and enhancement. *IEEE Computer, 21*(5), 61–72.

Bröhl, A. P., & Dröschel, W. (1993). *Das V-Modell—Der Standard für die Softwareentwicklung mit Praxisleitfaden*. Munich, Germany: Oldenburg-Verlag.

Burd, E., & Munro, M. (1997). Investigating the maintenance implications of the replication of code. In *Proceedings of IEEE International Conference on Software Maintenance* (pp. 322–329). Washington, DC: IEEE Computer Society Press.

Eick, S. G., Graves, T. L., Karr, A. F., Marron, J. S., & Mockus, A. (2001). Does code decay? Assessing evidence from change management data. *IEEE Transactions on Software Engineering, 27*(1), 1–12.

Lehner, F. (1991). Software lifecycle management based on a phase distinction method. *Microprocessing and Microprogramming, 32*, 603–608.

Mozilla. (2011). *Index of Firefox releases*. Retrieved on June 17, 2011, from http://ftp.mozilla.org/pub/mozilla.org//firefox/releases/

Naumann, J. D., & Jenkins, A. M. (1982). Prototyping: The new paradigm for systems development. *MIS Quarterly, 6*, 29–44.

Rajlich, V., & Bennett, K. H. (2000). A staged model for the software life cycle. *IEEE Computer, 33*, 66–71.

Rajlich, V., Wilde, N., Buckellew, M., & Page, H. (2001). Software cultures and evolution. *IEEE Computer, 34*, 24–29.

Sneed, H. M. (1989). *Software engineering management* (I. Johnson, Trans.). Chichester, West Sussex, U.K.: Ellis Horwood. (Original work published 1987)

Tamai, T., & Torimitsu, Y. (1992). Software lifetime and its evolution process over generations. In *IEEE International Conference on Software Maintenance* (pp. 63–69). Washington, DC: IEEE Computer Society Press.

Chapter 3

Software Technologies

Objectives

In this chapter, you will review the common technologies that form the foundation for the rest of the book. After you have read this chapter, you will know:

- The role of programming languages and compilers in software engineering
- The role of object-oriented technology in the current software engineering practice
- The foundations of object-oriented technology: objects, classes, relationships of part-of and is-a, and polymorphism
- The principles of version control system

***

The prefix *techno-* of the word *technology* originates from old Greek and means art, skill, or craft, while the suffix *-logy* means method, system, or science. The combination of the two, hence, means a "system of an art" or a "science of a skill" or a similar combination. Software technologies are a mixture of skills, tools, and processes that programmers use while working with software.

As already mentioned in chapter 1, a technology used in a specific software project is an accidental property of the software. There is usually a selection of available technologies, each with its own advantages and disadvantages. The choice of a particular technology for a particular project depends on unique project circumstances. For example, people who are involved in the project have experience with a specific technology; therefore, this technology becomes the technology of the project by default. In other situations, a new technology offers superior productivity and superior product quality that makes retraining of everybody on the project team cost effective. Programmers and managers weigh the pros and cons of various technologies before the software project starts.

Software technologies include programming languages in which software engineers write software; the current programming languages are very often object oriented, and object orientation is briefly explained in this chapter. Other examples of technologies that are used in software projects include the compilers, version control systems, libraries of reusable software parts, software tools and environments that help in software project tasks, and so forth. There are proven software technologies of the present, dead but historically important technologies of the past, and promising technologies of the future.

Software technologies are a wide topic, and this chapter presents only a very small subset, the bare minimum that is necessary to illustrate the later topics of this book. These select technologies can be considered just an illuminating example or accidental property of this book. Sections 3.1 and 3.2 are a survey of the prerequisites of this book.

The rest of the book is applicable to other technologies that lie outside of the scope of this brief chapter. These other technologies still display the same fundamental properties, and that makes the rest of the book applicable to these other technologies as well.

3.1 Programming Languages and Compilers

As one of the first project decisions, programmers and their managers select the programming languages that are used in the software project. Programming languages are a bridge between the programmers and the computer, because they are understandable to programmers and, at the same time, they are executable by the computer. Some software projects use one programming language, while others use a combination of several.

Over the course of software history, a large number of programming languages have been created and used. Some of them were used only very briefly or within a small group of users, while others became widely popular and have been used worldwide for a long time. *COBOL* is the most successful programming language of all time and has been used in data-processing applications that handle large amounts of data; examples are company payrolls, banking systems, and so forth. *Java* is a programming language that is popular with academics and in web applications in recent years. *C++* has been a workhorse for the projects where the software engineers desire a particularly close control over the computer and its resources, for example, in real-time applications.

Software engineers must invest a considerable effort to become proficient in a particular programming language. They have to learn various language subtleties and quirks; therefore, programming language training and retraining represents a significant investment. In many instances, programming teams specialize in a specific programming language, and when the managers choose a team for a software project, they choose the team's programming language as well.

Software engineers write *source code* in a programming language, and computers then process and execute this source code. For the *compiled languages* like C++, the source code is divided into source files and the translation is done in two steps: In the first step, the *compiler* translates individual source code files into *object files*. In the second step, the *linker* links all object files into one executable file for the whole program. Please note that the notion *object file* is used just as an accident of history and does not have anything in common with the objects of the real world or the object-oriented technology that is explained later in this chapter. Other technologies, for example, *interpreters*, do the processing of the source code differently; the compiler produces *bytecode* that is then executed by an *interpreter*.

Compilers are the tools that cover the first step of translation. For the popular languages and popular hardware, there are usually several compilers available, and software engineers can choose the most appropriate one. The issue that they sometimes face is the issue of compatibility, which arises when software was written and translated by one compiler, but now it must be transferred to a different one. That happens with long-living projects where the original compilers are no longer available, or where compiler vendors produce a new compiler version.

Incompatibilities among compilers exist despite the fact that the popular programming languages are standardized. The standards do not cover everything, and different compiler writers make different choices for the items that are missing in the standard. The other source of incompatibility is the deviation from the standards; the compiler writers sometimes implement subsets or supersets of the standard language, and these omissions or extensions are also a source of incompatibility. When software engineers move from one version of compiler to another, they must make sure that the differences between the compilers do not introduce bugs; they have to retest the whole software thoroughly. It is a good software engineering practice to know which features of the programming language are likely to cause problems when compilers are changed, and as a precaution, to avoid using these features.

Programming languages are accompanied by reusable *libraries*, which are collections of frequently used modules, and they usually are bundled with the compiler. The libraries contain ready-made functions like sine and cosine, or frequently used data structures like queue and stack, or elements of user interfaces like buttons and menus, and so forth. Programmers incorporate these modules into their source code, and these libraries save them a substantial effort.

The linker takes object files produced by the compiler and creates a single executable program. The reusable libraries are usually a collection of object files, and they are linked into the executable file by the linker.

Each version of the project consists of the complete set of source files, object files, and the executable file, as depicted in Figure 3.1.

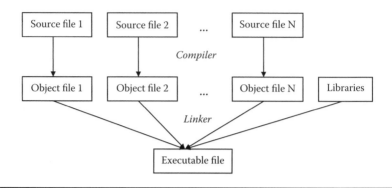

Figure 3.1   Code of a version of a software project that uses compiled language.

3.2 Object-Oriented Technology

Object-oriented technology is a mainstream software technology of today, and the most popular current programming languages are object oriented. It uses abstraction as a technique to deal with the complexity of the programs. This abstraction is done in two steps: First, there are software objects that share the select properties with their counterparts in the real world, and then there are classes that share the properties of similar objects.

3.2.1 Objects

Objects in software represent the objects of the real world. For example, in banking programs, the application domain contains customers and their accounts; therefore, the program will also contain customers and accounts as objects. Objects of the domain have properties: An account has a balance, and a customer has a name; therefore, the corresponding software objects have the same properties. These properties are called the attributes of the object. Also, the domain objects perform certain actions, like customers depositing and withdrawing money from their accounts, and the corresponding software objects perform the same actions; they are called object functions or object methods.

There are advantages in using objects as an organizing principle of programs. Everybody who understands the domain and its objects can understand the software objects; therefore, they can understand how the object-oriented program is organized.

Another advantage of objects is in the fact that objects present themselves to the outside as being simpler than they truly are. This property is called *information hiding*. The objects hide complicated and messy details inside, while to the outside they present a clean and simple interface. As a result, the interactions between objects are simpler, helping again with the comprehension of software.

A real-life example of information hiding is a cook, who takes several neatly wrapped ingredients like meat, flour, spice, and salt, and then disappears behind the kitchen door. After a while, the cook emerges from the kitchen with an elegantly arranged plate of a tasty meal. The kitchen with its table, stove, sink, refrigerator, grinder, mixer, garbage can, and other devices is hidden from sight, and the customers only see neatly wrapped ingredients going in and tasty meals going out.

A more software-oriented example is an object that stores phone numbers. When it receives a name or nickname, it returns the phone number. The functionality visible from the outside is simple: Name goes in, phone number goes out. However, there is a complicated functionality inside that deals with ambiguous or misspelled names, converts cleaned-up names into a key, searches the databases for the key and retrieves the record, extracts the phone number from the record, and then returns it.

3.2.2 Classes

Classes are modules of the source code that define the properties of several objects. For example, there may be banking customers Jacob and Joseph, and each of them owns one account at a bank, and they deposit and withdraw money from the account. They both also have a name and an address. In the banking application, there will be two objects, jacob and joseph, and they both will belong to the same class Customer. The class Customer implements all attributes and functions that jacob and joseph share. The functions implemented by classes are sometimes called *class methods;* both class attributes and class methods are called *class members.*

In a generic object-oriented language, a declaration of class Customer generally looks like this:

```
class Customer
      {
      // methods
      public:
            open_account();
            deposit(int deposit_amount);
            withdraw(int withdrawal_amount);
      // attributes
      private:
            String name;
            String address;
            int account_number;
            int balance = 0;
      };
```

The attribute name contains the customer's name, address contains the customer's address, account _ number contains the identification number of the customer's account, and balance contains the balance in the account; when the account is created, the balance is originally set to $0. The method deposit(int deposit _ amount) deposits the specified amount to the customer's account, and the method withdraw(int withdrawal _ amount) withdraws the amount specified from the customer's account. Opening the account is handled by the method open _ account(). The keyword public means that the following class members are visible from outside of the class, while the keyword private means that the class members are invisible from the outside and can be used only inside of the class. This control over the visibility of the class members implements information hiding that provides a simpler interface to the outside and keeps the complex details inside.

In the program, objects are declared in the following way:

```
Customer jacob, joseph;
```

Once objects jacob and joseph exist, they can perform various methods that class Customer provides. For example, consider the following code segment:

```
jacob.open_account();
jacob.deposit(100);
jacob.withdraw(10);
```

In this code segment, customer Jacob first opens an account, then deposits $100 to this account, and finally withdraws $10 from the account. This code segment uses only the public data members. It is easy to comprehend and illustrates that a well-written object-oriented code with well-chosen names has self-documenting properties that help the programmers to write, read, and comprehend it.

Coding conventions facilitate this understanding. Traditionally, class names are nouns and start with an uppercase letter, while object and attribute names are nouns that start with a lowercase letter. Method names are usually verbs. It is very important to choose meaningful names for classes, class members, and objects. Whenever classes and objects correspond to classes and objects of the program domain, the names from the program domain should be used. Ambiguous names or names that are too general should be avoided. For example, if the class represents a banking customer, its name should be Customer rather than the less specific Person, in order to help the understanding.

If there is a need to use more than one word in naming a class or object or class member, composite names are used; the composites either capitalize second and following words, the so-called camelCase, as in

```
firstCustomerWithdrawal
```

or separate the words by underscore, as in

```
first_customer_withdrawal
```

Consistent rules on how names are created is an important early project decision that should be made before the project starts and should be used consistently by all programmers through the whole duration of the project. This will make the reading of the code easier and it will help future software evolution.

3.2.3 Part-Of Relationship

In the real world, some objects are made of other objects. For example, a car consists of wheels, engine, hood, and so forth. We say that the car is a *composite*, and the wheels, engine, and hood are the *components*. The relationship of a car and a hood is called a *part-of* relationship because, in our everyday language, we can say: "a hood is part of a car."

In object-oriented technology, composite classes have attributes that are of the type of component classes. Consider, for example, a small store where inventory is part of the store:

```
class Store
      {
      private:
            Inventory inv;
      };
```

Thus we say that class Store has a component Inventory, or that Inventory is a part of Store.

3.2.4 Is-A Relationship

In the real world, some classes are more general than other classes. For example, class "Person" is a more general class than class "Bank customer" because each bank customer is a person, while there are persons who are not bank customers. The relationship of a bank customer and person is called an *is-a* relationship because, in our everyday language, we say, "A bank customer is a person."

The same is-a relation is also a part of object-oriented technology and is called a relationship of *inheritance*. It is based on the observation that some classes share common members. For example, both the banking customers and banking tellers share a name and an address. When such situations appear, the programmers use inheritance.

Inheritance is a relation between two classes: one called *base class* or *superclass* that defines the *base type* and the other called *derived class* or *subclass* that defines the *derived type*. The base class defines class members that are shared among all derived classes, while derived classes contain members that are specific to that particular class. An example of base class and derived class is the following:

```
class Person
      {
      private:
              String name;
              String address;
      };
class Customer: public Person
      {
      public:
              open_account(int account_number);
              deposit(int deposit_amount);
              withdraw(int withdrawal_amount);
      private:
              int account_number;
      };
```

Another example of inheritance is geometric two-dimensional shapes, like a rectangle, triangle, circle, and so forth. The data that all shapes share is a location of the shape in the drawing canvas, given by two coordinates (see Figure 3.2). The shape can be moved to a different location in the canvas by a method that changes this location. These shared data and methods are a part of the base class Shape:

```
class Shape
      {
      public:
              move(int new_x, new_y);
      private:
              int x,y;
      };
```

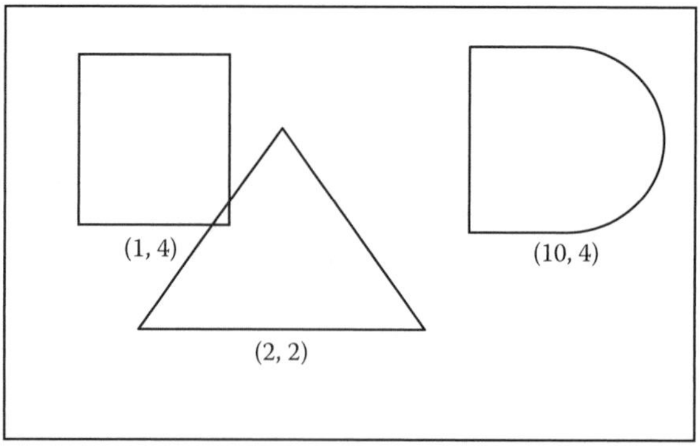

Figure 3.2   Figures in a drawing canvas.

The figures then inherit both the coordinates x and y, and the method move. An example is a rectangle of the following definition:

```
class Rectangle: public Shape
     {
     public:
              draw(int x, int y, int width, int height);
     private:
              int width,height;
     };
```

In this example, class Rectangle inherits from class Shape the variables x and y, that determine the position of the lower left corner of the rectangle on the canvas, and the method move that moves the rectangle to a different location with a different location of the lower left corner. Moreover, the class contains two additional data parameters, width and height, that determine the size of the rectangle, and the method draw that draws a rectangle of the specified width and height at the location given by coordinates x and y.

3.2.5 Polymorphism

Polymorphism is a construct of object-oriented technology that allows the use of a derived type in the place of the base type, for example, in a variable declaration, function parameter, and so forth. A way to view polymorphism is to see it as an implicit switch statement. The programmers write the code where the base type appears in the source code, but the implicit switch checks which actual derived object is being invoked, and based on that, it takes the appropriate action that belongs to the derived type. This implicit switch works during run time, since the compiler usually cannot decide which derived type will be used. The derived type will be decided during run time, and the mechanism that supports it is called *late binding* or *dynamic binding*.

In C++, the polymorphism is expressed with the help of pointers and virtual methods. Virtual methods are present in the base class, but when virtual methods are called and the object that calls it is of the derived type, then the derived type's method is called instead of the base type's method.

The following example deals with farm animals (base type) and cows and sheep (derived types). The base class has a virtual method makeSound(), but when that method is called, cows and sheep make different sounds:

```
class FarmAnimal
     {
     public:
              virtual void makeSound() {}
     };
```

```
class Cow : public FarmAnimal
        {
        public:
                void makeSound() {cout<<" Moo-oo-oo";}
        };
class Sheep : public FarmAnimal
        {
        public:
                void makeSound() {cout<<" Be-e-e";}
        };
```

The classes are used in the following code fragment, which describes a farm with three animals:

```
FarmAnimal* ourAnimal[3];
ourAnimal[0] = new Cow;
ourAnimal[1] = new Sheep;
ourAnimal[2] = new Cow;
for(int i = 0; i < 3; i++)
{
        ourAnimal[i] -> makeSound();
};
```

This code fragment will print out Moo-oo-oo Be-e-e Moo-oo-oo; in the loop body, when a cow is the animal, cow's makeSound() is called, while when a sheep is the animal, sheep's makeSound() is called.

3.3 Version Control System

A version control system is a tool that supports project versions and collaboration in the programming team. Each project consists of multiple source files, object files, and executable files. Each of these files has multiple versions that differ from each other by the changes that the programmers made during the stages of software evolution or servicing. Keeping the order among these files while the programmers work on them is a challenge. A version control system helps programmers to keep up with that challenge by maintaining the *repository* in which all project files are stored and can be retrieved on demand.

The most important project version is the *baseline*: It is the current version of the project, and it is the center of the activities of the team. The baseline consists of a specific version of all source files, object files, and the version's executable file. The software engineers are making parallel changes in the various files of the baseline, and when these changes have been completed, the new version will be produced by a *build* process that compiles, links, and tests these newest versions and produces the new baseline. This process requires a considerable level of cooperation so that the team members do not hinder each other's progress or destroy each other's work, and a version control system supports such cooperation.

While the repository is stored on a central server for the whole team, individual team members have a *private workspace*: the disc space on their computer. They can download the files of the current baseline and modify them. After the modifications, they test them in their private workspace, and if everything is all right, they return them back to the repository, as shown in Figure 3.3. Then the team performs a build and creates a new baseline that consists of the newly updated files and also contains the old files of the previous baseline that have not been updated.

3.3.1 Commit

Version control systems help programmers prevent conflicts where two programmers update the same code in two different ways at the same time. This is accomplished in two different ways. An older way is based on the ideas of *checkout*. The programmer can copy any file from the repository in two different ways: as read only, or as a file that will be updated. If the programmer copies a file from the repository in order to update it, nobody else will be able to do the same until the programmer returns the file back to the repository; returning an updated file is

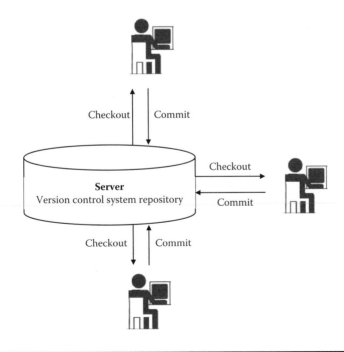

Figure 3.3 Version control system.

called a *commit*. It is analogous to checking a book out of the library; a customer checks out a book and that book is not available to anybody else until the programmer returns the book. Only then can it be checked out by a different customer. Of course, if the book is already checked out, the customer has to wait until it is returned. The idea of file checkouts protects the programmers from the situation where two of them update the same file in two different ways.

The disadvantage of checkouts is that, very often, programmers have to wait for each other to complete their tasks; laggards who keep the files checked out for a long time are a particular annoyance to the others, exactly like library customers who keep the books for an excessively long time. For that reason, new version control systems are based on a different idea: They allow several programmers to work on the same file, then identify what the programmers actually changed, and then produce a new file that has the changes from all programmers in it.

There are two software tools that support that process: The tool *diff* identifies differences between two files and produces a *patch file* that contains a list of changes that are needed to turn the first file into the second one. The other tool is tool *merge* that takes an original file and a corresponding patch file and makes all the changes that the patch files requests.

In the simplest process, the commit works in the following way: A programmer checks out the latest version of file X, edits it and makes all necessary changes, and then commits the modified file X to the repository. The commit is usually done with a help of the diff tool. It produces a patch that identifies what changes the programmer made in the file by comparing the modified file X against the original file in the repository. After that, the merge tool merges the changes into the old file and thus creates the new file.

If two programmers, programmer A and programmer B, update the same file X in parallel and each of them changes a different part of the file X, then both changes are committed without a problem. However if the second programmer B changes something in the file X that the first programmer A also changed, the version control system does not allow the second programmer B to commit. If that happens, the second programmer B has several options. The easiest one is to undo some changes to stay away from the areas that the first programmer A changed, and then to commit. If that is not possible, then another more arduous option is to restart with the file that was modified by programmer A and redo the changes in this modified file again, and then commit.

Finally, the last option is to convince programmer A to undo the changes that stand in the way of the changes done by programmer B. This last option is taken usually when changes by programmer A are smaller or less significant than the changes made by programmer B. This last option, of course, requires collaboration and the good will of both programmers; the programmers must avoid misunderstandings and hard feelings that can arise during this process. Fortunately, this last option is relatively rarely used, and that allows this process to be used successfully by most teams.

3.3.2 Build

After the programmers of the team have committed their updated files, it is time to create the new baseline by the build process. During the build, the programmers compile all files, link them together, and then create and test the new version. If everything goes smoothly, the build creates a new baseline that will be used from then on.

For large systems, the build can take a long time and may require overnight work. The programmers have a deadline by which they must commit, and if they miss the deadline, the build process starts without their updates. The updates have to wait until the new deadline and the next baseline.

This process sometimes produces infamous broken builds; if a programmer, Fred, committed buggy code and the new baseline cannot be created by the build, then this situation creates an emergency because the progress of the project is now threatened. If the team identifies Fred's commit early in the build process as a culprit, it may reject Fred's commit and restart the build. However, in the worst case, the whole build process has to be abandoned and the team has to return to the old baseline because the new baseline was not created or is unusable. For large teams and projects, this can be a considerable expense. Needless to say, breaking a build does not enhance Fred's reputation within the team or with the management.

If a project does such builds rarely, there is a larger accumulation of work to be processed by the build, and that makes the expense of a broken build larger. Moreover, it increases the risk that something will go wrong and result in a broken build. Because of this, some authors advocate frequent builds, even several times a day.

Even when a build is successful, it still may represent a step in the wrong direction, where the software before the changes was better than the software after. In this situation, the repository allows retrieving older baselines and restarting the project from one of them. Hence, the repository provides the option of a large project "undo" where it is possible to roll back to some earlier baseline.

Summary

Software technologies are accidental properties of the software projects. Very often, the projects can choose from several competing technologies. Programming languages, their compilers, and libraries are one class of such technologies, and they support the coding on the project. Object-oriented technology presently occupies a central stage among software technologies. It gives programmers effective tools to express their intent, and many current programming languages use object orientation as a conceptual foundation. It deals with software objects that simulate objects of the real world. It also deals with classes and relationships among the classes that include part-of and is-a relationships. Polymorphism is a special feature of object orientation that allows substituting a derived type for the base type in situations where this action is appropriate.

Version control system tools are another class of technologies that support collaboration on the project. They support a central repository of project files and commits of updated files by the programmers. Version control system tools also support resolution of the conflicts created when two programmers update the same file in contradictory ways.

Further Reading and Topics

The software projects of today use a wide range of diverse technologies, and this brief survey addresses only a very few of them. Interested readers can find more about programming languages in the work of Sebesta (2009) and about compilers in a work by Wilhelm and Maurer (1995). Numerous books deal with object-oriented technology. The part-of relation that we used in this chapter is a special case of a more general has-a relation that is discussed, for example, by Booch et al. (2007). A more sophisticated use of class relationships than the ones presented in this chapter is explored in *Design Patterns* by Gamma, Helm, Johnson, and Vlissides (1995).

One popular approach divides programs into *tiers*, where each tier plays a different specialized role. Three tiers in particular stand out, and the corresponding program organization is called *three-tier architecture*. A *presentation tier* implements the communication of the program with the environment. In interactive programs, the user interacts with the program through the presentation tier, which is called a *graphical user interface*, or GUI. The next tier is the *algorithmic* or *business logic* tier, where the program does all its computations. Finally, there is the *data tier* that stores all relevant data. For example, in a point-of-sale program, the GUI supports the menus that the cashier or store manager can use to select the particular program features, the algorithmic tier supports calculations of sales tax and other similar algorithms, and the data tier keeps the inventory, cashier records, and so forth.

Programmers often use different technology for each of the three tiers. The mainstream programming languages like C++ or Java support the algorithmic tier. GUI technologies support the creation of the presentation tier (Dix, Finlay, Abowd, & Beale, 2004; Shneiderman, Plaisant, Cohen, & Jacobs, 2009). Databases also have a selection of available technologies (Teorey, Lightstone, Nadeau, & Jagadish, 2005). For historical reasons, these technologies are considered separate academic disciplines, covered in separate textbooks and taught in separate courses. However, all tiers are parts of the same software projects, and the programmers have to be fluent with the technologies for all tiers.

Version control system systems are described by Tichy (1995) and by Pilato, Collins-Sussman, and Fitzpatrick (2008).

The Hype Cycle

Innovators are the first people to adopt a brand-new technology, sometimes at a considerable risk. Some observers noticed a fickle behavior of the innovators and described it by the so-called hype cycle (Fenn and Linden 2005).

The hype cycle starts with a *technology trigger* when a new technology appears on the scene. The technology trigger is often accompanied by hyped up publicity in mass media that extols the advantages of the new technology and glosses over the drawbacks and unfinished issues. Some naïve innovators buy into these excessive expectations, and the popularity of the technology soars until it reaches a *peak of inflated expectations*. However, at this point, many innovators realize that the path to maturity of the technology is much more arduous than originally expected, and they become disillusioned and abandon the technology. The popularity of the technology sinks to what is called a *trough of disillusionment*. Only the hardiest of the innovators are willing to stick with the technology through this time. However, if the technology has a true potential and is more than empty hype, it starts a steady growth from this point and ultimately delivers on its promise.

As noted by Fenn and Linden (2005), the peak of inflated expectations in 2005 was occupied by Intelligent Agents, while the trough of disillusionment was occupied by Handwriting Recognition. Object-oriented technology was beyond these ups and downs and occupied a spot with the steady growth in popularity.

New technologies continually appear in software engineering, but the introduction of new technologies into practice is a protracted process (Rogers, 1995; Pfleeger & Menezes, 2000). At the very beginning, the technology is unproven, and very few people can use it effectively; the *innovators* are the first group of users who are willing to assume the risks and use an unproven technology in their projects. *Early adopters* are the next group that draws on innovators' experience. *Majority adopters* accept the new technology when its advantages are proven and well understood. *Late adopters* accept the technology when there is no longer any significant doubt about the technology's superiority. Finally, *laggards* join in when they have no other option, when not using the now well-established technology is risky and can leave them behind. An important milestone in this process is the moment when the technology reaches majority adopters. There can be a substantial time lag before a technology reaches that point; in some instances, it may take more than 10 years (Redwine Jr. & Riddle, 1985).

Exercises

3.1 In compiled languages, what are the steps programmers have to make to create an executable file?

3.2 Are program libraries used in the form of source file or object file? Why?

3.3 What is the role of version control system in software projects?

3.4 Explain what a baseline is.

3.5 How does the program version in the private workspace differ from the baseline?

3.6 Let there be two files that contain the following code:

```
foo()
    {
    j = 1;
    k = 2;
    }
```

and

```
foo()
    {
    j = 1;
    k = 3;
    }
```

What information does *diff* tool produce after reading these two files?

3.7 What does *merge* tool do?

3.8 What is the conflict between two updates of a file? How does it arise and how is it resolved?

3.9 What is the build and what is the result of a build?

3.10 Write a class that supports course grading; it contains an array where each student is identified by an integer and has a course grade. There is also a method that can change the student grade and a method that computes the grade point average for the class.

3.11 What is three-tier architecture?

3.12 How long does it typically take a technology to reach majority adopters?

3.13 What is inheritance in object-oriented technology? Give an example.

3.14 What is the difference between an object and a class in OO technology?

3.15 Describe the role of polymorphism in object-oriented technology. Give an example.

3.16 Describe the role of "information hiding" in program comprehension.

References

Booch, G., Maksimchuk, R., Engle, M., Young, B., Conallen, J., & Houston, K. (2007). *Object-oriented analysis and design with applications* (3rd ed.). Reading, MA: Addison-Wesley Professional.

Dix, A., Finlay, J., Abowd, G., & Beale, R. (2004). *Human-computer interaction*. Harlow, England: Pearson Education.

Fenn, J., & Linden, A. (2005). *Gartner's hype cycle special report for 2005*. Retrieved on June 16, 2011, from http://www.gartner.com/DisplayDocument?doc_cd=130115

Gamma, E., Helm, R., Johnson, R., & Vlissides, J. (1995). *Design patterns: Elements of reusable object-oriented software*. Reading, MA: Addison-Wesley.

Pfleeger, S.L., & Menezes, W. (2000). Technology transfer: Marketing technology to software practitioners. *IEEE Software, 17*(1), 27–33.

Pilato, C. M., Collins-Sussman, B., & Fitzpatrick, B. W. (2008). *Version control with subversion* (2nd ed.). Sebastopol, CA: O'Reilly Media.

Redwine Jr., S. T., & Riddle, W. E. (1985). Software technology maturation. In *Proceedings of International Conference on Software Engineering* (pp. 189–200). Washington, DC: IEEE Computer Society Press.

Rogers, E. M. (1995). *Diffusion of innovations* (4th ed.). New York, NY: Free Press.

Sebesta, R. W. (2009). *Concepts of programming languages* (9th ed.). Reading, MA: Addison-Wesley.

Shneiderman, B., Plaisant, C., Cohen, M., & Jacobs, S. (2009). *Designing the user interface: Strategies for effective human-computer interaction.* Reading, MA: Addison-Wesley.

Teorey, T. J., Lightstone, S. S., Nadeau, T., & Jagadish, H. V. (2005). *Database modeling and design: Logical design* (4th ed.). San Francisco, CA: Morgan Kaufman.

Tichy, W. (1995). *Configuration management.* New York, NY: John Wiley & Sons.

Wilhelm, R., & Maurer, D. (1995). *Compiler design.* Reading, MA: Addison-Wesley.

Chapter 4

Software Models

Objectives

In this chapter, you will learn about software models. Software models present a simplified view of software that concentrates on the important issues and omits the clutter that complicates our understanding; they are useful tools that help programmers to deal with software complexity. After you have read this chapter, you will know:

- The software models that are used in the context of software design, analysis, and architecture
- UML class and activity diagrams
- Class dependency graphs
- Contracts among suppliers and clients, preconditions, and postconditions

***

Software engineers create models in different *contexts*. One class of models is created up-front, before the software implementation starts. The up-front models are called *designs*, and they capture the main characteristics of the future program. They give software engineers a first glimpse of what is to be done, identify the potential risks and the hurdles of the project, and suggest how to plan the time and resources of the project.

Another class of models is *extracted models*, which are used when software already exists and software engineers need to analyze its properties. To simplify the analysis, the models ignore the details that are not needed in the given context. Different questions about the same system may require different extracted models.

Finally, there are *prescriptive models* that also correspond to the existing program and its code, and they are equivalent to a set of rules that have to be observed during the software evolution. Software engineers must guarantee that the model remains valid even after they make changes in the code. These prescriptive models define *constraints* that have to be preserved during the evolution; an example is a constraint that allows only several special classes to have access to the database. No other class may gain this access through an inadvertent update.

Models can be useful if they reflect correctly the important properties of the software, but they can also be misleading. The key to successful modeling is always to understand which details are essential and which ones are insignificant. The essential details have to be retained by the model, otherwise the model loses its validity and gives the wrong answer to the question asked by the modeler. For example, some up-front designs may miss features that are crucial for the success of the project, thereby presenting a simplistic view of the system that sweeps some significant problems under the rug, and will not help the developers. This danger is common to all modeling efforts in all technical or scientific fields, and led statistician George Box to quip, "All models are wrong, but some are useful."

4.1 UML Class Diagrams

One of the most popular modeling tools for software systems is the *Unified Modeling Language* (UML). UML is a visual modeling language that describes various aspects of the software system; the visual aspect helps in the comprehension of the models. The current version, UML 2, consists of 13 different types of diagrams that belong to two groups: structure diagrams that model the static structure of the software system and behavior diagrams that model system behavior or the behavior of software users. An example of a structure diagram is a class diagram, and an example of a behavior diagram is an activity diagram. Small subsets of these two diagrams are explained in this chapter. However, because of the huge popularity and impact of UML, it is recommended that the readers not limit their knowledge to just this subset, but instead acquire a more complete knowledge of UML beyond what is used in this book.

UML class diagrams model the classes of the system and their relations. They can be used on different levels of precision and completeness. They are so general that they can be used in the modeling of systems that use widely different technologies, ranging from object-oriented programs to relational databases. This book uses UML class diagrams as a graphical representation of object-oriented programs.

4.1.1 Class Diagram Basics

Each class is represented as a rectangle with three compartments. In the left part of Figure 4.1, only the name of the class is filled in. If more details about the class are desired, all three compartments can be filled in, as shown in the right part of Figure 4.1. The top compartment contains the class name Inventory, the middle compartment contains the *class attributes*, which are implemented in object-oriented languages as class data members. In Figure 4.1, there is one data member i of the type int. The bottom compartment contains the *operations*, which are implemented in object-oriented languages as methods. In Figure 4.1, there is one method update(). The sign "–" means that the class member is private and invisible from the outside, while the sign "+" means that the class member is public. Class Inventory of Figure 4.1 represents the following class:

```
class Inventory
      {
      public:
              void update();
              ...
      private
              int i;
              ...
      };
```

Classes relate to each other by *associations* that are graphically represented by lines. In Figure 4.2, there is an association between classes Store and Inventory. The presence of an association between two classes means that there is some relationship between them. There is also a more specific association between classes Item and Price, with *one-way navigation* symbolized by an arrow; it means that class Item has access to the public members of class Price, but not the other way around.

Some class diagrams describe the relationship between two classes more specifically. Figure 4.3 contains two classes and an association between them that is adorned by a black diamond. This represents a part-of or composite-component relationship that was discussed in section 3.2.3 and was described by the following code fragment:

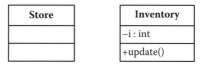

Figure 4.1   UML representations of a class.

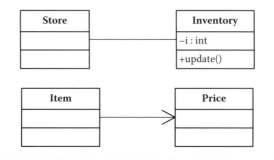

Figure 4.2 **Association**

Figure 4.3 **Part-of relationship between classes.**

```
class Store
      {
      ...
      Private:
            Inventory inv;

      ...
      };
```

Similarly, the is-a relationship (or inheritance) that was discussed in section 3.2.4 is denoted by an empty triangle that points from the more specific to the more general class, as depicted in Figure 4.4. The corresponding code fragment is

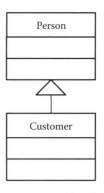

Figure 4.4 **Is-a relationship between classes.**

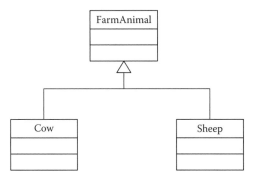

Figure 4.5 Is-a relationship of multiple classes.

```
class Customer: public Person
        {
        . . .
        };
```

UML class diagrams do not make a distinction between an is-a relationship with or without polymorphism. Figure 4.5 contains an example that can be described by the following code from chapter 3:

```
class FarmAnimal
        {
        . . .
        };
class Cow : public FarmAnimal
        {
        . . .
        };
class Sheep : public FarmAnimal
        {
        . . .
        };
```

UML class diagrams may have a number of additional properties, but this subset is sufficient for the models that are used in this book. An example of a class diagram of a small application is in Figure 4.6. It omits class attributes and methods and represents only classes of the program and their is-a and part-of associations.

Figure 4.7 presents an even more abstract UML class model of the same program that omits composite-component adornments, and the inheritance is the only adornment that the figure retains. The reader must guess that the associations in Figure 4.7 are in reality part-of and that the composite-component associations are mostly top down or from the center out, but there can be exceptions. This

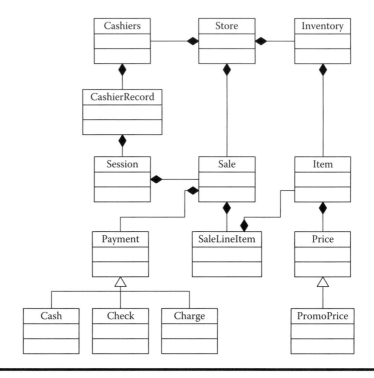

Figure 4.6 UML class diagram of point-of-sale application.

figure illustrates a general rule that UML class diagrams are allowed to miss some information: Such a diagram is not incorrect; it is only more abstract. However, for many tasks, the missing information is of crucial importance, and the practice of ignoring the composite-component adornments is not recommended.

UML class diagrams have an advantage in that both programmers and the users easily understand them, and they can serve as a means of communication between these two stakeholder groups. They are widely used and serve as a default modeling tool whenever there is a need to capture the static relations among the modules of the software.

4.2 UML Activity Diagrams

Activity diagrams are another widely used type of UML diagrams. Activity diagrams model dynamic aspects of programs; they model the *activities* and decompose them into smaller units called *actions*. The activities describe the work of computers, human users, human-computer combinations, controlled systems, and so forth.

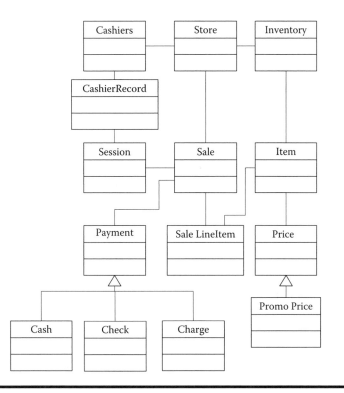

Figure 4.7   UML class diagram of point-of-sale application with missing composite-component adornments.

Activity diagrams contain several different types of nodes. Among them, *action nodes* represent atomic units of work. Actions follow each other in a certain order, and that order is defined by *control flow*. The control flow starts at the *initial node*, which is denoted by a black circle, and ends at the *final node* that has the shape of a target, which is a white circle with a black concentric circle inside (see an example in Figure 4.8).

Another part of activity diagrams are *decisions*. Decisions have several output edges, and only one of them is traversed after the decision is reached and evaluated. The different branches are then merged in *merge nodes*. An example is shown in Figure 4.9.

Sometimes the actions take place in parallel. This is described by a combination of a *fork* and *join*, both represented by a fat horizontal line (see Figure 4.10). Actions that follow fork run in parallel, and join means that when all previous parallel actions have finished, the action that follows join takes place.

Activity diagrams can also contain *swim lanes*. Swim lanes are used when there are several actors present that jointly perform the activity. The actions of each actor are grouped into a single swim lane. Figure 4.11 is an example of an activity diagram with swim lanes.

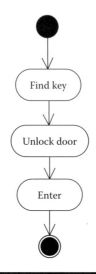

Figure 4.8 **Example of an activity diagram.**

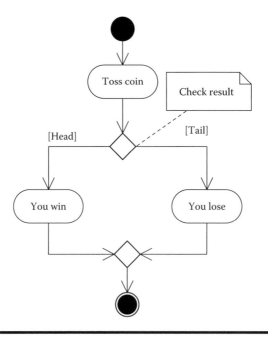

Figure 4.9 **Decision and merge nodes.**

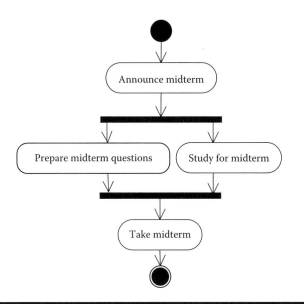

Figure 4.10 **Fork and join activities representing parallel actions.**

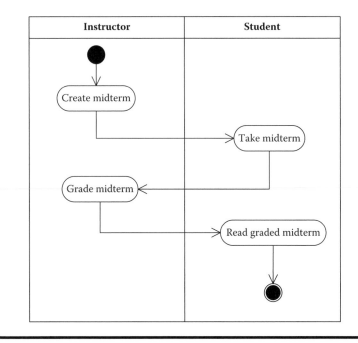

Figure 4.11 **Midterm process: example of swim lanes.**

4.3 Class Dependency Graphs and Contracts

Besides UML class diagrams, there are other class models that differ from class diagrams in seemingly small but significant details. Class dependency graphs are one such model.

An important notion in the context of software modules and especially object-oriented classes is the notion of *responsibility* (sometimes called *functionality*). Each module (class) in the program plays a certain unique role, or in other words, assumes a certain responsibility. For example, the class Item in the point-of-sale program is responsible for items sold in the store. It implements their properties and everything that may change these properties, like additions of new kinds of items to the store, selling and ordering the items, a track record of the customer complaints about the item, and so forth.

Sometimes a class cannot handle all expected responsibility, and it asks other classes, the *suppliers*, for help. For example, class Item has a supplier class Price that assumes the responsibility for price of the item, including price changes and sale prices on certain dates, and so forth. Class Item asks this supplier class Price for help whenever the issue of the price comes up. The opposite of suppliers is *clients*; for example, clients of class Item are all the classes that depend on Item for help with their responsibilities. In general, class A *depends on* class B if class B is a supplier of class A (and that means that class A is a client of class B). We call it a *dependency* between A and B and denote it by a couple, <A,B>.

A *class dependency graph* is a directed graph where nodes are all classes of the program and edges are all dependencies. Figure 4.12 contains a graphical notation for a dependency graph of the same program that is represented by a UML class diagram in Figure 4.6. The notation uses the same symbols for classes as the UML class diagram and uses broken arrows for dependencies. Examples of dependencies are the following: If there is a part-of relation between classes A and B, there is also a dependency <A,B>. If there is a nonpolymorphic inheritance of X from Y, then <X,Y> is a dependency. If there is a polymorphic inheritance between X and Y, then both <X,Y> and <Y,X> are dependencies. Additional dependencies among the classes are discussed in the literature that is listed in the "Further Reading" section.

Since both UML class diagrams and dependency graphs are similar, software engineers sometimes use the more popular UML class diagrams in the style of Figure 4.6, or an even less accurate UML class diagram in the style of Figure 4.7, in situations where class dependency graphs are more appropriate. However, in that case, they should make sure that they correctly translate the associations of Figure 4.6 or Figure 4.7 into the dependencies.

The concept of suppliers and clients extends to their respective transitive closures. The *supplier slice* is the set of all suppliers, suppliers of suppliers, and so forth. As an example, for class Item in Figure 4.12, the supplier slice is S(Item) = {Item, Price, PromoPrice, SaleLineItem} (see Figure 4.13). The *client slice* is complementary to the supplier slice, and it is the set of all clients, clients

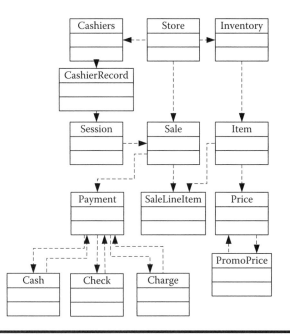

Figure 4.12   Dependency graph of point-of-sale application.

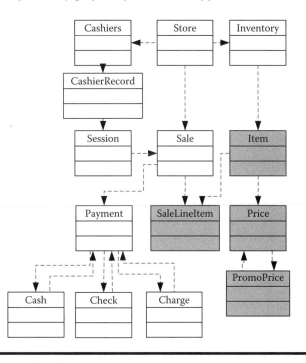

Figure 4.13   Supplier slice of class Item.

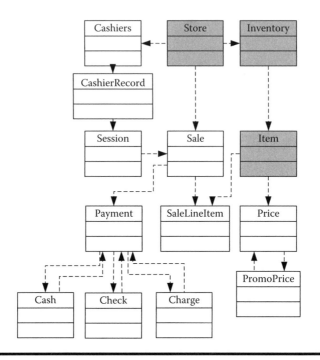

Figure 4.14 Client slice of class `Item`.

of clients, and so forth. As an example, for a program represented by the dependency graph of Figure 4.14, the client slice is C(`Item`) = {`Item`, `Inventory`, `Store`}.

For the readers who like the formal definitions, let G = (C,D) be a dependency graph, that is, a directed graph where C is the set of classes and D is a set of dependencies. For class A ∈ C, the supplier slice is S(A) = {X | X = A or there is a dependency <Y, X> ∈ D such that Y ∈ S(A)}. The client slice is C(A) = {X | X = A or there is a dependency <X,Y> ∈ D such that Y ∈ C(A)}.

Bottom classes of the program are classes that do not have any suppliers, and *top classes* are the classes that do not have any clients. The program code that a customer uses always has just one top class where the execution of the program starts. However, programmers working on a project sometimes develop a code that has several top classes, each supporting a different variant of the program; some of them are the variants that are used for testing.

A class assumes two separate responsibilities. Alone and unaided, the class assumes the *local responsibility*, while the whole supplier slice assumes the *combined responsibility*. As mentioned earlier, the class itself may be unable to implement everything that is expected from it by the clients. In that case, it delegates some of the responsibilities to the suppliers. In the example of Figure 4.13, class `Item` assumes some responsibility on its own, but it delegates some of it to classes `Price`,

PromoPrice, and SaleLineItem; the client Inventory receives all this combined responsibility without distinguishing what class Item does on its own and what it delegates to the classes of the supplier slice.

Combined responsibilities are sometimes expressed by *contracts* between a class and its clients. If clients request something, then they have to make the request within reasonable bounds; for example, they cannot request properties of items that the store does not sell. These bounds are described by the *precondition* that the clients must guarantee. If the precondition is satisfied, the class fulfills its responsibility and takes the expected action; the results of the action are described by the *postcondition*. The following are examples of contracts:

Precondition: A nonempty list of student names and grades; *postcondition*: the grade point average

Precondition: A valid checking account number, the amount A to be withdrawn, and the current balance in the account is greater than A; *postcondition*: the printed check, the new balance in the account

Precondition: A nonempty list of the festival events and their descriptions, ordered by the time of their beginning; *postcondition*: printout of the last event

Depending on the circumstances, the contracts are described with different levels of formality and precision. The highest precision is achieved when the contracts are described by formal logic or special assertion language. An informal description of the contracts is done in plain English, as in the previous examples. A common, although not recommended, practice is that the contracts are only tacit, not recorded anywhere, and all programmers who deal with the class must rediscover them on their own; this situation may lead to misunderstandings and errors.

Ariane 5 Disaster

Ariane is a series of rockets that were developed as a part of the European space program. On June 4, 1996, Ariane 5 crashed shortly after launch, causing a loss of approximately a half billion dollars. Because of the large loss, a special international board conducted an inquiry into the causes of the disaster.

The board found that the cause of the disaster was a software error in a subsystem called the Inertial Reference System (IRS). The IRS is a supplier to the rest of the software control system and deals with "horizontal bias." The precondition for the correct functioning of the IRS was that the value of the horizontal bias must fit within a 16-bit integer. The IRS was used in the earlier versions of Ariane without any problems.

However, the clients of IRS in the control software in Ariane 5 violated this precondition and sent IRS a value that was larger than what can fit into a 16-bit integer. The IRS could not handle this large value and malfunctioned. This malfunction crashed the whole Ariane 5 control software and caused the half billion dollar loss.

The experience of Ariane teaches the lesson about the contracts between software suppliers and clients. These contracts are an important ingredient of the correct functioning of the software, and their violations can be expensive. The programmers have to understand them well to avoid bugs similar to the one that doomed Ariane 5 (Jézéquel & Meyer, 1997).

Summary

Software models help to deal with software complexity; the models omit details and are simpler than the software they reflect. Programmers use the models in several contexts: Models serve as designs that precede and guide software coding, or programmers extract models from the already existing software to better understand important properties, or they use them as a prescriptive set of rules that have to be followed during software evolution. The most popular models are based on the Unified Modeling Language (UML), which models either static structure (for example, with class diagrams) or dynamic properties (for example, with activity diagrams). Software evolution uses dependency diagrams that reflect delegation of responsibilities among the classes. The contracts are a description of these delegations of responsibilities and they consist of preconditions and postconditions; they can be either formal or informal.

Further Reading and Topics

The role of models in software engineering is discussed by Seidewitz (2003). Besides the models described in this chapter, there are several other models used in this book, and they are introduced in the context of the problem that they address.

UML is an extensive modeling language, and besides class and activity diagrams, it has numerous additional diagrams. Moreover, both class diagrams and activity diagrams have additional features beyond the ones covered in this chapter. Classes also can be represented by a simple rectangle with just the name of the class in it. An interested reader can find more about UML in the works of Rumbaugh, Jacobson, and Booch (1999), and Arlow and Neustadt (2005), and many other publications. When reading this additional literature, please note that the term *dependency* in UML class diagrams has a different meaning than the meaning that is presented in section 3.3 in relation to class dependency graphs.

Class dependency graphs are extracted from the code through program analysis that is either static or dynamic (Binkley, 2007; Ernst, 2003; Gallagher & Lyle, 1991). The static analysis explores the source code, while dynamic analysis deals with the execution traces of the programs. Program analysis is a large field that presents numerous analysis algorithms that result in a wide variety of models. Some of these models are suitable for software evolution, while others are more suitable for compiler construction. An example of a model that is closely related to a class dependency graph is an object relation diagram (Milanova, Rountev, & Ryder, 2002). A different kind of model that is also used in software evolution is the class interaction graph, which is explained in chapter 7.

Software modeling is done on a certain *granularity*. This book deals mostly with the granularity of classes, where a class is the smallest unit of the code that the model deals with. However, in some tasks, a finer granularity than the class level is necessary. In that case, a finer granularity level of class members or program language statements has to be considered (Petrenko & Rajlich, 2009).

Contracts and responsibilities are covered in detail by Meyer (1988) in conjunction with an object-oriented programming language, Eiffel, that has special language constructs for the description and enforcement of the contracts. Preconditions and postconditions are special cases of *invariants*, which are statements related to certain points in the code, and they should always be true when computation reaches that point (Floyd, 1967). Dynamically generated invariants are described by Ernst, Cockrell, Griswold, and Notkin (2001).

Prescriptive software models are often a part of software architectures, and there is a sizeable amount of literature that deals with architectures (Shaw & Garlan, 1996; Bass, Clements, & Kazman, 2003; Perry & Wolf, 1992). Some architectures consist of *tiers*, where each tier plays a specialized role. As mentioned in chapter 3, many applications have three tiers: The presentation tier supports interaction with the user; the logic tier does all calculations that the application requires; and the data tier stores data (Ramirez, 2000).

Model driven architecture (MDA) relies on the fact that software models consist of a subset of the source code information. That offers an opportunity to reorganize the source code in such a way that the software model will be one explicit part of it, and the remaining information will be the other part (Kleppe, Warmer, & Bast, 2003).

Exercises

4.1 Draw a class diagram of a small banking system showing the associations between three classes: the bank, customer, and the account.

4.2 Draw a class diagram of a library lending books using the following classes: Librarian, Lending Session, Overdue Fine, Book Inventory, Book, Library, Checkout System, and Library Card.

4.3 Draw an activity diagram of pumping gas and paying by credit card at the pump. Include at least five activities, such as "Select fuel grade" and at least two decisions, such as "Get receipt?"

4.4 Draw a class dependency graph of a software for a library lending books.

4.5 Explain how a class dependency graph differs from a UML class diagram.

4.6 Suppose that you have two classes: class A that is responsible for reading an address provided by a user, and its supplier class B that verifies whether a user-provided ZIP code is located within the user-provided state. Write the contract between classes A and B in plain English.

4.7 For a program represented by the class dependency graph of Figure 4.12, write a contract between classes Sale and Payment in plain English.

4.8 Why does each contract have to specify preconditions?

4.9 Explain the meaning of the activity diagram in Figure 4.15.

4.10 In the class dependency graph of Figure 4.16, define both supplier slices and client slices of classes B, C, D.

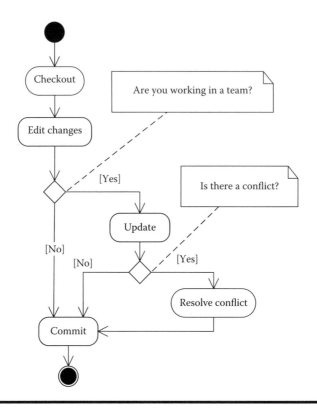

Figure 4.15   An activity diagram.

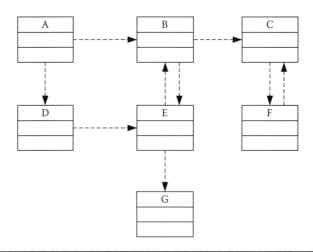

Figure 4.16   A class dependency graph.

References

Arlow, J., & Neustadt, I. (2005). *UML 2 and the unified process*. Upper Saddle River, NJ: Addison-Wesley.

Bass, L., Clements, P., & Kazman, R. (2003). *Software architecture in practice*. Upper Saddle River, NJ: Addison-Wesley.

Binkley, D. (2007). Source code analysis: A road map. In *Proceedings of Future of Software Engineering Conference* (pp. 104–119). Washington, DC: IEEE Computer Society Press.

Ernst, M. D. (2003). Static and dynamic analysis: Synergy and duality. In *WODA 2003: ICSE Workshop on Dynamic Analysis* (pp. 24–27). Retrieved June 16, 2011, from http://www.cs.washington.edu/homes/mernst/pubs/staticdynamic-woda2003.pdf

Ernst, M. D., Cockrell, J., Griswold, W. G., & Notkin, D. (2001). Dynamically discovering likely program invariants to support program evolution. *IEEE Transactions on Software Engineering, 27*(2), 99–123.

Floyd, R. W. (1967). Assigning meanings to programs. In *Proceedings of Symposium on Applied Mathematics: Mathematical Aspects of Computer Science* (pp. 19–32). Retrieved on June 16, 2011, from http://www.cs.virginia.edu/~weimer/2007-615/reading/FloydMeaning.pdf

Gallagher, K. B., & Lyle, J. R. (1991). Using program slicing in software maintenance. In *IEEE Transactions on Software Engineering* (pp. 751–761). Washington, DC: IEEE Computer Society Press.

Jézéquel, J. M., & Meyer, B. (1997). Design by contract: The lessons of Ariane. *IEEE Computer, 30*, 129–130.

Kleppe, A. G., Warmer, J., & Bast, W. (2003). *MDA explained: The model driven architecture: Practice and promise*. Boston, MA: Addison-Wesley Longman.

Meyer, B. (1988). *Object-oriented software construction*. Upper Saddle River, NJ: Prentice Hall.

Milanova, A., Rountev, A., & Ryder, B. (2002). Constructing precise object relation diagrams. In *Proceedings of International Conference on Software Maintenance* (pp. 586–595). Washington, DC: IEEE Computer Society Press.

Perry, D. E., & Wolf, A. L. (1992). Foundations for the study of software architecture. *ACM SIGSOFT Software Engineering Notes, 17*(4), 40–52.

Petrenko, M., & Rajlich, V. (2009). Variable granularity for improving precision of impact analysis. In *Proceedings of International Conference on Program Comprehension* (pp. 10–19). Washington, DC: IEEE Computer Society Press.

Ramirez, A. O. (2000). Three-tier architecture. *Linux Journal, 75*. Retrieved on June 16, 2011, from http://www.linuxjournal.com/article/3508

Rumbaugh, J., Jacobson, R., & Booch, G. (1999). *The unified modelling language reference manual*. Essex, U.K.: Addison-Wesley Longman.

Seidewitz, E. (2003). What models mean. *IEEE Software, 20*(5), 26–32.

Shaw, M., & Garlan, D. (1996). *Software architecture: Perspectives on an emerging discipline*. Upper Saddle River, NJ: Prentice Hall.

SOFTWARE CHANGE

II

Contents

This part of the book deals with software change, which is a foundation of most of the software engineering processes. The book first explains the classification of changes, followed by the explanation of the requirements, their analysis, and the product backlog. Software change consists of several phases, and the first one is the selection of a specific change request from the product backlog. This is followed by the phase of concept location, where the programmers find what specific software module needs to be changed. Then impact analysis decides on the strategy and extent of the change. Actualization implements the new functionality and incorporates it into the old code. Refactoring reorganizes software so that the change is easier (prefactoring) or cleans up the mess that the change may have created (postfactoring). Verification validates the correctness of the change. Change conclusion creates a new baseline, prepares software for the next change, and possibly releases the latest version to the users. This part of the book establishes a foundation on which the next part, software processes, builds.

Chapter 5

Introduction to Software Change

Objectives

A change in existing software is an important software engineering process. After you have read this chapter, you will know:

- The characteristics of software change
- The phases of a typical software change
- The product backlog
- The requirements analysis and prioritization
- The change initiation

***

Software changes are by far the most common software engineering tasks. The key stages of software life span, software evolution, and servicing consist of repeated software changes. There is a wide variety of software changes, and their characteristics and phases are explained in this chapter.

5.1 Characteristics of Software Change

Software changes differ from each other by their purpose, their impact on software functionality, their impact on the code, their strategy, the form of the modified code, and so forth.

5.1.1 Purpose

Software changes are characterized by their *purpose* and, from this point of view, *perfective changes* are the most common. They introduce new functionality and increase the value of software. An example is the introduction of a credit card payment to the point-of-sale system that had only cash payment before; such a change extends the functionality of the program and increases its value.

The surveys found that perfective changes constitute approximately two-thirds of all software changes. The large share of perfective changes is not surprising, because they are the response to volatility of the requirements. This volatility drives software evolution and, as a result, most of the evolution changes are perfective. Note that products other than software rarely experience perfective changes and, once delivered to the users, their functionality usually remains stable. It is very rare to do perfective changes on cars, appliances, shoes, or similar products.

Another category of changes are *adaptive changes* that adapt software to new circumstances within which the software operates. An example of such circumstances is a new version of the operating system or a new compiler used in the project, and so forth. The Y2K change that is discussed in the sidebar is an example of an adaptive change. The purpose of adaptive changes is to protect the existing value of the program. If nothing was done in the changed circumstances, the value would greatly decrease or completely disappear.

Y2K Software Change

Perhaps the most famous software change in history was the so-called Y2K change. Y2K is an abbreviation of the "Year 2000," and it became a commonly known acronym. The Y2K change was caused by the fact that programmers in the last century represented years by the last two digits; for example, the year 1997 was represented by "97." The computer assumed that the two digits representing the year are always preceded by an additional two digits: "19."

There was a reason why programmers made this choice. During the early years of software, computer memory was very expensive, and using the extra two digits for a year seemed like a waste of this expensive resource. Later, when memory became more affordable and there was no longer an economic imperative behind this choice, the programmers continued with this practice partially out of inertia and partially out of the belief that the life span of software would be short. They did not believe that their software would still be used in the year 2000.

The two-digit year representation worked fine through most of the 1900s, but as January 1, 2000, was approaching, many people realized that the software systems would interpret the date represented by the combination "01, 01, 00" as January 1, 1900, instead of January 1, 2000, resulting in some potentially serious complications. As the fateful date approached, many speculators in mass media wondered what was going to happen if software malfunctioned on a massive scale. There were even suggestions that civilization might collapse because of the possible malfunctions of finance, trading, transportation, electrical grids, and other essential components of the economy that are supported by software. Because of this widespread fear, the effort to fix the Y2K bug was coordinated at the highest levels by the President's Council on Year 2000 and through the International Y2K Cooperation Center (IY2KCC).

Note that the required change belonged to the category of adaptive changes. There was no need for any new functionality; there was only a need to extend the current software functionality beyond January 1, 2000. Also note that, in isolation, to change the year representation from two digits to four digits is a relatively minor exercise; the hardest part of this exercise is to look up the additional quirks of the Gregorian calendar that are not covered by the two-digit representation. This change, when handled in isolation, is presented as Exercise 5.11 of this chapter, and it is not harder than other exercises in this book. Then why did Y2K turn into such a gigantic task?

The answer is that the date has been handled in the old software in various obscure places and contexts. The code supporting the dates was interleaved with code that was doing something else, and when the code was changed it had to be revalidated to make sure that no bugs were introduced. In the context of the old code, this relatively simple exercise became a formidable task. This is often the case with software changes where functionally simple tasks are made complex by the context of the old code. Therefore, we have to study various phases of software change like concept location, impact analysis, and so forth.

In the end, the Y2K change was done on time; there was no collapse of civilization, but the cost was considerable. It was estimated that worldwide, 45% of all software applications were modified, and 20% were completely replaced, at a total cost ranging somewhere between $375 and $750 billion (Kappelman, 2000).

There are also *corrective changes* that correct software bugs and malfunctions. These bugs and malfunctions are deviations from the intended functionality and impact the users in often unexpected ways. An example from a point-of-sale system may be that, under a certain configuration of sold merchandise, the total on the receipt is incorrect.

Another category of changes are *protective changes* that are invisible to the user, and they shield the software and its value in a proactive way. Examples of such changes are changes that improve the structure of software to make the future changes easier, and hence, they represent an investment that will pay off over time. Other changes in this category are transfers to a new technology that promises a longer life span of the software, or proactive improvements in the security of software.

Note that the purposes of a change are not mutually exclusive, and there are no sharp boundaries. Some changes can be categorized in different ways; for example, what some programmers may consider to be a bug, other programmers may consider an adaptation, and so forth.

5.1.2 Impact on Functionality

From the point of view of functionality, *incremental changes* add new functionality to software. An example of incremental change in a point-of-sale system is adding support for credit card payments, which was missing in the previous versions. Incremental changes increase the business value of software because they provide a new functionality that was not available before.

The opposite of incremental changes are *contraction changes* or *code pruning*, where some obsolete functionality is removed from software. However, very often, programmers are reluctant to remove this obsolete functionality, arguing that this removal may inadvertently damage some useful parts of the code. To guarantee that code pruning does not introduce bugs requires substantial work and thorough verification of the software afterwards.

The programmers often argue that this obsolete functionality should stay in the code because its removal does not increase business value, while requiring substantial extra work. However, unwanted obsolete functionality left in the code clutters the code and makes the code unnecessarily large and complex. The programmers must remember that there are parts that are no longer active, and they must treat these parts with caution; these parts can become a source of problems if somebody inadvertently activates them. Thus, a bloated code can become a long-term problem and should be pruned from time to time.

There are *replacement changes* that replace an existing functionality with another one. This is very common in debugging, where an unwanted functionality, a bug, must be replaced by a correct one. In reality, very often, incremental change is also a replacement change, where a sophisticated functionality replaces an old primitive one.

Refactoring is a type of change that substitutes the obsolete structure of the program by a better one, without changing program behavior. Refactoring does not increase the business value of software, and there may be a reluctance to invest too much effort into it; nonetheless, it is essential for the long-term health of the code.

Although incremental changes may be the main goal of software evolution, refactoring plays an important supporting role that keeps the system in shape for future incremental changes. Incremental changes often contain refactoring phases that prepare the code for the specific change in the functionality, or clean up the residual problems in the code after the change.

5.1.3 Impact of the Change

The smallest changes are *localized;* they impact only one module of the code or a handful of closely related modules. These changes are relatively easy to implement, and the consequences of such changes are likely to be predictable.

Advanced software technologies support logical structuring of software that limits the consequences of the changes. For example, object-oriented technologies allow programmers to construct software from objects that correspond to the objects of the domain. Hence, when a change is related to just one domain object, chances are that the corresponding change will also affect just one software object or a small group of closely related objects.

Unfortunately, not all changes are localized. There are *massively delocalized changes* that, when undertaken, mean a review and update of a substantial part of the code. Changes in technologies, operating systems, user interfaces, and other delocalized software properties belong to this category. These changes are expensive and risky because every single code file that is changed can introduce bugs into the software; therefore, there is a potential that these changes will create large problems. These changes must be undertaken with caution. Fortunately, these massive changes are relatively rare.

In the middle of the scale, there are changes that affect a medium but significant number of classes. Typically, these changes introduce a new and substantial functionality into software. Although they are rarer than small changes, medium changes still are frequent enough that every software engineer should know how to deal with them. This knowledge is an important part of a software engineer's skills. There may be several viable strategies to implement these changes, and the programmers should be able to identify the appropriate strategies, identify their impact, and select the most appropriate ones.

Software changes impact not only the code, but other artifacts as well; for example, they impact software models, manuals, documentation, and so forth. If the documentation or software models are to remain valid and useful, they have to be updated whenever changes in the code are made.

5.1.4 Strategy

Software change can be done as an emergency quick fix or as a long-term investment in software quality. In the former case, it is sometimes possible to find various shortcuts, but software may carry the scars of these hasty actions. The only acceptable circumstance for a quick fix during the evolution stage is in the situation of an emergency, where human life or a substantial value is at stake; thus, the fix has to be done quickly, and the speed outweighs every other consideration.

The quick fix is a common strategy of change during the servicing stage; the software value at that point is low; there are no plans for future evolution; and the fixes just keep it afloat. In this situation, there is no reason for any gold plating, and the change is done as cheaply as possible. The patchwork left in the wake of quick fixes does not matter because the value of the software is low anyway, and any additional lowering of the software value is inconsequential.

These exceptional circumstances have one common characteristic: The long-term cost of the resulting patchwork is lower than the benefit of the fast change. In all other circumstances, software change should be done with the highest professional workmanship. The change should be well designed, executed well, and add value to software in all respects. Everything that the change touches should end up upgraded rather than degraded, whether it is the quality of the code at the center of the change, quality of the distant code that was touched by the change, software documentation, and so forth.

5.1.5 Forms of the Changing Code

Changes in the source code are much easier than changes in the executable code; therefore, an overwhelming number of changes are done in the source code. The programmers use code editors to make these changes and then recompile the code. This is how software engineers work most of the time.

Changes in other code forms, for example, in executable code or bytecode, are done only under unusual circumstances. They happen mostly when source code is not accessible and executable code is the only available form. Occasionally they also are made in emergencies when the compilation is too long and programmers do not have the time to wait, or when the compiler produces unacceptable code.

When software engineers do these changes, they are giving up all human-oriented aspects of the source code like meaningful names, comments, and so forth, and are dealing only with binaries, and that makes the changes much harder. These changes also lead to differences between source and executable code, and the source code is no longer the basic document that reflects the system behavior. Therefore, the value of the source code is substantially diminished, and any subsequent changes also may have to be done on the executable code. Because of all these problems, this kind of change should be done only in very exceptional circumstances.

5.2 Phases of Software Change

There are a wide variety of software changes, and the software change process resembles a kit with building blocks; each specific change is assembled from these blocks. The building blocks are called *phases*, and a specific software change consists of some combination of these phases. Figure 5.1 describes the phases of a typical midsized software change. The next chapters of the book describe these phases in more detail.

Software change starts with *initiation*, where the programmers decide to implement the change in the software. The next phase is *concept location* that finds in the software the code snippet that must be changed or the module that must be updated. This module is the place where the new functionality or the bug correction will reside. Concept location may be a small task in small programs, but it can be a very difficult task in very large programs.

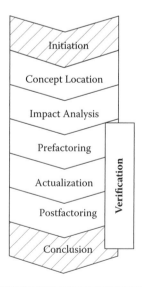

Figure 5.1   Phases of a mid-sized software change.

Very often, software change is not localized in a single program module, but it affects other parts of the software. *Impact analysis* is a phase that determines all these other parts. It starts where concept location stopped, that is, it starts with the modules identified by concept location as the places where the change should be made. Then, it looks at the related modules and decides to what degree they are also affected. Impact analysis together with concept location constitute the design of software change, where the strategy and extent of the change is determined, and precede the phases where the code is actually modified.

The real code modifications consist of phases of prefactoring, actualization, postfactoring, and verification. These phases are the core of software change. *Actualization* is the phase that implements the new functionality. The new functionality is implemented either directly in the old code, or it is implemented and tested separately and then integrated with the old code. In either case, the change can have repercussions in other parts of software. Change propagation identifies these other parts, making the secondary modifications. Methodologically, change propagation is similar to impact analysis because the same process of identifying the other affected parts is made; only this time, the actual code modifications are implemented.

Refactoring, as mentioned previously, changes the structure of software without changing the functionality. During the typical software change, refactoring can be done as two different phases: before the actualization and after. When it is done before the actualization, it is called *prefactoring*. Prefactoring prepares the old code for the actualization and gives it a structure that will make the actualization easier. For example, it gathers all the bits and pieces of the functionality that is going to change and makes the actualization localized, so that it affects fewer software modules. This makes the actualization simpler and easier. The other refactoring phase is called *postfactoring*, and it is a cleanup after the actualization; the actualization can make a mess, and postfactoring cleans it up.

Verification is the phase that aims to guarantee the quality of the work, and it interleaves with the phases of prefactoring, actualization, postfactoring, and conclusion. Although no amount of verification can give a 100% guarantee of software correctness, numerous bugs and problems can be identified and removed through the systematic verification. The verification uses various strategies and techniques.

Conclusion is the last phase of software change. After the new source code is completed and verified, the programmers commit it into the version control system repository. This can be an opportunity to create the new baseline, update the documentation, prepare a new release, and so forth.

If there is a team that works on a software project and the change is done by a programmer within that team, then both the change initiation and conclusion are team activities, and they may differ, depending on the team process. Because they involve an interaction of the whole team, they are highlighted in Figure 5.1. We will revisit them when the software processes are discussed. The remaining phases are usually done by an individual programmer.

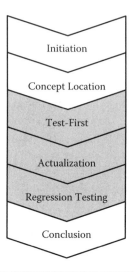

Figure 5.2 Process of localized software change with test-driven development strategy.

A variant of the software change process is depicted in Figure 5.2. The phases of initiation, concept location, and change conclusion are the same as in the process of Figure 5.1. However, the middle phases of the software change process are specialized variants, and these are shaded in Figure 5.2.

In this process, the verification is divided into two parts: one that precedes the actualization and one that follows it. The tests for the future code are written first, and they are based on the contract with the new code. During the actualization, the new code is written and immediately tested, and the actualization is complete when the newly written code passes the tests. After that, regression testing guarantees that those parts of the code that were not touched by the change still work.

The rest of this chapter deals with change requirements in general and change initiation in particular.

5.3 Requirements and Their Elicitation

The *requirements* describe the desired software functionality. They request a perfective change in existing software; or they propose an adaptation of software to new circumstances; or they propose a protective change. These requirements typically take the form of a sentence or a paragraph, written in plain English. An example of such a requirement is: "Implement a price variation of an item in a store. There can be a price increase or decrease on a specific date."

In other situations, they report a bug in the software. An example of such a bug report is, "An error appears when attempting to get credit card authorization." The bug report usually describes the symptoms of the bug, a sample of the input and output data that demonstrates the bug, the software configuration within which the bug is demonstrated, and so forth. This description will help the programmers to reproduce the bug and decide how to fix it.

Requirements originate from the users, who may desire a new functionality or an improvement in the current functionality, or they can originate from the programmers who thought of an improvement or found a bug, or managers who want to meet a competitor's new functionality, and so forth.

Larger requirements are sometimes called *user stories*. A user story describes new functionality from the point of view of the prospective users. Because a user story is the communication between users and programmers, it must be easy to understand and simple. To limit the complexity of the story and potential for misunderstanding, it is frequently required that the user story fit into a previously specified space, for example, a 3-in. × 5-in. card. If a new functionality cannot be described in such a small place, it has to be divided into several user stories. User stories written on the cards constitute a deck that can be reshuffled; new stories can be added or deleted, and old user stories can be rewritten when additional knowledge is acquired by the users, or when additional clarification is needed by the programmers.

There is rarely only one change requirement present; usually there is a whole set of requirements that programmers have to manage. The set of requirements is stored in a *product backlog*. The product backlog is also called a *requirements database*, and in other contexts it is called a *project wish list* because it lists desired future product properties and functions.

The product backlog describes a shared vision of the project stakeholders for the future of the product. Figure 5.3 depicts the product backlog that corresponds to the desired future code. The code, the product backlog, the software models that programmers may use, and the documentation that is discussed in chapter 11 belong to the category of software *work products*, and as the project progresses, programmers repeatedly update all these work products.

The product backlog is created and incremented in a process of *requirements elicitation* that is depicted in Figure 5.4. Some of the requirements are contributed

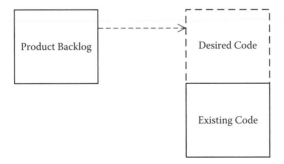

Figure 5.3   Relation of product backlog and the code.

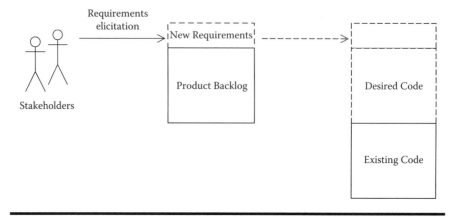

Figure 5.4   Requirements elicitation.

by the stakeholders on their own initiative. However, if that initiative fails, the programmers must go out of their way to get the requirements from the stakeholders.

Some elicitation techniques originate from other fields, and they include the use of questionnaires, interviews, surveys, and so forth. Focus groups, which are commonly used in the social sciences, are also used for requirements elicitation, and they prompt the users to express their desires for the product.

5.4 Requirements Analysis and Change Initiation

The raw requirements often require additional work, and that work is called *requirements analysis*. Resolving inconsistencies and prioritization are the important issues of requirements analysis.

5.4.1 Resolving Inconsistencies

The requirements come from different sources of variable reliability, and therefore, it is not surprising that they are often burdened by inconsistencies. The following are examples of inconsistencies:

Contradiction is the most glaring inconsistency; there may be requirements in the product backlog that directly contradict each other. An example is two different formulas for how to calculate an insurance premium, where each formula comes from a different stakeholder. The contradicting requirements have to be reconciled, possibly by a negotiation with the stakeholders until a consensus is reached, or by managerial decision.

Inadequacy is another inconsistency; some requirements can be too terse, and the programmers are left guessing what is really required. These requirements need to be expanded so that the programmers are sure what functionality is expected. The opposite is *overspecification*, where the requirements contain things that should be decided by programmers during the implementation, for example, what data structures, algorithms, or elements of the user interface should be used, and so forth. These requirements need to be pruned, and the parts that cause the overspecification need to be deleted.

Ambiguity describes requirements that can be interpreted in more than one way. These requirements need to be reconsidered and clarified. The requirements can even be *unintelligible*, and in that case, they have to be replaced by better-formulated ones.

Noise is an irrelevant requirement that is not related to the system's purpose. The stakeholders who provided this requirement may not understand the purpose of the system. These requirements are deleted from the product backlog.

Unfeasibility describes requirements that cannot be done with current technology or by the current project team, or they do not fit within the constraints of the budget. These requirements also should be dropped.

5.4.2 Prioritization

The programmers choose the requirements for their changes from the product backlog. Their selection is greatly simplified if that product backlog is sorted by priority. Both programmers and project managers cooperate in determining the priority of requirements. There are several—sometimes synergistic but sometimes conflicting—criteria to prioritize the requirements.

In the case of bug reports, the *severity* of the reported bug drives the prioritization. Very often, industrial firms develop their own standards to help the stakeholders in assigning the bug severity. For example, an industrial company in Cleveland, OH, uses four severity ranks for each bug (White, Jaber, Robinson, & Rajlich, 2008):

1. Fatal application error
2. Application is severely impaired (no workaround can be found)
3. Some functionality is impaired (but workaround can be found)
4. Minor problem not involving primary functionality

Severity rank 1 requires immediate attention and, if necessary, all ongoing work has to be stopped and the bug has to be fixed immediately. There may be some breathing space with bugs of severity rank 2, and their fix may be postponed if it would be too costly to do it immediately; but these bugs impair the application seriously, and they will rank either at the top or close to the top on the priority list. The bug ranks 3 and 4 are a subject of further analysis, where the cost of fixing the bug is compared to the inconvenience of having the bug in the project. In this analysis, the bugs compete with other requirements for the priority rankings.

Another criterion is the *business value* of the requirement. Some requirements are essential to the users, while other requirements are of only a marginal interest. Using the same scale of four priority values, the following are the four priorities from the point of view of business value:

1. An essential functionality without which the application is useless
2. An important functionality that users rely on
3. A functionality that users need but the program is useful without it
4. A minor enhancement

Another criterion is the *risk reduction*. Every project faces numerous risks that threaten its success. They range across the wide spectrum that includes technical, personal, business, or even political issues. An example of a technical issue is an untried technology that is to be used in the project, and there is no guarantee that the technology will work as intended for this particular project. An example of a personal issue is a key team member who may leave. Without that member, the project may be in jeopardy. An example of a business issue is the time to market; if the product is not out in the market before a competing product, the market may shrink and the project may be cancelled. An example of a political issue is the venture funding; if the venture capitalists do not "see something" by a certain date, they will withdraw their support. The requirements in the product can be rated from the point of view of how they resolve these risk issues. Again on a scale of 1 to 4, the following are the ratings of the risk that the requirements represent:

1. A serious threat, the so-called showstopper; if unresolved, the project is in serious trouble
2. An important threat that cannot be ignored
3. A distant threat that merits attention
4. A minor inconvenience

Another priority is the *process needs*. Some requirements must be implemented before the others; otherwise, the rework that the future changes require would be too large. For example, an application stores information in a database. The requirements that emphasize the database may have higher process priority than other requirements that define some other features. On a scale of 1 to 4, the process priority requirements are rated as follows:

1. A key requirement; if not implemented in advance, practically all code that was implemented up to that point will have to be redone
2. An important requirement that, if postponed, will lead to large rework
3. A nontrivial rework will be required if this requirement is postponed
4. A minor rework will be triggered

There are also lesser criteria that usually come into play after the highest priorities, according to the previous criteria, have been resolved. Some requirements cause *analysis problems*; for example, there can be requirements that contradict each other. Until the analysis problems are resolved, it does not make sense to prioritize these requirements, and it is better to postpone them. There are also *easy requirements* that can be implemented quickly. There is a certain cost of keeping requirements in the product backlog, reprioritizing them, and so forth. Some requirements are so simple that they can be implemented at the same or even lesser cost than keeping them in the product backlog, and they should be given a high priority.

The factors that affect prioritization often contradict each other, and it is the judgment of the project programmers and managers to decide on the final prioritization. Some projects assign specific weights to the individual factors and use formulas that compute the prioritization.

The processes of requirements analysis and prioritization can be done on the whole product backlog, and with large product backlogs it can be a formidable task. However some requirements have an obviously low priority, and their analysis can be postponed. In that situation, the analysis and prioritization are intermingled and done on an as-needed basis. The process then consists of the repetition of the following steps:

■ Estimate the highest-priority requirements
■ Analyze these requirements
■ Prioritize the analyzed requirements

5.4.3 Change Initiation

The change initiation is the selection of a specific requirement from the product backlog for implementation. This requirement is also called the *change request*. If the product backlog is analyzed and prioritized, it means to select the highest-priority requirement. Sometimes the product backlog is neither analyzed nor prioritized, and in that case all relevant analysis and prioritization must be done as a part of change initiation.

After the change initiation, the selected requirement is deleted from the product backlog and, during the subsequent change, implemented as new code, as shown in Figure 5.5. In the meantime, new requirements may come in, forwarded by the project customers or other stakeholders. Hence, the product backlog is undergoing constant alteration.

The product backlog is often supported by software tools that add/delete/modify requirements, re-sort the priority queue based on the priorities provided by the programmers, and so forth.

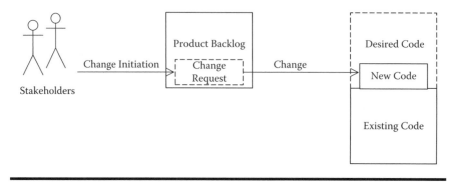

Figure 5.5 Change initiation.

Summary

Software change is the foundation of software evolution and servicing, and it is the most common task that programmers do. Software changes are classified by their purpose (perfective, adaptive, corrective, and protective), their impact on functionality (incremental, contraction, replacement, and refactoring), their impact on the code (from small to massive), their strategy (from quick fix to high workmanship), and the impacted code form (source code or compiled code).

Software changes typically consist of several phases (initiation, concept location, impact analysis, prefactoring, actualization, postfactoring, verification, and conclusion). They deal not only with the code, but also with the product backlog that consists of the requirements that have been elicited from the stakeholders and then analyzed. They are prioritized by various criteria that include severity for bugs, business value for enhancements, risk, process needs, and other criteria. A highest-priority requirement is selected as a change request, and that initiates the software change.

Further Reading and Topics

The importance of software change is confirmed by surveys that indicate that up to 80% of all software engineering work is spent in software changes (Carroll 1988). A classical survey from the 1980s introduced the classification of software changes by purpose (Lientz & Swanson 1980). A more recent taxonomy of the changes appeared in a paper by Buckley, Mens, Zenger, Rashid, and Kniesel (2004).

The remaining phases of software change are described in chapters 6 through 11, and an example is presented in chapter 17. Software changes are a part of the software processes that are described in chapters 12 through 15, and an example is presented in chapter 18. This change-process model was also published by Buchta and by Petrenko, Poshyvanyk, Rajlich, & Buchta (2007). An alternative model of software changes is presented by Yau, Nicholl, Tsai, and Liu (1988) and by Aldrich, Chambers, and Notkin (2002).

Requirements analysis and prioritization are parts of the field of requirements engineering. Numerous publications deal with that, for example, Robertson and Robertson (1999) and Van Lamsweerde (2009). Examples of highest priority bugs are presented by Neumann (1995, p. 169). The risk criterion for prioritization is discussed by Boehm (1991).

Changes are also initiated by user stories (Cohn 2006), use cases (Cockburn 2000), scenarios (Carroll 1995), and several other notations or techniques.

Exercises

5.1   How are software changes classified by their purpose? What is the most common purpose of the change?

5.2   How do software changes impact functionality of software? What is the classification from this point of view?

5.3   When is it permissible to do quick-fix changes?

5.4   Name and give the order of at least five phases of software change.

5.5   What is a product backlog?

5.6   What is prioritization of requirements in a backlog? What are the changes with the highest priority?

5.7   Explain the severity ranks of the bugs.

5.8   Consider a class `DateToDay` that contains a method `char* convert(int,int,int)`. It converts the date into day, and the precondition is that all three integers of the date are two-digit integers, representing the month, day of the month, and a year (see the enclosed code). Change the precondition of `convert` in such a way that the year is a four-digit integer, like 2010. Take into account the corresponding quirks of the Gregorian calendar.

```
class DateToDay {
public:
  char* convert(int dd,int mm,int yy){
   if (!(dd > 0 && dd <= lengthOfMonth(mm,yy) && mm >0 &&
     mm < 13))
     throw;

   int dayNumber = dd%7;
   for (int y = 0; y <yy; y++)
     dayNumber = (dayNumber + 365 + isLeapYear(y)) %7;
   for (int m = 1; m < mm; m++)
     dayNumber = (dayNumber +lengthOfMonth(m,yy)) %7;

   switch(dayNumber) {
     case 0:
       return("Sunday");
       break;
     case 1:
       return("Monday");
       break;
```

```
       case 2:
        return("Tuesday");
        break;
       case 3:
        return("Wednesday");
        break;
       case 4:
        return("Thursday");
        break;
       case 5:
        return("Friday");
        break;
       case 6:
        return ("Saturday");
        break;
       default: throw;
     }
   }

private:
  int lengthOfMonth(int mm, int yy) {
    switch(mm) {
      case 4: case 6: case 9: case 11:
        return(30);
      case 2:
        if (isLeapYear(yy) )
          return(29);
        else
          return(28);
      default:
        return(31);
    }
  }
  int isLeapYear(int yy){
    return ((yy%4 == 0) && (yy != 0));
    }
};
```

5.9 You are the manager of a business software; you distribute 3-in. × 5-in. cards to your users and encourage them to write requests for new functionality to your software. A user of your software calls one day and says, "I can't fit my user story on these small cards. I'm going to submit a 10-page user story." What should you tell this user? Why?

5.10 In the point-of-sale software, two types of payment are accepted: check and charge. Write three new user stories for three additional types of payment.

References

Aldrich, J., Chambers, C., & Notkin, D. (2002). ArchJava: Connecting software architecture to implementation. In *Proceedings of 24th International Conference on Software Engineering* (pp. 187–197). Washington, DC: IEEE Computer Society Press.

Boehm, B. W. (1991). Software risk management: Principles and practices. *IEEE Software, 8*, 32–41.

Buchta, J. (2007). *Incremental change and its application in software engineering courses.* M.S. thesis, Computer Science, Wayne State University, Detroit, MI. Retrieved June 16, 2011, from http://digitalcommons.wayne.edu/dissertations/AAI1442892/

Buckley, J., Mens, T., Zenger, M., Rashid, A., & Kniesel, G. (2004). Towards a taxonomy of software change. *Journal of Software Maintenance and Evolution: Research and Practice, 17*, 309–332.

Carroll, J. M. (1995). *Scenario-based design: Envisioning work and technology in system development.* New York, NY: John Wiley & Sons.

Carroll, P. B. (1988, January 22). Computer glitch: Patching up software occupies programmers and disables systems. *Wall Street Journal*, pp. 1, 12.

Cockburn, A. (2000). *Writing effective use cases.* Reading, MA: Addison-Wesley Longman.

Cohn, M. (2006). *Agile estimating and planning.* Upper Saddle River, NJ: Prentice Hall Pearson Education.

Kappelman, L. A. (2000). Some strategic Y2K blessings. *IEEE Software, 17*(2), 42–46.

Lientz, B. P., & Swanson, E. B. (1980). *Software maintenance management: A study of the maintenance of computer application software in 487 data processing organizations.* Reading, MA: Addison-Wesley.

Neumann, P. G. (1995). *Computer-related risks.* Reading, MA: Addison-Wesley.

Petrenko, M., Poshyvanyk, D., Rajlich, V., & Buchta, J. (2007). Teaching software evolution in open source. *Computer, 40*(11), 25–31.

Robertson, S., & Robertson, J. (1999). *Mastering the requirements process.* Upper Saddle River, NJ: Addison-Wesley.

Van Lamsweerde, A. (2009). *Requirements engineering: From system goals to UML models to software specifications.* New York, NY: Wiley.

White, L., Jaber, K., Robinson, B., & Rajlich, V. (2008). Extended firewall for regression testing: An experience report. *Journal of Software Maintenance and Evolution: Research and Practice, 20*, 419–433.

Yau, S. S., Nicholl, R. A., Tsai, J. J. P., & Liu, S. S. (1988). An integrated life-cycle model for software maintenance. *IEEE Transactions on Software Engineering, 14*, 1128–1144.

Chapter 6

Concepts and Concept Location

Objectives

When programmers decide to implement a specific software change, the first step is to find which part of the code needs to be modified. Concept location is the technique that allows one to identify the code that needs to change. After you have read this chapter, you will know:

- The concepts and their importance in software change
- The concept name, intension, and extension
- Significant concepts of a change request
- Concept location by grep and by dependency search

***

To find what to change in small and familiar programs is easy, but it can be a formidable task in large software systems, which sometimes consist of millions of lines of code. *Concept location* is the phase that finds a code snippet that the programmers will modify; it follows the change initiation (see Figure 6.1).

To explain concept location, we have to understand that in this phase, the programmers deal with two separate systems: One is the *program*, and the other is the *discourse* about the program. This discourse consists of everything that stakeholders say or write about the program, and change requests belong to this discourse. The stakeholders are programmers, users, managers, investors, and other interested

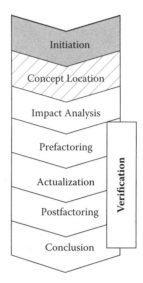

Figure 6.1 Concept location as part of software change.

parties. The bridge between these two worlds, the program on one hand and the discourse on the other hand, consists of *concepts*.

6.1 Concepts

The notion of a concept is used in linguistics, mathematics, education, philosophy, and other fields; it applies to the discourse about the software as well. Each concept has three facets, depicted symbolically by a triangle in Figure 6.2. One facet is a *name*, represented by the top vertex of the concept triangle; some concepts may have a single-word name like "payment," and other concepts have a more complex name that consists of several words, like "credit card payment." The use of concept

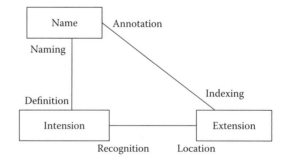

Figure 6.2 Concept triangle and directions of comprehension processes.

names allows people to communicate about the concepts of the world, of the program, or of the program domain.

The lower left vertex of the concept triangle represents the *intension* of the concept; it is the list of the concept properties and relations. For example, the intension of the concept named "dog" is, according to a Merriam-Webster dictionary, "a highly variable domestic mammal (*Canis familiaris*) closely related to the gray wolf."[1] Another name sometimes used for intension is "definition" or "account."

Spelling, Watchmaker Anecdote

The word "intension" is not misspelled; according to the Merriam-Webster dictionary:

Intension \in-'ten(t)-shən\ synonym CONNOTATION, (a) the suggesting of a meaning by a word apart from the thing it explicitly names or describes, (b) something suggested by a word or thing — W. R. Inge> an essential property or group of properties of a thing named by a term in logic.[1]

The more common word with the same pronunciation but slightly different spelling has a different, although overlapping meaning:

Intention \in-'ten(t)-shən\ synonyms INTENT, PURPOSE, DESIGN, AIM, END, OBJECT, OBJECTIVE, GOAL mean what one intends to accomplish or attain. INTENTION implies little more than what one has in mind to do or bring about <announced his intention to marry>. INTENT suggests clearer formulation or greater deliberateness <the clear intent of the statute>. PURPOSE suggests a more settled determination.[1]

Concept location is shorthand for "location of a significant concept extension in the code." The following anecdote illustrates the importance of concept location in a different setting that also deals with complexity:

A customer asks a watchmaker to fix a watch. The watchmaker opens the watch, looks at the tiny wheels and screws with magnifying glass, then takes one of the small screwdrivers, tightens one of the tiny screws, and hands back the repaired watch. The customer asks: "How much is that going to cost?" The watchmaker answers: "$20." The customer starts complaining that to tighten one small screw cannot cost that much, to which the watchmaker answers: "To tighten the screw costs $1, but to know which screw to tighten costs an additional $19!"

Many software changes are similar to the repair of the watch in this anecdote, and concept location is their most important part.

The *extensions* of a concept are things in the real world that fit the concept intension. Examples of an extension of a dog are real dogs like Fido, the pictures of dogs in family photos, Lassie from the TV series and movies, Buck in Jack London's book *Call of the Wild*, and so forth.

The relations among the vertices of the concept triangle are many-to-many. A name can mean several different intensions (homonyms), or the same intension can be named by several names (synonyms). Each intension or concept name can have several extensions, and each thing in the world may fit several intensions or several concept names.

The software code also contains the concept extensions; these extensions simulate the concepts of the domain. For example, the concept named "payment"

---

[1] With permission. From *Merriam-Webster's Collegiate® Dictionary, 11th Edition* ©2011 by Merriam-Webster, Inc. (www.merriam-webster.com).

belongs to the domain of point-of-sale; in the software system, it has an extension in the form of a statement `int paymt`. This variable `paymt` contains the amount a customer pays for the merchandise, and it is an extension of the concept "payment" the same way as a photograph of Fido is an extension of the concept "dog."

Figure 6.2 depicts not only the three facets of the concept, but also six comprehension processes. They are:

- *Location*: intension → extension
- *Recognition*: extension → intension
- *Naming*: intension → name
- *Definition* (or *account*): name → intension
- *Annotation*: extension → name
- *Indexing*: name → extension

Location is one of these six processes, and the purpose of the concept location is for a given concept intension to find the corresponding extension in the code. It is a phase of the software change; the modification of this extension will be the start of the change. Concept location is a prerequisite for the rest of the software change.

The other comprehension processes also may occasionally appear in a software engineering context. *Recognition* is the opposite of location, and it recognizes an extension in the code ("this code does credit card payment!") and finds the corresponding intension. *Naming* gives a name to an intension. The opposite process is *definition* that, for a given name, finds the corresponding intension. The relation between names and intensions is many-to-many; therefore, the naming and definition have to deal with homonyms and synonyms. Next, there is *annotation* that recognizes an extension and gives it a name. The opposite is *indexing* that for a given name finds corresponding extensions. All of these six processes are important when a programmer tries to understand the code, but concept location is the most important of them when dealing with the software change.

6.2 Concept Location Is a Search

The concept extensions in the program appear as variables, classes, methods, parts of a method body, or other code fragments. The programmers must find these code fragments. It can be easy in small programs or in the programs that the programmer knows well, or in special situations when the concept extension is obvious in the code, for example, when a concept extension is implemented as a whole class and the class has a name that corresponds to the name of the concept. However it can be hard when the program is large, the programmers are not familiar with it, or the concept extensions are implemented in an obscure way. For some software changes, it can be the hardest part of the change, a proverbial search for a "needle in a haystack."

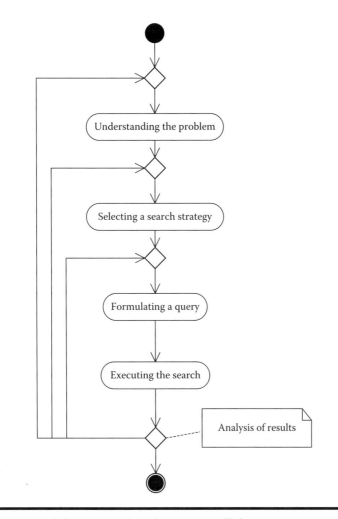

Figure 6.3 Search for concept location. From Rajlich, V. (2009). Intensions are a key to program comprehension. In Proceedings of IEEE International Conference on Program Comprehension (pp. 1–9). Washington, DC: IEEE Computer Society Press. Copyright 2009 IEEE. Reprinted with permission.

There are several concept-location techniques, and they share a common characteristic: The concept location is an interactive search process in which the search target is the code snippet that the programmers will modify in response to the change request. It is an interactive process, in which the programmers make decisions about how to conduct the search, and the tools play a supportive role. Searching for concepts in the source code is in many ways similar to searching for information on the Internet. The process of the search consists of the actions of Figure 6.3. The actions are:

- *Understanding the problem.* The programmers must understand the terminology used in the change request.
- *Selecting a search strategy.* The programmers choose the appropriate search strategy from the available assortment.
- *Formulating a query.* Each search requires a query that uses names of the concepts related to the change request.
- *Executing the search.* Programmers conduct the search with the help of supporting tools.
- *Analysis of results.* If the programmers find the concept location, the search ends successfully. However, if the search was unsuccessful, the programmers analyze the results and learn additional facts about the software system they are searching. They will use this new understanding to choose a better search strategy or to formulate a better query.

The programmers rarely find the significant concept extension with a single search; they often have to repeat the search several times.

The search starts with the concept intensions and ends with the corresponding concept extensions in the program. Figure 6.2 suggests two possible strategies of the search: Some strategies go directly from intensions to extensions, and the programmers use their understanding of concept intensions; others take a detour and identify the concept names first, and then look for these names in the code. The search space also may differ. The strategies search the static code, or external documentation, or preprocessed code, or execution traces.

The concept extensions that the programmers search for are either *explicit* or *implicit*. *Explicit concept extensions* directly appear in the code as fields, methods, code snippets, or classes. For example, the page count of a word processing document is explicitly present in the code as an integer, and the concept location is a search for this integer.

Implicit concept extensions, on the other hand, are only implied by the code, but there is no specific code snippet that implements them. Using the same word processor example, most word processors authorize any user to access any word processor file. The authorization to open files is an implicit concept extension that the source code does not explicitly implement; it is present in the code as an assumption that underlies the part of the code that is opening word processing files. To locate such implicit concept extensions, programmers must find related explicit concepts extensions that are close to these desired implicit concept extensions, or they have to find the code snippet that makes that implicit assumption. Some concept-location strategies are suitable for finding implicit concept extensions, while others are not.

6.3 Extraction of Significant Concepts (ESC)

A gateway to the search process is to formulate the query that will lead to the location of the concept. When programmers receive a change request, they analyze the change request and identify the appropriate concepts and their names. Concept names may appear in the change requests as nouns, verbs, or clauses. The change request can have many such nouns, verbs, or clauses. The programmers extract significant concepts (ESC) through the following steps:

- Extract the set of concepts used in the change request.
- Delete the *irrelevant concepts* that are intended for the communication with the programmers and do not deal with the requested functionality.
- Delete the *external concepts* that are unlikely to be implemented in the code, like concepts related to the things that are outside of the scope of the program or concepts that are to be implemented from scratch.
- Rank the remaining concepts—the *relevant concepts*—by the likelihood that they can be located in the code. The highest ranked concept is the *significant concept*.

As an example, suppose that the programmers deal with the point-of-sale system, and the change request is, "Implement a credit card payment." We can identify the following concepts: "Implement," "Credit card," "Payment."

The concept "Implement" is the communication with the programmers, unrelated to the code; therefore, it is not relevant. The concept "Credit card" is the new concept to be implemented from scratch; therefore, it is unlikely to be present in the current code. The relevant concept is the concept "Payment"; it is likely that some form of payment already exists in the old program, and this implementation is to be found in the program. It is the only relevant concept and, therefore, it is also a significant concept; its extension in the code is where the change will start. The software change will expand this extension to also include payment by credit card. The ESC process is presented in Figure 6.4.

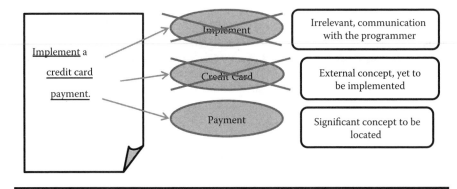

Figure 6.4 Extraction of significant concepts.

The process sometimes has to be expanded by the consideration of homonyms and synonyms. For example, the concept "Payment" can be called in the code by a synonym "Expense," "Imbursement," or various abbreviations like "Pmt" or "Paymt," and the query formulation must consider this. The "Payment" can also be a homonym for several intensions; the programmers look for the intension "Payment as an expense for goods or services" rather than "Payment as a punishment for a misdeed."

6.4 Concept Location by Grep

A popular concept location technique uses the tool "grep." It assumes that the concept extensions in the code are labeled by concept names; the concept name may be used as an identifier, or as a part of an identifier, or as a part of a code comment. The tool grep finds this concept name in the code, so in terms of Figure 6.2, the grep process follows the path intension → name → extension, and combines naming of the concept with the indexing of the name in the code.

The word "grep" is originally an acronym of the original "global/regular expression/print." The word "grep" outgrew its acronym status and programmers widely use it now both as a noun and as a verb.

Using grep, programmers formulate queries (i.e., regular expressions or "patterns"), then query the source code of a software system and investigate the results. If a line of code contains the specified pattern, it is called a "match." For example, when looking for the concept "payment," programmers may choose as a pattern to look for the original word ("payment") or various abbreviations and variants (pmt, paymt, pay_1, and so forth).

The grep tool produces a list of the code lines and the files where the specified pattern appears. There may be several matches; the programmers read the code that surrounds these matches and look for evidence of the presence of the concept extension. Based on this reading, they determine where the concept is located.

The query can fail in several different ways. One possible failure is that the set of matches is empty, and this indicates that the sought word is not used in the code. In another situation, the word is used in the code with a different meaning (as a homonym), and its occurrence does not indicate the significant concept location. In both of these cases, the programmers have to use a different query and repeat the search. In formulating such a query, they often use the new knowledge they learned while they inspected the results of the previous unsuccessful queries.

Sometimes the query produces too many matches, and it is not practical to go through all of them. In this situation, the programmers can formulate an additional query and do another search, this time searching only the set of the earlier matches. In this way, they get a set-theoretical intersection of the results of the two queries, and this resulting set of matches is smaller than the earlier large set.

The grep tool is quick and easy to use and, as such, it is very often used as the first strategy for concept location. However, a grep search often fails, and if the query does not produce a result, it may not be clear how to continue. In addition, grep often fails in a search for implicit concepts; their names usually do not appear in the code because there is no code, identifier, or comment that indicates the presence of the concept extension. In the situations where grep does not work, programmers must use other concept location techniques.

The programmers, when writing the code, can make the life of future programmers easier by selecting good identifiers and comments in the code that will lead to the concept extensions; the naming conventions can greatly enhance or hinder the grep search. Selection of the appropriate naming conventions is one of the most important early decisions of the project team.

6.5 Concept Location by Dependency Search

Dependency search is another technique of concept location. It uses local and combined responsibility of program modules to guide the search. Section 4.3 explained the local and combined responsibility, and we will revisit them briefly here.

Program modules implement concept extensions, for example, the class Pay implements concept "pay by cash" and possibly some other concept extensions. All concept extensions that the class Pay implements are part of the *local responsibility* of class Pay. When the programmers search for the concept "pay by cash," they want to find the class that is responsible for its extension.

The direction of the search is guided by *combined responsibility*. Combined responsibility is the complete responsibility that the module assumes on behalf of its clients, and it includes not only the concept extensions implemented locally by class Pay, but also all concept extensions implemented in the classes of the supplier slice. Figure 6.5 shows the concepts that are a part of the local and combined responsibility of module X. In the figure, the extension of concept A is present in both local and combined responsibility of X, while the extension of concept B is present only in the combined responsibility. Still, the module X delivers both extensions of concept A and concept B to its clients.

The top module of the program has the whole program as its supplier slice. The client of the top module is the user, and all modules of the program are supplying various responsibilities to the top module. Hence, the top module is responsible for all concepts of the whole program, and they are part of its combined responsibility. However, the top module does not implement all these concepts, but rather delegates most of them to its suppliers. These suppliers in turn delegate them further to other suppliers deeper down in the class dependency graph, and so forth.

The programmer who searches for a significant concept needs to recognize the presence of the concept extensions in both local and combined responsibility. Figure 6.6 contains the activity diagram of the concept location by dependency search.

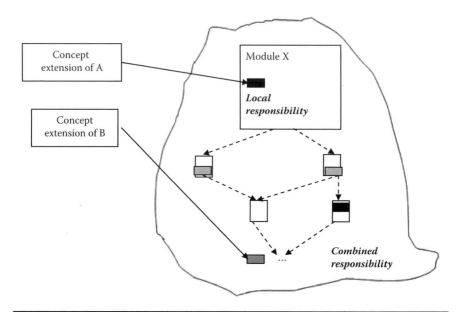

Figure 6.5 Concept extensions in the local and combined responsibility.

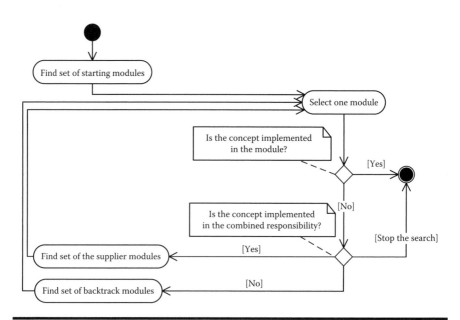

Figure 6.6 Concept location by dependency search. From Rajlich, V. (2009). Intensions are a key to program comprehension. In Proceedings of IEEE International Conference on Program Comprehension (pp. 1–9). Washington, DC: IEEE Computer Society Press. Copyright 2009 IEEE. Reprinted with permission.

The search starts with a set of possible starting modules. This could be the single top module, but in some situations, there are several top modules in the program, and the programmer selects the most relevant one.

Then the programmer decides whether the selected module implements the significant concept as its local responsibility. If this is the case, this class is the location of the concept, and the search ends successfully.

If the concept is not a part of the local responsibility, the programmer has to determine whether the concept is implemented in the combined responsibility. For that, the programmer uses various clues like the identifiers, comments, relations to other concepts, and so forth. Usually, there is no need to read the details of the code of the whole supplier slice; it is sufficient to make a rough guess. If the guess turns out to be wrong, it will lead to a later backtrack. This backtrack does not invalidate the search; it only makes it a little bit longer.

If the programmer concludes that the concept is implemented in the combined responsibility of the module, then the programmer selects the most likely supplier module and checks whether it contains the concept, and the search continues through the supplier slice of this module. However, if the programmer concludes that the concept is not present in the combined responsibility, it means that a wrong turn has been taken sometime before. The programmer then must backtrack to a previously visited client and take a different direction. If the programmer concludes that the search is leading nowhere, the search terminates unsuccessfully. The search must restart with another significant concept or another search technique.

Concept location by dependency search uses class dependency graphs; however, programmers often use the Unified Modeling Language (UML) class diagrams as a substitute. Strictly speaking, UML class diagrams contain ambiguities that can complicate the search. Nevertheless, because the search techniques allow the possibilities of backtracks that correct various errors, UML class diagrams often provide a sufficient support for dependency search. The next example of Violet illustrates a dependency search. An additional example appears in chapter 17.

6.5.1 Example Violet

Violet is an open-source UML editor that supports drawing several UML diagrams, including class diagrams. It contains approximately 60 classes and 10,000 lines of code (Horstmann, 2010). An example of the user interface of Violet is shown in Figure 6.7.

The change request is: "Record the author for each class symbol in the class diagrams." After this change, Violet will provide information about the authors who created a class symbol to everyone who needs it.

The change request contains the concepts "record," "author," "class symbol," and "class diagram." Of these concepts, "record" is a communication with the programmer and is therefore, irrelevant; "author" is an implicit concept that is to be implemented from scratch and is unlikely to be present in the current code; "class

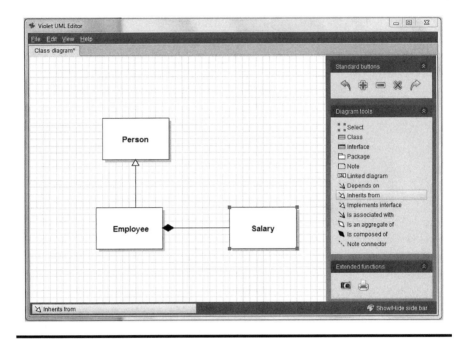

Figure 6.7   User interface of Violet.

diagram" is a background concept, but it is not the specific concept that needs to be changed. The "class symbol" is the significant concept the programmers will try to locate. A dependency graph of the top modules (classes) of the Violet code is in Figure 6.8.

The search starts at the top module UMLEditor. The inspection of this module revealed that it does not contain the significant concept within the local responsibility.

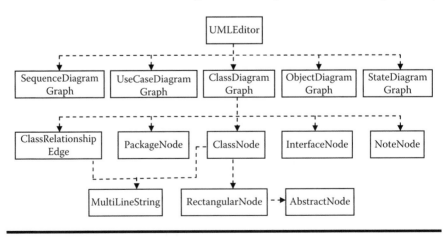

Figure 6.8   Partial class dependency graph of Violet.

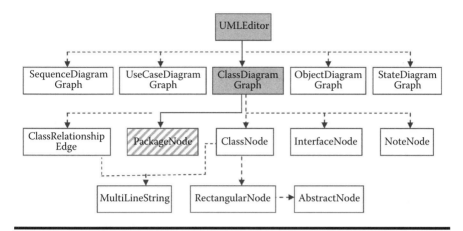

Figure 6.9   Wrong turn in dependency search.

There are several suppliers of this module, including `SequenceDiagramGraph`, `UseCaseDiagramGraph`, `ClassDiagramGraph`, and so forth. Of them, `ClassDiagramGraph` is an obvious choice for the inspection because it is most likely that the concept "class symbol" is in its combined responsibility.

The suppliers of `ClassDiagramGraph` are `ClassRelationshipEdge`, `PackageNode`, `ClassNode`, and several additional modules, some of them represented in Figure 6.8. The programmers inspected the module `PackageNode` but determined that the concept is not in its combined responsibility. Figure 6.9 shows the current state of the dependency search: Inspected modules where the programmer believes that the concept is in combined responsibility are gray; the module where the concept is not in combined responsibility is hatched.

The next step in the search is a backtrack to a previously inspected client that has the concept in its combined responsibility, in this case `ClassDiagramGraph`, and select a different supplier for the continuation of the search. The programmers selected `ClassNode` as the next supplier and determined that the concept is in both its combined and local responsibility; hence, the concept location has been found (see Figure 6.10). In it, the concept location is `ClassNode`, and previously inspected modules are filled with gray; an unsuccessful visit and inspection is represented by a hatched rectangle.

At this point, the search is complete and can stop. The significant concept has been located, and the change can be completed by adding the properties of an author to the module `ClassNode`. However, the class `ClassNode` inherits from class `RectangularNode`, which further inherits from `AbstractNode`. If the concept "author" is implemented there, the authorship of not only class symbols, but also package symbols, interface symbols, and so forth, will be recorded. This exceeds the change request and makes the change even more powerful and useful

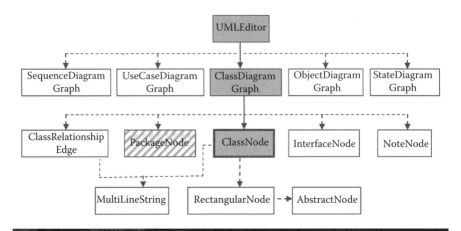

Figure 6.10   Location of concept "class."

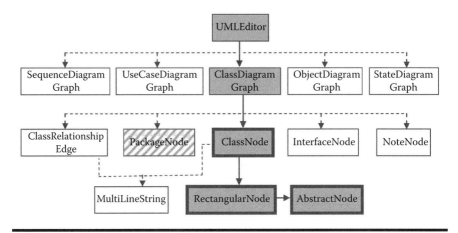

Figure 6.11   Alternative locations of the more abstract concept.

than the original change request. The final figure for this search with three options for the concept location is in Figure 6.11.

6.5.2 An Interactive Tool Supporting Dependency Search

An interactive tool takes over a part of this process. The UML activity diagram in Figure 6.12 contains two swim lanes: one for the tool (computer) and one for the programmer. It represents the cooperation of the computer and the programmer and captures their complementary roles. The computer finds all top modules of the program, finds the set of supplier modules, and keeps track of all previously inspected modules for a possible backtrack. The programmer decides the direction of the search.

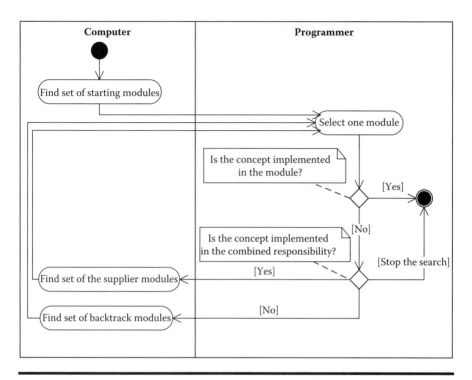

Figure 6.12   Concept location by dependency search using analysis tool.

Summary

Concepts are bridges between discourse about the program (that includes a change request) and the program itself. Concepts have three facets: name, intension, and extension. When a change request arrives, the programmers must find the significant concept and then its extension in the code; that is where the code modification will start. This process is called concept location. Different search strategies are available for concept location. The grep search strategy seeks the name of the concept in the identifiers and comments of the code and considers them as an indication of the presence of the concept extension. Dependency search utilizes local and combined responsibilities of the program modules and searches the code based on these responsibilities.

Further Reading and Topics

Classic literature that deals with concepts includes the work of Wittgenstein (1953), de Saussure (2006), and Frege (1964). The notions of extensions and intension used in this chapter were coined by Frege. How concepts apply to the issues of program comprehension and concept location are discussed by Rajlich (2009) and by Rajlich and Wilde (2002).

Searches in an electronic environment have been discussed by Marchionini (1997). A grep search is described by Petrenko, Rajlich, and Vanciu (2008), and the original description of the dependency search was provided by Chen and Rajlich (2000). These two concept-location techniques, described in this chapter, do not require any special preprocessing of the code; therefore, they are easy to use, even when the code is incomplete. There is a large set of other techniques that do require code preprocessing; see, for example, information retrieval techniques similar to the ones that are used to search in a natural language text or on the Internet (Marcus, Sergeyev, Rajlich, & Maletic, 2004).

In the software engineering literature, some authors replace the word *concept* with the word *feature* and use these two words as synonyms. However, there is a subtle difference that was discussed by Rajlich and Wilde (2002): Features are special concepts that are controlled by the software users, who can choose whether or not to execute them. An example of a feature is "cut and paste" in a word processor. The users can choose to use it but do not have to; it is their decision whether this feature is executed. On the other hand, an example of a concept that is not a feature is the opening window of the word processor. Whenever the users run the word processor, the windows appears, so the users do not have control over this, and hence, it is not a feature. The difference between concepts and features is an important consideration when using the dynamic concept location that uses execution traces to locate a concept (Wilde & Scully, 1995).

Indexing links play a similar role as an index in a book (Antoniol, Canfora, Casazza, De Lucia, and Merlo, 2002): They list the concept names, and for each name, they have an address of the corresponding concept extension in the code. When indexing links are available, they make the process of concept location much easier. In the literature, indexing is often called traceability.

Information about the extraction of significant concepts from the requirements appears in the literature in many contexts. Abbott (1983) wrote an early paper on the topic about the use of extraction in a context of software specifications and design. However, for some changes, concepts related but not actually present in the change request must be used in the query, and hence, a broader context of the change request must be considered (Petrenko et al., 2008).

Note that the concept location does not have to identify complete concept extension in the code; it is sufficient to identify only a part. The rest of the concept extension and possible secondary code modifications are found by impact analysis, which is described in the next chapter. Also note that some authors deal with "concerns" that have a substantial overlap with notion of "concept" (Robillard & Murphy, 2002).

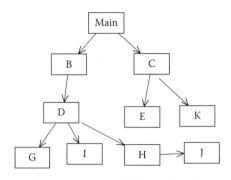

Figure 6.13 **A class dependency graph.**

Exercises

6.1 Find a significant concept in the following change request: "To the color palette in your application, add 'amber.'"

6.2 For the concept named "color amber," find intension and some real-world extensions.

6.3 What are the basic steps of the search for concept location? Draw the diagram.

6.4 Extract the significant concepts from the following change request: "The application allows the users to draw only two figures: circles and rectangles. Allow the user to draw triangles." Justify your answer.

6.5 What is the difference between grep and dependency search in concept location? What are the advantages and disadvantages of the two techniques?

6.6 Describe a situation when a grep search fails. What would you do if this happened to you?

6.7 Explain the difference between local and combined responsibility.

6.8 Which parts of the concept location by dependency search are done by the programmer, and which parts are done by the computer?

6.9 Suppose that your program has the class dependency graph of Figure 6.13. What is the first class you have to inspect during concept location by dependency search? Suppose that after inspecting a class, you always decide correctly which is the next inspected class. What is the maximum number of classes to be inspected?

References

Abbott, R. J. (1983). Program design by informal English descriptions. *Communications of the ACM, 26*, 882–894.

Antoniol, G., Canfora, G., Casazza, G., De Lucia, A., & Merlo, E. (2002). Recovering traceability links between code and documentation. *IEEE Transactions on Software Engineering, 28*, 970–983.

Chen, K., & Rajlich, V. (2000). Case study of feature location using dependence graph. In *Proceedings of International Workshop on Program Comprehension* (pp. 241–249). Washington, DC: IEEE Computer Society Press.

de Saussure, F. (2006). *Writings in general linguistics*. Oxford, UK: Oxford University Press.

Frege, G. (1964). *The basic laws of arithmetic: Exposition of the system*. Berkeley: University of California Press.

Horstmann, C. (2010). *Violet UML editor*. Retrieved on June 17, 2011, from http://source-forge.net/projects/violet/

Marchionini, G. (1997). *Information seeking in electronic environments*. Cambridge, England: Cambridge University Press.

Marcus, A., Sergeyev, A., Rajlich, V., & Maletic, J. (2004). An information retrieval approach to concept location in source code. In *Proceedings of the 11th IEEE Working Conference on Reverse Engineering* (pp. 214–223). Washington, DC: IEEE Computer Society Press.

Petrenko, M., Rajlich, V., & Vanciu, R. (2008). Partial domain comprehension in software evolution and maintenance. In *Proceedings of IEEE International Conference on Program Comprehension* (pp. 13–22). Washington, DC: IEEE Computer Society Press.

Rajlich, V. (2009). Intensions are a key to program comprehension. In *Proceedings of IEEE International Conference on Program Comprehension* (pp. 1–9). Washington, DC: IEEE Computer Society Press.

Rajlich, V., & Wilde, N. (2002). The role of concepts in program comprehension. In *Proceedings of International Workshop on Program Comprehension* (pp. 271–278). Washington, DC: IEEE Computer Society Press.

Robillard, M. P., & Murphy, G. C. (2002). Concern graphs: Finding and describing concerns using structural program dependencies. In *Proceedings of International Conference on Software Engineering* (pp. 406–416). New York, NY: ACM.

Wilde, N., & Scully, M. (1995). Software reconnaissance: Mapping program features to code. *Journal of Software Maintenance: Research and Practice, 7*, 49–62.

Wittgenstein, L. (1953). *Philosophical investigations*. New York, NY: Macmillan.

Chapter 7

Impact Analysis

Objectives

This chapter introduces impact analysis—a phase that predicts the full extent of the required modifications and selects between different strategies of the change. It is the phase that immediately follows concept location.

The chapter explains the process of iterative impact analysis. After you have read this chapter, you will know:

- Initial and estimated impact sets of a change
- Interaction graphs and their support for impact analysis
- An iterative process of impact analysis that uses interaction graphs
- Marks used in the iterative impact analysis
- The alternatives in software change implementation
- The role of the supporting tools

***

In the process of software change, impact analysis starts where concept location lets off. The division of labor between concept location and impact analysis is depicted in Figures 7.1 and 7.2. While concept location finds the location of the relevant concept extension in the code, the impact analysis goes beyond that and determines the full effect of the change to the software system, including secondary changes in distant modules. The first notion that is covered in this chapter is the notion of the impact set.

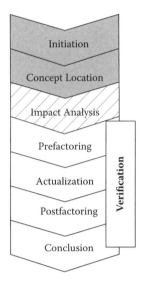

Figure 7.1   Impact analysis in the software change process.

7.1 Impact Set

Concept location gives the programmers a foothold in the code, the modules where the primary code modifications will appear. The modules that are identified during concept location constitute the *initial impact set*. If the modifications are small, the initial impact set contains all modules that will be impacted by the change.

However, there are large software changes that are not limited to the modules of the initial impact set. Code modifications that spread to other modules are called *secondary* modifications. The task for the impact analysis is to find these other changing modules and create the *estimated impact set*. The initial impact set and its relation to the estimated impact set is depicted in Figure 7.2. Later, when the change is implemented, the *changed set* is the set of modules that the programmers actually modify. The success of impact analysis is measured by how closely the estimated impact set matches the changed set.

There is a reason why concept location and impact analysis are separate phases during software change, although they work very closely together. These two phases are methodically very different. As an example of the differences, concept location finds a specific location, and the programmers repeat it until a correct location is found. On the other hand, impact analysis methodically visits the neighboring modules, but it is more difficult to know whether the entire estimated impact set has been found. Hasty programmers can miss some impacted modules, and there is no warning that would prompt them to repeat impact analysis.

The progress of the impact analysis is based on the module interactions, and some authors call this process the "ripple effect" of a change. A stone thrown into a pond

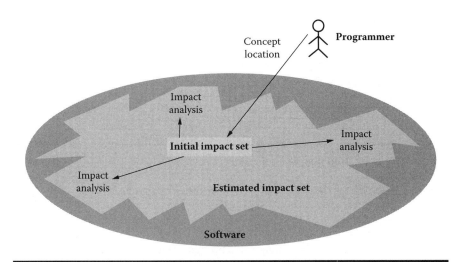

Figure 7.2 Concept location and impact analysis. From Rajlich, V. (2006). "Changing the paradigm of software engineering." Communications of ACM, 49, 67–70. Copyright 2006 by ACM. Reprinted with permission.

causes a ripple effect that spreads further and further; similarly, a large software change also causes a ripple effect that spreads further and further through the interactions among the modules. We illustrate the impact analysis process in the following example.

Interacting People and Their Schedules

There are two close friends, Jacob and Henry, who meet regularly every Tuesday night at 7 p.m. for a glass of beer and gossip. They have been doing it for several years, and they look forward to this Tuesday night meeting; it has become a fixed part of their lives.

However, there is a sudden change in Jacob's life: He becomes engaged to Emma, and Emma's parents, John and Mary, invite him to their home for dinner every Tuesday, an invitation that is impossible to refuse. Therefore, he has to change his schedule. This change in Jacob's schedule is the initial impact set of this case. Jacob wants to keep meeting with Henry, and after some discussion, Henry agrees that they will switch the regular meetings to Thursday night; hence, the change now propagates from Jacob's to Henry's schedule.

Further, Henry has been regularly meeting with another friend, Chuck, on every Thursday evening for a tennis game. Now, that has to be rescheduled. Chuck agrees to move the tennis game to Tuesday night, so the change now propagates to Chuck's schedule also. Figure 7.3 keeps track of all these interactions that are taking place.

Chuck promised his nephew Bobby that he would take him to a movie on Tuesday two weeks from now, and Bobby is looking forward to this event. Chuck and Bobby agree that they will go to the movies on Saturday afternoon instead, but this is the time when Bobby regularly cleans his room under the supervision of his mom, Jane, so the cleaning has to be rescheduled to Friday afternoon. Bobby also meets his friends James and Pat on Saturday mornings at 10 a.m., and this meeting is not impacted by the modification in the schedule.

The primary change originated in Jacob's schedule, and secondary changes impacted a number of other people; the estimated impact set includes the schedules of Jacob, Henry, Chuck, his nephew Bobby, and Bobby's mom Jane. It does not matter that Jane has never heard of Jacob or his engagement; her schedule is still impacted by this change. The initial impact set is highlighted in dark grey in Figure 7.3, and the estimated impact set is highlighted in both dark and light gray. The schedules of James and Pat are not impacted and are left blank.

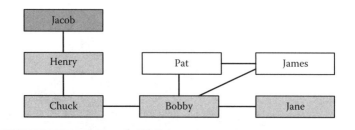

Figure 7.3   Impact on people's schedules.

7.1.1 Example: Point-of-Sale Software Program

Software systems consist of tightly interdependent software classes. When a change appears in one of the classes, it may trigger secondary changes in interacting classes. An example is a variant of a point-of-sale program that supports a small store and keeps track of an inventory of items by item name, price, tax, available quantity, cashiers who are authorized to sell in the store, and so forth. The Unified Modeling Language (UML) class diagram for this program is in Figure 7.4.

The classes in the program are `Store`, which is the top class of the application; class `Cashiers`, which contains a list of cashiers; class `Inventory`, which supports the inventory for the store; class `Item`, which contains data of a specific item that is being sold in the store; and class `Price`, which contains the price of an item. The code of class `Price` assumes that there is only a single price for every item, and as a result, class `Price` is very simple; it contains just one integer for the price and `getPrice()` and `putPrice()` methods that return and set the price of the item, respectively.

A software change to be done is described by the following change request: "Support price fluctuations; the users of the program should be able to set prices of items in advance and be able to change the item prices on selected dates. For

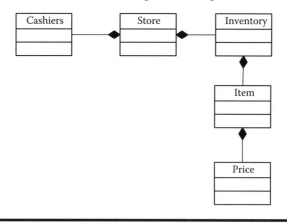

Figure 7.4   Small point-of-sale program.

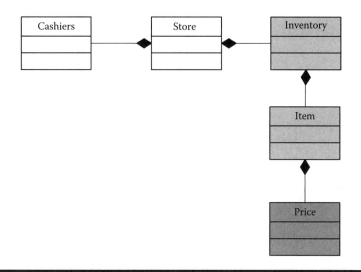

Figure 7.5   The initial and estimated impact set of the price fluctuations.

example, there can be sales periods where on certain dates the price is lower, while after these dates it returns to the previous level."

This change requires an overhaul of the class Price that adds a new functionality that deals with the price changes on specific dates. As a result, getPrice() and putPrice() methods will have an extra parameter "date" that the clients of class Price have to use when calling these methods. Classes Item and Inventory will be affected and become members of the estimated impact set. Figure 7.5 contains the dark-shaded class Price, where the change starts and which constitutes the initial impact set, and the light-shaded estimated impact set.

7.2 Class Interaction Graphs

The previous example illustrates the processes that find the estimated impact set. This section describes a graph-theoretical model that underlies the example and that is used in impact analysis. It is another software model, slightly different from the models that are explained in chapter 4. It is based on two kinds of class interactions: dependencies and coordinations.

7.2.1 Interactions Caused by Dependencies

The dependencies and accompanying contracts among the classes were previously described in section 4.3. As a reminder, class A is a client of class B, and class B is a supplier of class A if some of the responsibility of class A is delegated to B. In such a situation, classes A and B interact through a contract, and a modification in one

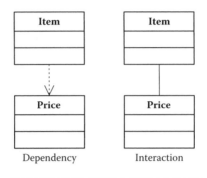

Figure 7.6   Each dependency (left) is also an interaction (right).

of them that changes the contract may propagate to the other one. The interactions are symmetric because the supplier can change the contract and cause secondary modifications in the client, and vice versa.

An example of such a situation is the class `Price`, which is a supplier to class `Item` and supplies the price of a store item. If class `Price` changes and now supplies the price on a specific date, this change causes secondary modifications in class `Item`. Figure 7.6 models the relation of two classes as a dependency on the left and as interaction on the right.

7.2.2 Interactions Caused by Coordinations

There is also another kind of interaction that is called *coordinations*. Even if two classes do not have a contract between them, they still may interact in a way that is similar to the people coordinating their schedules in this chapter's sidebar. If one party changes the agreed-upon meeting time, the other party is affected.

Another example of coordination in software is the classes that coordinate the coding of colors, where 0 is the code for red, 1 is the code for yellow, and 2 is the code for green. Because of the coordination, the classes send these codes to the other classes and are sure that each class interprets them the same way. As a more complete example, suppose class A contains the member function `int A::get()` that receives a choice of a color from the user and converts it into the code. Class B contains member function `void B::paint(int)` that receives the color code as an argument, decodes it, and paints the screen with the corresponding color. Class C is a client of both classes A and B, and it contains the following code fragment that establishes how the color code gets from A to B:

```
class C { …
  A a;
  B b; …
  void foo() { …
    b.paint(a.get());
```

```
    ...
    }
};¹
```

The interaction graph that represents the classes of this code is in the right part of Figure 7.7. The interaction between A and B in Figure 7.7 is caused by the coordination of the color code. Note that if the color code changes in A, it must also change in B, while class C does not change at all. The interactions of classes C with A and C with B are dependencies, and for comparison, the dependency graph is in the left part of Figure 7.7.

7.2.3 Definition of Class Interaction Graph

A class interaction graph captures these class interactions, whether the interactions are based on dependencies or coordinations. Formally, a class interaction graph is an undirected graph $G = (X,I)$, where X is a set of classes, and for two classes $A \in X$, $B \in X$, if class A interacts with class B, then there is an edge $(A,B) \in I$.

When comparing class interaction graphs with UML class diagrams, contracts typically are depicted in UML class diagrams as associations, but some of the interactions, particularly the coordinations among classes, are often missing. In spite of that, the programmers often substitute UML class diagrams for interaction graphs, but they should be aware that the missing interactions pose a risk that some secondary modifications will also be missed. Figure 7.8 uses a UML class diagram that substitutes for the interaction graph.

An important notion in the interaction graphs is the notion of neighborhood. The *neighborhood* of class A is a set of all classes that interact with it: $N(A) = \{B\ (A,B) \in I\}$. In Figure 7.8, neighborhood of class Item is $N(Item) = \{Inventory, Price\}$. Classes Inventory, Price are also called *neighbors* of class Item.

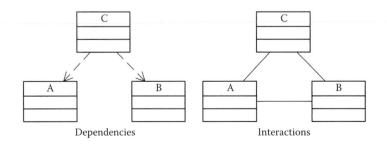

Figure 7.7 Dependencies (left) and interactions (right) among the classes of the color example.

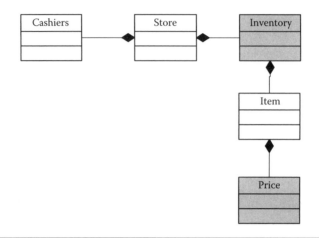

Figure 7.8 **Neighborhood of class Item.**

7.3 Process of Impact Analysis

Impact analysis is the process that finds the estimated impact set. Large estimated impact sets cannot be determined in a single step. The programmers work step by step and trace how the code modifications propagate through class interactions.

To facilitate impact analysis, programmers use *marks* that indicate the status of the individual classes. Table 7.1 contains the five basic marks that the classes can receive. Figure 7.9 contains the activity diagram of the impact analysis with these marks.

Initially, all classes of the program receive the Blank status. The class identified during concept location receives the Changed status, and after that, all Blank neighbors are marked Next.

Then, the programmers select one of the Next classes, inspect it, and decide on its mark. If the programmers conclude that the selected class is going to change, they mark it Changed and then mark all its Blank neighbors as Next. If the programmers conclude that the selected class is not going to change, they mark it Unchanged and they select another Next class for inspection. If there are no Next classes to select from, the process of impact analysis is completed; all classes marked Changed constitute the estimated impact set.

Figure 7.10 presents a simple example of impact analysis. In the figure, Blank classes are left blank; Changed classes are shaded black; Next classes are diagonally shaded; and Unchanged classes are indicated by the letter *U*. The mark Propagates is described in the next section and is not used in this figure.

The process of impact analysis starts with the snapshot at the top of Figure 7.10, with all classes having the mark Blank. The fat top-down arrows of Figure 7.10 indicate the progress from one snapshot to the next one.

Table 7.1   Status of Classes in Impact Analysis Process

Mark	Meaning
Blank	Unknown status of the class; the class was never inspected and is not currently scheduled for an inspection.
Changed	The programmers inspected the class and found that it is impacted by the change and thus belongs to the estimated impact set. All formerly Blank neighbors of the Changed class will be marked Next.
Unchanged	The programmers inspected the class and found that it is not impacted by the change. It also does not propagate the change to any of its neighbors.
Next	The class is scheduled for inspection.
Propagating	The programmers inspected the class and found that it is not impacted by the change, but the neighbors of this class may still change; the class propagates the change although it does not change itself. All formerly Blank neighbors of the Propagating class will be marked Next (see the explanation in section 7.4).

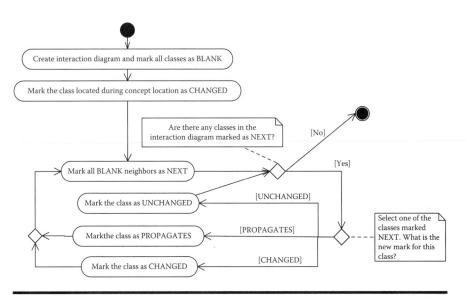

Figure 7.9   Activity diagram of impact analysis.

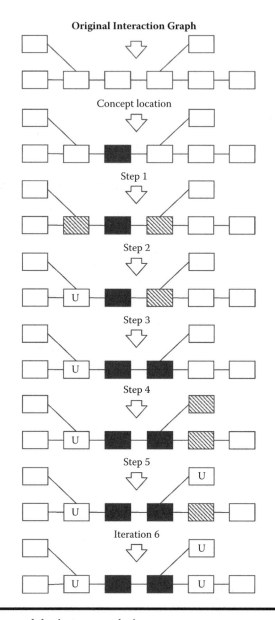

Figure 7.10 Steps of the impact analysis.

The class identified during concept location receives the Changed mark (denoted by black shading), indicating that it will change. After Step 1, all its neighbors will receive the Next mark (see diagonal shading in Figure 7.10). In Step 2, programmers inspect one of the Next classes and mark it as Unchanged, as indicated by the letter *U*.

During Step 3, the second Next class is inspected and marked as Changed; consequently, in Step 4, its two Blank neighbors are marked as Next. In Steps 5 and 6, the programmers inspect these two classes and mark both of them as Unchanged. At this point, there are no remaining classes marked Next, and the impact analysis is complete. The estimated impact set contains two classes.

7.4 Propagating Classes

Table 7.1 and Figure 7.9 contain one additional mark for Propagating classes. This is a mark for classes that do not change themselves, but propagate the change to their neighbors; therefore, their neighbors have to be inspected by the programmers.

The propagating classes, for example, can be the classes that just deliver a message from one class to another, and although they are in the middle of the propagating change, they do not need to change themselves. For the programmers, it is important to remember the existence of the propagating classes and take the appropriate precautions.

Propagating Class Analogy: The Mail Carrier

A real-life counterpart of a propagating class is a mail carrier. John loaned a small amount of money to Paul, but now he needs the money back. He writes a letter to Paul requesting the money; a mail carrier takes the letter from John to Paul. Now, Paul must get a part-time job to pay back the loan, so there is a big change that propagated from John to Paul.

In this example, there are two interactions: John interacts with the mail carrier, and the mail carrier interacts with Paul. The change originated with John and propagates through the mail carrier to Paul. The mail carrier is in the middle of the propagation but does not have to change anything; just keeps delivering the letters from one person to another. Figure 7.11 contains the interaction graph; the shaded rectangles represent the people who modify their activities (John and Paul), while the mail carrier in the middle does not need to modify anything and delivers letters like before.

Figure 7.12 is an example that includes a Propagating class that is labeled by the letter *P*. The example starts again with concept location that identifies the first class labeled Changed. In Step 1, the programmers inspect the Next class, and they conclude that it is propagating; therefore, they label it by *P*. After that, all its currently Blank neighbors have to be re-marked Next, as done in Step 2 of Figure 7.12. In the Step 3, the programmers inspected one of the Next classes, decided that it changes, and marked it Changed. In the final step, Step 4, they inspected the last remaining Next class and concluded that it does not change and also that it does not propagate the change and thus marked it Unchanged. This concludes the impact analysis, since there are no longer any classes marked Next; the classes shaded black are the estimated impact set.

Figure 7.11　Interactions between John, mail carrier, and Paul.

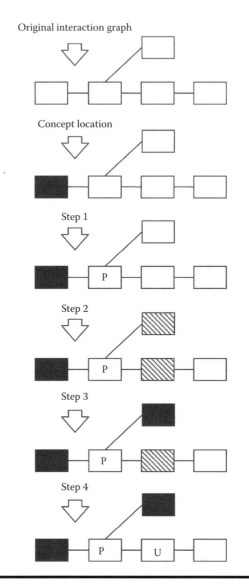

Figure 7.12   Impact analysis with propagating class.

7.5 Alternatives in Software Change

Programmers often can implement changes in several different ways. An example is a program that is displaying a temperature in Fahrenheit, and the required change is to display it in Celsius instead. In the program, two separate locations deal with the temperature: one where the temperature is calculated from the sensor data and the other one where it is displayed to the user. One way to make the change is to change the logic, that is, to change the temperature calculation. The other one is to keep the calculation intact and adjust only the display of the temperature in the user interface by a conversion formula there. Impact analysis weights these alternatives and decides which strategy of the change is better.

The criteria that help to decide what is a better strategy are the required effort and the clarity of the resulting code. Very often, these two criteria contradict each other; the easier change may negatively impact the clarity of code and vice versa. In the previous example, it is easier to adjust the temperature by employing a simple conversion formula in the user interface. However, for the future clarity of the code, it is better to have all calculations of the temperature in one place and therefore, do the conversion in the place where the temperature is calculated from the sensor data. The first approach makes the future evolution more difficult, because the future programmers will have to identify two locations in the code that participate in the temperature calculations rather than just one.

It is tempting to choose the change strategy that completes the change quickly and ignores the consequences. This is a classic conflict between short-term and long-term goals. The true professionals should resist temptations to solve today's problems at the expense of the future. In the end, project managers who are trained in the evaluation of such trade-offs should evaluate the existing options.

Impact analysis is carried out not only in the source code, but other artifacts may also be involved, like the tests, external documentation, and so forth. These auxiliary documents also need to be updated during the change, as the change propagates to them through their interactions with the source code.

The estimated impact set can be prepared for a single software change, for a sequence of several changes, or for a completely new release that consists of a large number of changes. The size of the estimated impact set is one of the criteria that lead to a selection of the appropriate change strategy.

7.6 Tool Support for Impact Analysis

Tools have been developed to support the impact analysis process, and the programmers can delegate some actions to these tools. These actions include the extraction of the class interaction graph from the code, and keeping the marks of the various classes that are involved in the impact analysis process.

The activity diagram of Figure 7.13 represents the division of labor between the tool and the programmer. This activity diagram contains the same actions as the earlier activity diagram of Figure 7.9; however, there is an addition of two swim lanes, one for the computer and one for the programmer. The computer swim lane contains all actions that the tool/computer performs. These actions are easy for the tool and difficult or onerous for the programmer, such as keeping track of the classes, their interactions, and their marks during the iterative impact analysis process. The tool automatically creates a class interaction graph and assigns the

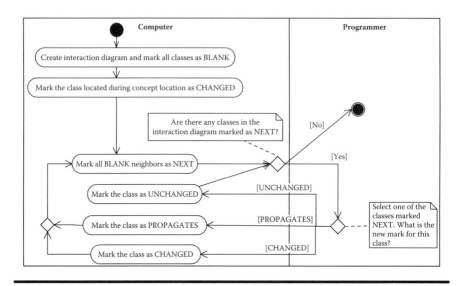

Figure 7.13 **Activity diagram of interactive impact analysis. From Petrenko, M., & Rajlich, V. (2009). Variable granularity for improving precision of impact analysis. In Proceedings of IEEE International Conference on Program Comprehension (pp. 10–19). Washington, DC: IEEE Computer Society Press. Copyright 2009 IEEE. Reprinted with permission.**

original Blank mark to all classes. Furthermore, the tool assigns the mark Next to the neighbors of the Changed and Propagating classes, and detects the situation where there are no longer any Next marks, which signals that the process of the impact analysis is finished.

The programmer swim lane contains all actions that are hard for the tool; hence, they still have to be done by the human programmers. The programmers conduct the inspections of the classes marked Next and, based on the results of these inspections, they assign marks Changed, Unchanged, and Propagating.

Summary

Impact analysis starts with the result of the concept location—that is, with the initial impact set—and produces an estimated impact set that consists of classes that will be modified due to secondary modifications. It uses class interaction graphs that represent all class interactions that include dependencies and coordinations between the classes. The programmers trace the change using these interaction graphs and use the marks to remember the status of the classes in this process. The neighbors that interact with a changed class have to be inspected by the programmer, who decides whether they will also change. There are also propagating classes that do not change themselves but propagate the change to their neighbors. The impact analysis also decides on the strategy of the change. A supporting tool for impact analysis constructs an interaction graph, keeps marks of the classes in the process, and prompts the user to inspect classes marked for the inspection.

Further Reading and Topics

Early papers on impact analysis include works by Haney (1972) and Yau, Collofello, and McGregor (1978); a thorough survey of the early work is provided by Bohner and Arnold (1996). An interactive impact analysis and a preliminary set of marks and rules is described by Queille, Voidrot, Wilde, and Munro (1994). This model was further formalized and expanded by additional propagation rules and marks in works by Rajlich (1997, 2000). Further expansion of the model by Petrenko and Rajlich (2009) takes into account different granularities that the programmers may want to use. These granularities include the granularity of the classes, which is emphasized in this chapter, as well as additional finer granularities of methods and code segments. A tool based on these models of interactive impact analysis was described by Chen and Rajlich (2001), and later it was refined and implemented as a tool called JRipples (Petrenko, 2010). The JRipples tool implements the activities of the "computer" swim lane of Figure 7.13, and its user interface supports the activities in the "programmer" swim lane. In particular, it supports the presentation of the modules and their marks, and prompts the programmers to inspect the modules that are marked for inspection.

UML class diagrams were used in an impact analysis as a substitute for the interaction graphs by Rajlich and Gosavi (2004). Briand, Labiche, Yan, and Di Penta (2004) presented the results of an experiment that showed that the use of the Object Constraint Language (Warmer & Kleppe, 2003) can significantly increase the quality of impact analysis performed on UML models. The quality of impact analysis and change planning can increase if software maintainers are supplied with the design rationale for each module in the system (Abbattista, Lanubile, Mastelloni, & Visaggio, 1994).

Classification of class interactions into different categories can improve impact analysis (Kung, Gao, Hsia, & Wen, 1994). A classification that considers the effects of object-oriented dependencies such as inheritance and polymorphism on impact analysis was explored by Li and Offutt (1996). Coupling metrics were used to estimate the likelihood that a change would propagate through an interaction (Briand, Wuest, & Lounis, 1999). Dynamic analysis, which uses program execution traces to find the estimated impact set, has been explored in works by Law and Rothermel (2003) and Orso, Apiwattanapong, and Harrold (2003).

While the analysis of dependencies is fairly advanced, the analysis of coordinations among the classes still has very many open research problems. A certain class of coordinations called "hidden dependencies" is based on the data flows among the objects. These data flows carry encoded information from the generator to the recipients, and they both have to use the same encoding formula. If one changes, so must the other (Yu & Rajlich, 2001; de Leon & Alves-Foss, 2006).

Impact analysis often deals with code that uses various software technologies. Impact analysis in distributed databases was performed by Deruelle, Bouneffa, Melab, and Basson (2001). Impact analysis can also use only module interface information and does not necessarily consider the modules' content (Muller, Hood, & Kennedy, 1987).

Data-mining approaches for the software repository rely on the project's historical data for impact analysis (Ying, Murphy, Ng, & Chu-Carroll, 2004; Zimmermann, Weisgerber, Diehl, & Zeller, 2005). A common heuristic for this type of approach is that if two artifacts frequently changed together in the past, then there is a high probability that these two artifacts are interacting and will change together in the future. Information retrieval techniques that are combined with data mining proved to be particularly effective (Canfora & Cerulo, 2005).

Exercises

7.1 Section 7.1.1 discusses the impact analysis in the point-of-sale system. For each of the following software changes, determine the estimated impact set:
   a. Keep detailed sale records such as item sold and date/time of sale.
   b. Support multiple items per transaction.
   c. Expand cash payment to include cash tendered and return change.
   d. Implement payment by a check.

7.2 Describe at least two different diagrams or graphs that could be used in impact analysis and discuss their benefits and limitations.

7.3 What is the difference between initial impact set and estimated impact set?

7.4 Explain the difference between dependencies and coordinations. Give an example of each.

7.5 What is a propagating class? Give an example.

7.6 Consider the class interaction graph of a program in Figure 7.14. If the concept is located in A, and the change set is {A, E}, what components need to be inspected by the programmers during impact analysis? Justify your answer.

7.7 In the class interaction graph of Figure 7.15, the Propagating and Unchanged classes are denoted by P and U, respectively. Among the classes that are currently left blank, denote by C all classes that are Changed so that the process of impact analysis also produces the classes currently labeled by P and U.

7.8 In Figure 7.5, a UML class diagram is used for impact analysis; all class associations are, in fact, class dependencies. Create the corresponding interaction graph.

7.9 Change the activity diagram of Figure 7.13 in such a way that the classes marked Unchanged are inspected again if a class marked Changed becomes their neighbor.

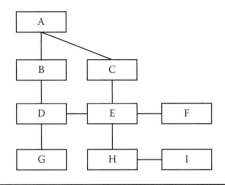

Figure 7.14 Class interaction graph.

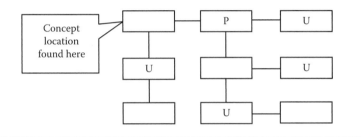

Figure 7.15 Class interaction graph.

References

Abbattista, F., Lanubile, F., Mastelloni, G., & Visaggio, G. (1994). An experiment on the effect of design recording on impact analysis. In *Proceedings of the International Conference on Software Maintenance* (pp. 253–259). Washington, DC: IEEE Computer Society Press.

Bohner, S. A., & Arnold, R. S. (1996). *Software change impact analysis.* Los Alamitos, CA: IEEE Computer Society Press.

Briand, L. C., Labiche, Y., Yan, H.-D., & Di Penta, M. (2004). A controlled experiment on the impact of the object constraint language in UML-based maintenance. In *Proceedings of IEEE International Conference on Software Maintenance* (pp. 380–389). Washington, DC: IEEE Computer Society Press.

Briand, L. C., Wuest, J., & Lounis, H. (1999). Using coupling measurement for impact analysis in object-oriented systems. In *Proceedings of IEEE International Conference on Software Maintenance* (pp. 475–483). Washington, DC: IEEE Computer Society Press.

Canfora, G., & Cerulo, L. (2005). Impact analysis by mining software and change request repositories. In *Proceedings of IEEE International Software Metrics Symposium* (pp. 29–38). Washington, DC: IEEE Computer Society Press.

Chen, K., & Rajlich, V. (2001). RIPPLES: Tool for change in legacy software. In *Proceedings of International Conference on Software Maintenance* (pp. 230–239). Washington, DC: IEEE Computer Society Press.

de Leon, D. C., & Alves-Foss, J. (2006). Hidden implementation dependencies in high assurance and critical computing systems. *IEEE Transactions on Software Engineering (TSE), 32*, 790–811.

Deruelle, H. L., Bouneffa, M., Melab, N., & Basson, H. (2001). A change propagation model and platform for multi-database applications. In *Proceedings of IEEE International Conference on Software Maintenance* (pp. 42–51). Washington, DC: IEEE Computer Society Press.

Haney, F. M. (1972). Module connection analysis. In *Proceedings of AFIPS Joint Computer Conference* (pp. 173–179). New York, NY: ACM.

Kung, D., Gao, J., Hsia, P., & Wen, F. (1994). Change impact identification in object oriented software maintenance. In *Proceedings of IEEE International Conference on Software Maintenance* (pp. 202–211). Washington, DC: IEEE Computer Society Press.

Law, J., & Rothermel, G. (2003). Whole program path-based dynamic impact analysis. In *Proceedings of 25th International Conference on Software Engineering* (pp. 308–318). Washington, DC: IEEE Computer Society Press.

Li, L., & Offutt, J. (1996). Algorithmic analysis of the impact of changes on object-oriented software. In *Proceedings of International Conference on Software Maintenance* (pp. 171–184). Washington, DC: IEEE Computer Society Press.

Muller, H. A., Hood, R., & Kennedy, K. (1987). Efficient recompilation of module interfaces in a software development environment. In *Proceedings of ACM SIGSOFT/SIGPLAN software engineering symposium on practical software development environments* (pp. 180–189). New York, NY: ACM.

Orso, A., Apiwattanapong, T., & Harrold, M. J. (2003). Leveraging field data for impact analysis and regression testing. In *Proceedings of the 9th European Software Engineering Conference held jointly with ACM SIGSOFT International Symposium on Foundations of Software Engineering* (pp. 128–137). New York, NY: ACM.

Petrenko, M. (2010). *Jripples*. Retrieved on June 18, 2011, from http://jripples.sourceforge.net/

Petrenko, M., & Rajlich, V. (2009). Variable granularity for improving precision of impact analysis. In *Proceedings of IEEE International Conference on Program Comprehension* (pp. 10–19). Washington, DC: IEEE Computer Society Press.

Queille, J., Voidrot, J., Wilde, N., & Munro, M. (1994). The impact analysis task in software maintenance: A model and a case study. In *Proceedings of International Conference on Software Maintenance* (pp. 234–242). Washington, DC: IEEE Computer Society Press.

Rajlich, V. (1997). A model for change propagation based on graph rewriting. In *Proceedings of international conference on software maintenance* (pp. 84–91). Washington, DC: IEEE Computer Society Press.

———. (2000). Modeling software evolution by evolving interoperation graphs. *Annals of Software Engineering, 9*(1–4), 235–248.

Rajlich, V., & Gosavi, P. (2004). Incremental change in object-oriented programming. *IEEE Software, 21*(4), 62–69.

Warmer, J., & Kleppe, A. (2003). *The object constraint language: Getting your models ready for MDA*. Boston, MA: Addison-Wesley Longman.

Yau, S. S., Collofello, J. S., & McGregor, T. M. (1978). Ripple effect analysis of software maintenance. In *Proceedings of IEEE Computer Software and Applications Conference* (pp. 60–65). Washington, DC: IEEE Computer Society Press.

Ying, A. T. T., Murphy, G. C., Ng, R., & Chu-Carroll, M. C. (2004). Predicting source code changes by mining change history. *IEEE Transactions on Software Engineering, 30*, 574–586.

Yu, Z., & Rajlich, V. (2001). Hidden dependencies in program comprehension and change propagation. In *Proceedings of IEEE International Workshop on Program Comprehension* (pp. 293–299). Washington, DC: IEEE Computer Society Press.

Zimmermann, T., Weisgerber, P., Diehl, S., & Zeller, A. (2005). Mining version histories to guide software changes. *IEEE Transactions on Software Engineering, 31*, 429–445.

Chapter 8

Actualization

Objectives

During the actualization phase, programmers modify the software and add the new functionality that the stakeholders requested. While previous phases planned the change, the actualization follows this plan and modifies the code and the program's functionality. After you have read this chapter, you will know:

- Differences between small and large changes
- Incorporation of a new responsibility through polymorphism
- Incorporation of a new supplier
- Incorporation of a new client
- Incorporation of a new responsibility through replacement
- Change propagation through the old code

***

Previous chapters explained the preparatory phases of change initiation, concept location, and impact analysis (see Figure 8.1). The actualization differs from these preparatory phases by the fact that it actually modifies the code and implements the new functionality. It may also be preceded by a phase of prefactoring that, together with postfactoring, is explained in the next chapter. It also overlaps and interleaves with verification, which is also presented in future chapters.

The actualization phase consists of the implementation of the new functionality, its incorporation into the old code, and change propagation that seeks out and updates all places in the old code that require secondary modifications. The size of

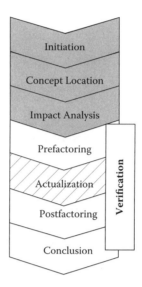

Figure 8.1   Actualization in the software change process.

the changes determines the process and the small changes are handled differently than the large ones.

8.1 Small Changes

For small changes, programmers add the new responsibility by modifying the appropriate code segment. As an example, consider a change where a five-digit zip code is replaced by a nine-digit zip code in a class `Address`. The old code is:

```
class Address
      {
      public:
            move();
      private:
            String name, streetAddress, String city;
            char state[2], zip[5];
      };
```

After the modification, the new code requires a nine-character array for the zip code; the modified code is in bold:

```
class Address
      {
      public:
            move();
```

```
private:
        String name, streetAddress, String city;
        char state[2], zip[9];
};
```

The change from a five-digit zip code to a nine-digit zip code also impacts the method move(), which is responsible for a person moving from an old address to a new one. This method is modified so that it can deal with a nine-digit zip code, while its old version dealt with a five-digit zip code only. The variable zip and method move() are members of the same class, and this change is completely contained within this class.

8.2 Changes Requiring New Classes

Larger changes may require new classes that are plugged into the old code by establishing associations between these new classes and the old code. The examples in this section include polymorphism, new suppliers, new clients, and replacement of old classes by the new ones. The subsections also explain when each of the techniques is applicable.

8.2.1 Incorporating New Classes Through Polymorphism

Polymorphism is a part of object-oriented technology that provides a convenient help to incorporate the medium-sized changes. An example of polymorphism is in section 3.4.5, and it is repeated here for the convenience of the reader:

```
class FarmAnimal
        {
        public:
        virtual void makeSound() {};
        };
class Cow : public FarmAnimal
        {
        public:
        void makeSound() {cout<<" Moo-oo-oo";}
        };
class Sheep : public FarmAnimal
        {
        public:
        void makeSound() {cout<<" Be-e-e";}
        };
```

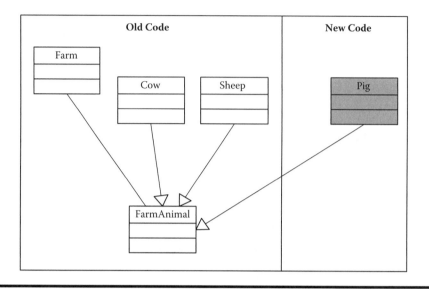

Figure 8.2   Addition of new class through polymorphism.

The change request is the following: Add a new farm animal Pig that makes the sound "Oink." The polymorphism makes this change easy; the programmers just add the following class:

```
class Pig : public FarmAnimal
    {
    public:
    void makeSound() {cout<<" Oink";}
    };
```

After this change, class Farm can declare objects of the type Cow, Sheep, or Pig; hence, the combined responsibility of Farm was extended by the concept Pig. The corresponding UML class diagram is in Figure 8.2, where the left part contains the old code and the right part contains the new class that is incorporated into the old code through polymorphism.

The incorporation of new functionality through polymorphism usually leads to small change propagation. This kind of incorporation should be used whenever polymorphism is available and the new responsibility meshes with it, as in the farm animal example.

8.2.2 Incorporating New Suppliers

If new responsibilities have no counterpart in the old code, then a viable way of implementing them is through new supplier classes. These new classes are developed as stand-alone classes (see Figure 8.3).

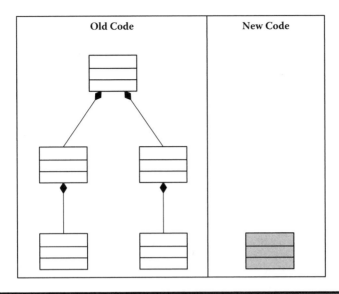

Figure 8.3 **New responsibility implemented as the local functionality of the new module.**

They are plugged in (incorporated) as new components into the appropriate place of the existing code through a declaration of a new object of the new class, as represented by Figure 8.4. Implicit concepts that were described in chapter 6 often must be incorporated as brand new component classes during actualization. The location that hosts the new objects is discovered by using concept location as described in chapter 6.

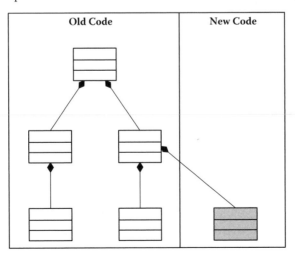

Figure 8.4 **New supplier incorporated as a component.**

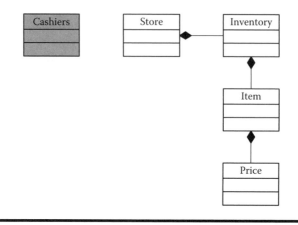

Figure 8.5   Class diagram of the existing point-of-sale; new class `Cashier`.

An example is an introduction of the cashier authorization into a point-of-sale. The old point-of-sale did not require authorization, and anyone was able to launch the application and use all of its functionality (see the classes in the right part of Figure 8.5 with blank fillings). The change request is to "create a cashier login that will control the user log in with a username and password."

A new class `Cashier` is created separately from the old code, and contains the new authorization responsibility. The new class has the fields `cashierId` and `password` and the methods `login()` and `logout()`. The integration of the new code with the old is based on the concept location that finds the best place in the old software for the new concept of `Cashier`, which is in the class `Store`.

After the creation of the object of type `Cashier` in the class `Store`, the relevant methods of class `Store` have to be updated. For example, the method that starts the application must be modified, because it has to invoke the method `login()`. The change in this example does not propagate to any additional classes (see Figure 8.6).

In other changes, incorporating new component classes often starts a large change propagation that propagates to other, sometimes distant classes. Chapter 17 contains a more complete example of incorporation of new component classes that triggers a large change propagation.

8.2.3 *Incorporating New Clients*

If the pieces of the new required responsibility already exist in the old code, then these pieces have to be collected and glued together. This leads to the implementation of the new responsibility as a new client (see Figure 8.7).

This new client is then plugged into the old code by the creation of a new object (see Figure 8.8). The location of this new object is again identified by a concept location. Sometimes a whole new application is created in this way, and the new client is the top module of this new application.

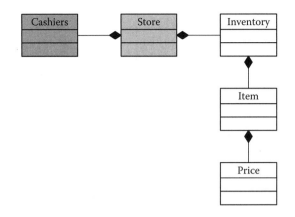

Figure 8.6   Implementation of a new client class.

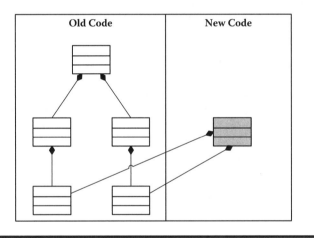

Figure 8.7   New responsibility incorporated as a new client.

An example is a point-of-sale program whose UML class diagram is in Figure 8.6. The new responsibility to be added is a daily report that summarizes what happened that day in the store. The report shows the state of the inventory at the end of the day and lists the cashiers who worked in the store on that day. The report is implemented by a new client DailyReport that uses the already existing suppliers Cashiers and Inventory. It is then plugged into the class Store as its component (see Figure 8.9).

8.2.4 Incorporation Through a Replacement

If an obsolete version of the required responsibility already exists in the old code and is being replaced by a new one, then the old module with obsolete responsibility is

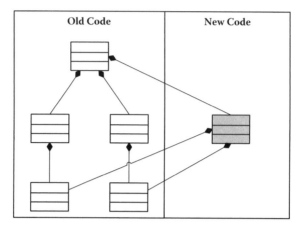

Figure 8.8   Class diagram of point-of-sale after incorporation of class Cashier.

replaced by a new module (see Figure 8.10). The replacement usually starts change propagation in all directions, because interactions with other modules have to be updated as well.

As an example, the point-of-sale program in Figure 8.6 contains the class Price that implements the price of an item. The old code assumes that there is only a single price for every item and, as a result, the class Price is very simple; it contains just one integer for the price along with methods getPrice() and setPrice() that return and set the price of the item, respectively. The change request is to support price fluctuations; the users of the program should be able to set prices of items in advance and be able to adjust the item prices on selected dates. For example, there can be sales periods where, on certain dates, the price is lower, while after these dates it returns to the previous level.

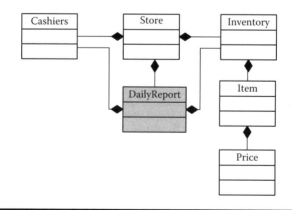

Figure 8.9   New responsibility incorporated as a new client.

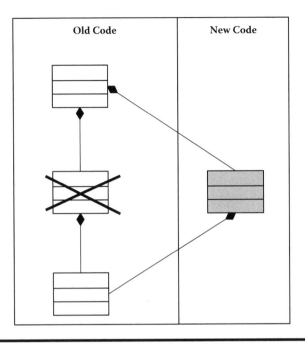

Figure 8.10 Obsolete composite/component class replaced by a new one.

This change requires a complete overhaul of the class Price. It adds new responsibility that deals with the successive dates and price adjustments and includes an algorithm that erases old prices on the dates past. This new class then replaces the old one.

8.3 Change Propagation

The code modifications, whether small or large in terms of the code size, often break the interactions among the classes. These broken interactions have to be repaired one by one, in a process that is similar to the process of impact analysis, but this time, the programmers do the actual code modifications. The secondary modifications are usually smaller than the primary modifications, and they are done directly in the old code. The set of all classes that are modified during the change are called the *changed set*.

In the previous example in Figure 8.6 and section 7.1.1, the constant price was replaced by a more complicated changing price that varies from day to day. The method getPrice() now has to have a new parameter that indicates the date on which the price is valid. That extra parameter causes modifications in the code of the classes Item and Inventory (see Figure 8.11).

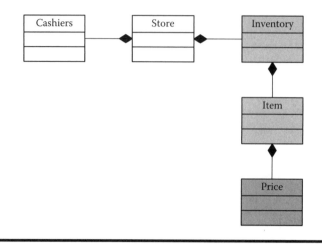

Figure 8.11   Change propagation for the sales price.

Deletion of obsolete responsibility also causes change propagation. Every location in the code that references the deleted responsibility must be inspected, and
the reference to it must be removed.

How Programmers at Ericsson Radio Underestimated the Impact Set

Impact analysis and change propagation go hand in hand; impact analysis estimates which
classes have to be modified, and change propagation modifies the code of the impacted classes.
Change propagation is the moment of truth for impact analysis; it confirms or refutes the predictions that impact analysis has made. As with all predictions, impact analysis is frequently less
then perfect.

The accuracy of impact analysis is important for software managers; they use the size of
the estimated impact set in their planning. Researchers at the Swedish company Ericsson Radio
Systems asked themselves how accurate the predictions of impact analysis are (Lindvall &
Sandahl, 1998). The data for both the estimated impact set and the actual changed set for a new
version of their project are presented in Table 8.1.

The data should be read in the following way: The total number of the classes in the system is
the sum of all numbers in the table, that is, the total = 42 + 0 + 64 + 30 = 136 classes. Of these
classes, 30 belong to the category of the classes that the programmers predicted would be modified, and, indeed, they actually were modified (lower right cell of the table). These classes are

Table 8.1   Accuracy of Impact Analysis Predictions

		Estimated	
		Unmodified	*Modified*
Actual	Unmodified	42	0
	Modified	64	30

Source: From Lindvall, M., & Sandahl, K. (1998). How well do experienced software
developers predict software change? *Journal of Systems and Software,*
43(1), 19–27. Copyright 1998 Elsevier. Reprinted with permission.

sometimes called *true positives*. On the other hand, there were zero classes that the programmers predicted would be modified but they were not; these classes are sometimes called *false positives*. The classes that the programmers predicted would not be modified and were not modified are called *true negatives*, and they are in the upper left cell of the table; there were 42 true negatives. Finally, *false negatives* are the classes that the programmers predicted would not be modified but that actually were modified; there were 64 false negatives.

The numbers in Table 8.1 are sometimes presented in terms of *precision* and *recall* (Baeza-Yates & Ribeiro-Neto, 1999), which are commonly used in the information retrieval. Precision indicates how many members of the estimated set are actually correct; that is, it is a ratio of (true positives)/(true positives + false positives). In the case of the engineers at Ericsson Radio Systems (Lindvall & Sandahl, 1998), precision = 30/(30 + 0) = 1 = 100%.

Recall indicates to what degree we retrieved everything that we need; that is, it is a ratio of (true positives)/(true positives + false negatives). In the case of Ericsson, recall = 30/(30 + 64) = 0.32 = 32%. In other words, the programmers estimated that the changes would impact only about one-third of all classes that actually were modified, and missed the other two-thirds. The managers who planned their effort got an estimate that was lower than reality by two-thirds!

The underestimation is very common in software engineering, perhaps because of the software invisibility, which is one of the essential software difficulties. However, software engineers are by no means the only people who underestimate the difficulties of the task they are facing. There are students who underestimate the difficulty of homework, book authors who underestimate the time necessary to write a book, and a long parade of others who find themselves in similar situations.

Summary

After the earlier preparatory phases, actualization modifies the code in such a way that the new requested functionality becomes a part of the code. Actualization of small changes is done directly by modification of the code in the location that was indicated by concept location. Actualization of larger changes is done by new classes that are incorporated into the old code. Polymorphism allows a straightforward incorporation of the new responsibility. Wherever the polymorphism cannot be used, then new responsibility can be introduced as a new supplier. If parts of the new functionality already exist in the code, then they can be glued together as a new client. If the old functionality needs to be upgraded, then it is incorporated through replacement. Secondary modifications then may propagate to other classes of the software.

Further Reading and Topics

There are numerous technologies that make the actualization easier. Polymorphism is one such technology, and its use in incorporation of new responsibilities was illustrated in section 8.2. Polymorphism and its theory are discussed in great detail by Cardelli and Wegner (1985).

Design patterns are precepts on how to use object-oriented technology, including polymorphism, in a sophisticated way to solve commonly occurring difficulties in class interactions. When properly used, they make incorporation of a new requested responsibility easier (Gamma, Helm, Johnson, & Vlissides, 1995; Stelting & Maassen, 2002).

Application programming interface (API) is a module that supports incorporation of composite clients. API is a supplier that provides a universal set of contracts for a specific problem area. When programmers need to create a new client, they use a combination of these contracts. They implement the new responsibility by finding the appropriate API and then gluing together the contracts offered by the API, by writing a minimal additional code. If they need to replace an obsolete client by an enhanced one, they use the same API and create the new client. API is a stabilized code, and ordinary changes do not propagate through API into the supplier slice; hence, change propagation is smaller. This greatly facilitates actualization of all changes that deal with the problems that are solved by API. An example of an elaborate API is in the *Eclipse Platform API Specification* (Eclipse, 2010).

Polymorphism, design patterns, and API belong to the category of *anticipated changes*. If programmers expect certain kinds of volatility, they can prepare software for it by using these techniques that make future changes easier. There are additional techniques that support anticipated changes, for example, *more general and complete class interfaces* (Parnas, 1979). However, all anticipatory approaches should be used with realistic expectations; the anticipation always codifies the past understanding of the system and past understanding of its evolution. There is no guarantee that the anticipated changes will actually arrive, while the unanticipated changes may hit with a vengeance. The anticipations also complicate the code and its comprehension by a new factor: The programmers have to guess what the original authors anticipated, and what they did not.

Among the additional technologies that support incorporation of new responsibilities into old programs, a widely used technology is *reflection* (Forman & Forman, 2004).

Some technologies support fast gluing of already-implemented responsibilities into a new composite client; they can be seen as a technological support of the incorporation of the composite client as described in section 8.2.3. Prominent among them are *scripting languages* (Ousterhout, 2002; Loui, 2008).

In certain situations where software cannot be stopped for the update, the incorporation is done dynamically while software is running (Hicks & Nettles, 2005).

Exercises

8.1 If you have a choice to incorporate your changes through polymorphism or through a component class, which one are you going to choose? Why?

8.2 Do changes done through polymorphism propagate to the clients of the base class?

8.3 How is the activity diagram of impact analysis in Figure 7.9 modified for change propagation?

8.4 What is the difference between small and medium size changes?

8.5 Give an example of the replacement of a component class by a class that contains new functionality.

8.6 Give an example of the replacement of the composite class by a class that contains new functionality.

References

Baeza-Yates, R. A., & Ribeiro-Neto, B. (1999). *Modern information retrieval*. Boston, MA: Addison-Wesley Longman.

Cardelli, L., & Wegner, P. (1985). On understanding types, data abstraction, and polymorphism. *ACM Computing Surveys, 17*, 523.

Eclipse. (2010). *Eclipse platform API specification*. Retrieved on June 18, 2011, from http://help.eclipse.org/helios/index.jsp?topic=/org.eclipse.platform.doc.isv/reference/api/overview-summary.html

Forman, I. R., & Forman, N. (2004). *Java reflection in action*. Greenwich, CT: Manning Publications.

Gamma, E., Helm, R., Johnson, R., & Vlissides, J. (1995). *Design patterns: Elements of reusable object-oriented software*. Reading, MA: Addison-Wesley.

Hicks, M., & Nettles, S. (2005). Dynamic software updating. *ACM Transactions on Programming Languages and Systems (TOPLAS), 27*, 1049–1096.

Lindvall, M., & Sandahl, K. (1998). How well do experienced software developers predict software change? *Journal of Systems and Software, 43*(1), 19–27.

Loui, R. P. (2008). In praise of scripting: Real programming pragmatism. *Computer, 41*(7), 22–26.

Ousterhout, J. K. (2002). Scripting: Higher level programming for the 21st century. *Computer,* 31(3), 23–30.

Parnas, D. L. (1979). Designing software for ease of extension and contraction. *IEEE Transactions on Software Engineering, SE-5*(2), 128–138.

Stelting, S., & Maassen, O. (2002). *Applied Java patterns*. Englewood Cliffs, NJ: Prentice Hall.

Chapter 9

Refactoring

Objectives

Refactoring is a phase of software change that improves the structure of the software while keeping the same functionality; the software has the same behavior before and after the refactoring. In this chapter, you will learn when and how to refactor the code so that evolution can continue unhindered.

After you have read this chapter, you will know:

- Prefactoring, which prepares the code for a specific change
- Postfactoring, which removes bad smells from the code
- Several specific refactorings, including function extraction, base class extraction, and component class extraction

***

An introductory example of a refactoring is "Rename an entity." Suppose that the programmers concluded that an identifier in the code is misleading and should be replaced by an improved one that better represents the concepts implemented by the entity. For example, the programmers may want to change the variable name money that is too generic to a more specific name salary.

In a simple context, renaming can be accomplished by a simple substitution of one string by another, but in the languages with complicated name spaces, like Java or C++, it can be a difficult task. The same name can be used in different contexts with different meanings. For example, names of methods can be overloaded, and the same name of a method with a different list of parameter types can have a different meaning. The programmers may desire to rename the identifier that has only one of these meanings. Therefore, often renaming is not just a simple string replacement, but it requires code analysis. Other refactorings are even more complex and change the software structure. Examples are merging and splitting classes, merging and splitting methods, moving a method from one class into another one, and so forth.

During the software change, refactoring is done both before and after the actualization, as indicated by Figure 9.1. Before the actualization, the programmers may want to reorganize software to make the following actualization easier; we call that *prefactoring*. After the actualization is complete, the programmers may want to clean up whatever problems the actualization caused, so that future programmers will encounter a clean and logical code structure; we call that *postfactoring*. It is a similar situation to home repair: Before adding a dishwasher to a kitchen, the repairman makes changes to the kitchen that give better access to the pipes and makes room for the dishwasher, without changing the kitchen's functionality (prefactoring). After the dishwasher has been installed, the repairman replaces all broken kitchen counter tiles, seals the holes around the pipes, cleans the debris, and so forth (postfactoring). If a repairman did not perform these tasks, you would consider it an incomplete or poor job; the same is true for software change.

The same set of refactoring transformations can be used in both prefactoring and postfactoring. For example, "Rename an entity," mentioned previously, is frequently used in postfactoring. The actualization that was just done in the software may mean that the entities of the program acquired new functionality and are no longer accurately identified by their old names; hence, they need renaming.

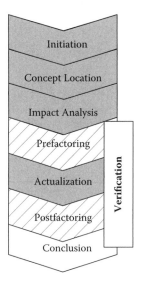

Figure 9.1   Refactoring in software change.

It can also be done during prefactoring when programmers decide to rename the entities in advance. There is a wide selection of refactoring techniques, and several frequently used refactorings are presented in the following sections. The last section of the chapter addresses the respective roles of prefactoring and postfactoring in the software change process.

9.1 Extract Function

During evolution, some functions grow too large because they acquire new responsibilities. When they reach a certain size, they need to be divided into smaller and more manageable parts that are easier to understand; "Extract function" refactoring accomplishes that. Sometimes a part of the function code is universal and can be used by other functions, and that is another reason to extract that code as a separate function. As an example, consider the following function:

```
void count_char_input(char c, int& count)
  {
int i, len;
char str[100];
cin.getline(str, 100);
len=strlen(str);
    count=0;
for(i=0; i<len; i++)
       if(str[i]==c)
             count++;
  }
```

The function count _ char _ input reads a string from input and then counts how many times the character specified as argument c appears in the string. The highlighted part of the function is doing the counting; this part of the code is universal and can be used in many different contexts, so it is a candidate for extraction as a new function count _ char _ str. After the extraction, function count _ char _ input calls this new function:

```
void count_char_input(char c, int& count)
  {
int len;
char str[100];
cin.getline(str, 100);
len=strlen(str);
    count_char_str(count,len,str,c);
  }

void count_char_str(int& count, int len, char* str, char c)
  {
```

```
int i;
count=0;
for(i=0;  i<=len;  i++)
            if(str[i]==c)
                    count++;
}
```

The functionality of the new and old code is the same; only the structure is different. The lines of code that were added during the function extraction are bold.

Function extraction consists of the following steps: First, the programmers select a block of code for extraction. The block must be syntactically complete; if there is a loop in the old function, it must be either completely inside or completely outside of the selection, and the same is true for other control constructs. Next, the programmer extracts the selected block as a new function body and replaces the selected block in the old function by the new function call. If the old function is a member of a class, the new function also becomes a member of the same class.

The variables that move from the selected block to the new function are turned into one of the following categories:

1. Local variables
2. Global variables
3. Parameters passed by value
4. Parameters passed by reference

The variable that is used only in the selected block and does not carry any information into or out of it becomes a local variable. That can occur even when the original variable is declared outside the selected block. A candidate for a local variable must be written before being read inside of the selected code, and it must not be accessed in the rest of the code; an example is the variable i in the previous code.

A variable will be passed as a value parameter to the new function if its value is used within the selected block, but either there is no modification to this variable in this block, or the modifications are not used elsewhere. This variable must be either local or passed by value in the original function; examples are variables len, str, and c.

If a variable is global in the original function, it remains global in the extracted function. The rest of the variables are passed as reference parameters; an example is the variable count in the previous code.

The programmers who want to separate a specific concept extension from the other concepts sometimes use function extraction. The opposite of extraction is macro expansion when the programmers replace function calls by the macro-expanded function body.

9.2 Extract Base Class

Programmers extract base classes whenever they want to prepare software for the incorporation of the new functionality through inheritance or polymorphism, as discussed in chapter 8. This is necessary whenever the programmers originally missed the opportunity to divide the responsibilities between the base and derived classes and created only one class instead. The need to separate derived and base classes becomes obvious later when a new change request demands a new functionality that has a large overlap with the functionality already implemented by an old class. If that happens, then the overlapping functionality should be extracted into the base class.

As an example of extracting a base class, consider a program that has a class `Matrix` that implements the concept "matrix" from the linear algebra; the matrix is implemented as a large array of 100 × 100 integers:

```
class Matrix
 {
      protected:
            int elements [100][100], columns, rows;
      public:
            Matrix();
            void inverse();
            void multiply (Matrix&);
            int get (int,int);
            void put(int,int,int);
 };
```

There is the following change request: "Add sparse matrix to the code." The reason for the change request is that the program is supposed to handle even larger matrices than 100 × 100, and there is a concern that the required memory size will be too large. Moreover, the data in the matrix are mostly zeroes, and therefore, the matrix can be implemented as a properly structured linked list where the nonzero elements are present as the nodes, and the zero elements are left out. For a better terminology, let's call this implementation *sparse matrix* and the original array implementation of the matrix to be *dense matrix*.

An analysis of the problem indicates that the only difference in the dense and sparse implementation of the matrix is the difference in the data structure that is used to represent the matrix. This difference is reflected in different access to the elements of the matrix, that is, in different implementations of the methods `get` and `put`. For the dense matrix, these methods are just reading and assigning an array element, while for sparse matrix they involve a search in the linked list that implements the matrix. At the same time, both sparse and dense matrices use the same algorithms for the matrix operations that constitute the bulk of the code, `multiply` and `inverse`. These algorithms originate from linear algebra; hence, it is not a surprise that they are the same for sparse and dense matrices. There is significant overlap between the old and new functionality; consequently, the situation is suitable for the addition of the new functionality through polymorphism, but that polymorphism has to be introduced into the program through prefactoring.

In the first step of the prefactoring, the programmers rename class Matrix to class DenseMatrix. The goal is to create several different classes that deal with matrices; therefore, each of them needs a more descriptive name. After renaming, the change is done in two steps: First, the base class AbstractMatrix is extracted from the DenseMatrix as in Figure 9.2. Later during actualization, the incorporation of the new functionality is done by polymorphism as in Figure 9.3. The shading in both figures represents the new class.

The extracting of the base class AbstractMatrix is done in the following steps:

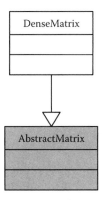

Figure 9.2　Extracting a base class.

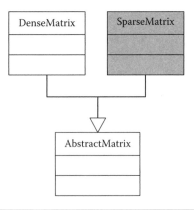

Figure 9.3　Incorporation of a new functionality in SparseMatrix.

- Create a new empty class `AbstractMatrix`
- Make `DenseMatrix` derived from `AbstractMatrix`
- Replace all references to the matrix elements in the code of `DenseMatrix` by `get` and `put` to avoid the direct references to the array implementation of the matrix
- Move variables `columns` and `rows` to `AbstractMatrix`
- Move methods `inverse` and `multiply` to `AbstractMatrix` and add virtual functions `get` and `put` into `AbstractMatrix`

After this refactoring, the code of the two classes is the following:

```
class AbstractMatrix
 {
      protected:
            int columns, rows;
      public:
            void inverse();
            void multiply (AbstractMatrix&);
            virtual int get (int,int)=0;
            virtual void put(int,int,int)=0;
 };
class DenseMatrix: public AbstractMatrix
 {
      protected:
            int elements [100][100];
      public:
            DenseMatrix();
            int get (int,int);
            void put(int,int,int);
 };
```

After this refactoring, the program has exactly the same behavior as before, but has a different class structure that is much more suitable for the addition of the `SparseMatrix`. Like `DenseMatrix`, the class `SparseMatrix` will contain the data structure that implements sparse matrix as a linked list as well as the functions `get` and `put` that access elements of the matrix. The complicated methods `multiply` and `inverse` will be inherited from the class `AbstractMatrix`, and this will greatly simplify the implementation and incorporation of `SparseMatrix`.

9.3 Extract Component Class

Programmers extract a component class when a primitive form of the concept extension is already present in the code, and it is to be modified and expanded in response to a change request. The old primitive concept extension does not have a

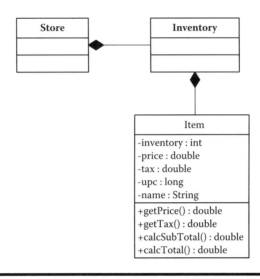

Figure 9.4   Point-of-sale before refactoring.

class of its own, but is a part of another class. The programmers extract it into a new class and, in this way, they prepare the software for the incorporation of the new functionality by replacement, as explained in chapter 8.

The point-of-sale example in Figure 9.4 contains three classes, and the concept "price" is implemented as a field and a method of the class Item. The old code assumes that there is only a single price for every item. The change request is to support price fluctuations and allow the users to set prices in advance and be able to change them on selected dates. For example, there can be sales periods where, on certain dates, the price is lower, while after these dates it returns to the previous level.

The prefactoring that prepares the program for this change creates the new component class Price and moves all related data fields and functions into it, as shown in Figure 9.5. It does not matter that this extracted class has very little responsibility, because it will be replaced anyway. During this class extraction, the field price and the method getPrice() are extracted and included in a new class called Price that is a component of the class Item.

The methods calcSubTotal and calcTotal that stay in the class Item are changed because they now have to deal with a component class. The commented-out code is deleted, and the code highlighted in bold is added to these two functions.

```
double calcSubTotal(int numberToSell)
   {
       if (numberToSell < 1) return 0.0;
       else
              // return numberToSell * price;
              return numberToSell * price.getPrice();
   }
```

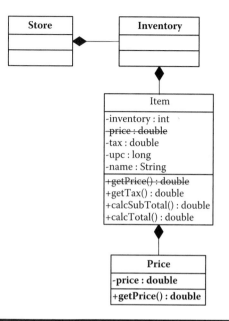

Figure 9.5   Extraction of the class Price.

```
double calcTotal(int numberToSell)
   {
        if (numberToSell < 1) return 0.0;
        else
        // return numberToSell * price *(1+tax);
         return numberToSell * price.getPrice() * (1+tax);
   }
```

After this refactoring, the code is ready for the incorporation of the new functionality. It is done through the replacement of the class Price by the new one that has the full functionality of price fluctuations.

Experience with Refactoring

Powertrain Engineering Tool (PET) is a program developed at Ford Motor Company to support the conceptual design of a car power train. The power train consists of the car engine, gear box, wheels, and so forth. The mechanical parts of the power train are described by physical parameters, and their interactions are modeled by equations that contain these parameters. Whenever a parameter value is changed, an inference algorithm traverses the equations and recalculates the values of all dependent parameters. The value of each calculated parameter must stay within certain constraints.

PET is implemented in C++, and every mechanical part is modeled as a C++ class. It is interfaced with other software, including optimization software and 3-D modeling software.

The object-oriented structure of PET was impacted by rapid evolution. PET started as a novel proof-of-concept tool, but it quickly developed a user community that used it to design the real power trains. Based on the experience from this use, user requirements substantially expanded. However, the structure of the code did not keep up with this rapid expansion. Some important concepts ended up sharing the same classes, which was not a problem with the original tool, but it became a problem once these classes grew. New programmers in particular had difficulty understanding and evolving this rapidly expanding system. With the growing size of the source code and confusing structure, further evolution became difficult.

One of the problems was the intermingling of two tiers: the graphics user interface through which the users communicate with the system and the algorithmic tier that handles the mechanical parts, the equations, and inference algorithm. This led to frequent situations where changes in user interface impacted the algorithmic part, and vice versa. To make the future changes easier, the programmers separated these two tiers, dividing the classes that intermingled the two tiers by "extract component" refactoring. That substantially improved the structure of the code and made further evolution easier, because the changes in the graphics user interface and changes in the algorithms no longer impacted the same code (Fanta & Rajlich, 1998).

9.4 Prefactoring and Postfactoring

Refactoring differs from actualization by the fact that it is hidden from the user, because no new functionality is added. This leads some programmers and managers to incorrectly conclude that refactoring does not add to the value of the software.

Among the refactorings presented in the previous two sections, both component and base class extractions are particularly suitable for prefactoring that prepares the software for a change actualization. These refactorings, if properly used, make the subsequent actualizations easier, and in fact they divide the implementation of the change into two smaller and easier steps: prefactoring and actualization.

Change actualization sometimes leaves messy code. The old code and the new code that was introduced by actualization may work correctly together, but the structure of the code may become confused and illogical. These deviations from the ideal have been called *bad smells*. Bad smells—if left untreated—will cause code decay and complicate future software evolution.

The purpose of postfactoring is to remove bad smells from the code. If the code contains functions that are too large, they are removed through "extract function." If the names used in the program become illogical, the problem is solved by renaming. If a class is too big, it is divided into smaller ones by class extraction, and so on. The postfactoring cleans up the code and makes future changes feasible.

While prefactoring has a clear goal, postfactoring's goal is a somewhat ambiguous "good code structure," and sometimes the question is raised how much code postfactoring is optimal. Obviously, insufficient postfactoring causes problems, and a certain portion of programming effort must be spent in postfactoring. The bad smells left in the code contribute to the code decay, and the code decay causes problems that were discussed in chapter 2 that ultimately lead to the loss of evolvability.

On the other hand, there is no such thing as perfect code, and excessive postfactoring can be a waste of resources. Small bad smells (small deviations from perfect) can be a matter of opinion, where different programmers may prefer different variants of the code structure. Excessive postfactoring or postfactoring that is not backed by a consensus of the programming team should be avoided.

Summary

Refactoring reorganizes the structure of software according to the needs of software evolution. It is done either before (prefactoring) or after (postfactoring) actualization. Prefactoring makes work on the change easier; hence, it is driven by the self-interest of the programmers. Postfactoring, on the other hand, makes work easier for future programmers; therefore, it requires a responsible attitude on the part of the programmers. There is a large selection of specific refactorings. Examples of important refactorings that were covered in this chapter are "Rename an Entity," "Extract a Base Class," "Extract Function," and "Extract Component Class."

Further Reading and Topics

There are as many different postfactorings as there are deviations from a good structure of the code. Beyond the refactorings that are presented in this chapter, numerous additional refactorings appear in a book by Fowler (1999). The same author also maintains a website that, at current count, contains 93 refactorings (Fowler, 2011). More advanced refactorings are refactorings to patterns (Kerievsky, 2005). Base class extraction of section 9.2 is from Opdyke and Johnson (1993).

Large-scale refactorings can be presented as transformations of dependency graphs; a survey of this approach is presented in a paper by Mens & Tourwé (2004).

Refactoring can be done by a standard editor, but in that case the bulk of the work is done by the programmers, and the code after refactoring must be thoroughly verified because the programmers can introduce bugs. Recent software environments contain a selection of refactoring tools that cover basic refactorings (Deva, 2009). They help the programmers to refactor and also to improve the correctness of refactoring results. Some of these tools are fully automatic, and they refactor the code correctly. After these refactorings, the code does not need retesting. An example of such refactoring tools includes those used for "Rename an entity."

Exercises

9.1 During the software change process, the programmer has already done refactoring during the prefactoring phase. Why is postfactoring needed?

9.2 Give three examples of refactoring. When should each of them be applied, and why are they important?

9.3 Associate the following types of refactoring with prefactoring and postfactoring. Justify each decision.

    a. Move function from one class to another

    b. Extract superclass

    c. Extract component class

    d. Merge classes

9.4 From the following function `printPosition()`, extract a new function that returns the position of the beginning of a given string in a given text.

```
void printPosition(){
  int i,j;
  char text[1024]="1234567890";
  int text_length = 10;
  char array_to_search1[4]="23";
  int array_to_search1_length = 2;
  int position1 = -1;
  for (i=0;i<text_length-array_to_search1_length+1;i++) {
      bool found = true;
      for (j=0;j<array_to_search1_length;j++)
          if(text[i+j]!=array_to_search1[j])
                found = false;
      if (found) {
          position1 = i;
          break;
      }
  }
  cout<<position1;
}
```

9.5 The following program calculates the square root of the absolute value of a given number. The program contains duplicate code, dead code, and variables without a meaning. Apply refactoring, and justify your decisions.

```
public class A {
  public static void main(String args[]){
          double c = Double.parseDouble(args[0]);
          if (c>0) {
                  double t = c;
                  double EPSILON = 1e-15;
                  while (Math.abs(t - c/t) > t*EPSILON) {
                          t = (c/t + t) / 2.0;
                  }
                  System.out.println(t);
          }
          else    {
                  double t = -c;
                  c = -c;
                  double EPSILON = 1e-15;
                  while (Math.abs(t - c/t) > t*EPSILON) {
                          t = (c/t + t) / 2.0;
                  }
                  System.out.println(t);
  }
          if ( c<0){
                  System.out.println(«Error: the number is
                                      smaller than 0»);
          }
  }
}
```

References

Deva, P. (2009). *Explore refactoring functions in Eclipse JDT.* Retrieved on June 20, 2011, from http://www.ibm.com/developerworks/opensource/library/os-eclipse-refactoring/index.html?ca=dgr-lnxw07Refractoringdth-OS&S_TACT=105AGX59&S_CMP=grlnxw07

Fanta, R., & Rajlich, V. (1998). Reengineering object-oriented code. In *Proceedings of International Conference on Software Maintenance* (pp. 238–246). Washington, DC: IEEE Computer Society Press.

Fowler, M. (1999). *Refactoring: Improving the design of existing code.* Reading, MA: Addison-Wesley.

———. (2011). *Refactorings in alphabetical order.* Retrieved on June 20, 2011, from http://www.refactoring.com/catalog/index.html

Kerievsky, J. (2005). *Refactoring to patterns.* Boston, MA: Addison-Wesley Professional.

Mens, T., & Tourwé, T. (2004). A survey of software refactoring. *IEEE Transactions on Software Engineering, 30*(2), 126–139.

Chapter 10

Verification

Objectives

Regardless of their size and scope, all changes in the code, even the smallest ones, have to be verified. After you have read this chapter, you will know:

- The reasons why programmers need to verify all their work
- The role of testing, its limits and strategies
- Unit testing and test-driven development
- Functional and structural testing
- The purpose of regression and system testing
- Verification of the code by inspections

***

Programmers are performing verification during phases of prefactoring, actualization, postfactoring, and change conclusion. Figure 10.1 shows the verification and the phases it overlaps with.

The reason for the need to verify programs lies in the essential difficulties of software that were described in chapter 1. Because of these difficulties, programmers very often produce imperfect work and commit various mistakes. These mistakes are called *faults*, *defects*, or *bugs*, and the purpose of the verification is to find and correct them. The bugs, when found, are either immediately fixed, or they are described in a bug report and recorded in the product backlog with the expectation that they will be fixed later.

Many techniques of software verification have been researched and proposed, but in current practice, testing and code inspection are the main techniques used.

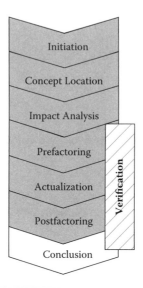

Figure 10.1   Software verification and its role in software change.

10.1 Testing Strategies

Software testing verifies the correctness of software through *tests*, which execute the program or its parts. Tests execute software with the specific input data, compare the outputs of the execution with the expected outputs, and report if there is a deviation. Tests are usually organized into a *test suite* that consists of several, often many, tests.

Although testing is the most common form of software verification, it has a serious weakness that has been summarized by the following observation: Testing can demonstrate the presence of bugs, but not their absence. No matter how much testing is done, residual bugs can still hide somewhere in the code, because they have not been reached and revealed by any of the current tests. No test suite can guarantee that the program runs without errors under all conditions; no matter how thorough it is, it cannot simulate all the circumstances under which the program or its parts operate.

There are deep theoretical reasons for this fact, as it is one of the consequences of the so-called *halting problem*. The halting problem states that it is impossible to create a tool that would analyze a program and determine whether the program contains an infinite loop or whether it always stops. Although the programmers can create tools that find some specific infinite loops, they cannot create tools that find all of them.

Because an infinite loop is a bug in many programs, it logically follows that it is impossible to create a perfect tool or perfect a test suite that would reveal all bugs. Programmers have been trying to do the best under the circumstances and have developed techniques of testing that—although they cannot and do not establish complete correctness of software—are nevertheless able to intercept a large number of bugs and satisfy reasonable stakeholder expectations.

When developing testing techniques, programmers face software discontinuity that is an essential difficulty of software and was discussed in chapter 1. Because of it, the software may give a correct result for a specific value, for example, for the value 1, but for the very next value, 0, it can have a bug because, in one of the statements somewhere in the code, it attempts to divide by this value.

There is a large variety of software testing techniques and contexts. The *tests of the new code* are created from scratch as a part of the software change. There is also the testing of the old code that was not supposed to be impacted by the change, and the tests make sure that this is indeed the case. These tests are called *regression tests*, because their purpose is to prevent regression of what was already functioning before. The *system tests* verify software comprehensively, without regard to what is new and what is old; they are done during the phase of change conclusion and verify the complete functionality of the software baseline.

Unit tests verify individual modules (units) of the program, for example, classes or class methods. *Functional tests* verify correctness of a specific functionality of the whole program. If the program has a graphical user interface (GUI), the features that are available to the user are tested in these functional tests. Furthermore, there are *structural tests* that guarantee that the tests executed certain parts of the programs, and the *testing coverage* specifies the parts that the structural tests must execute. The tests are aggregated into test suites that test various aspects of software and contain unit, functional, and structural tests.

There is a distinction between the *production code* and the *scaffolding* or *harness* code. Production code is part of the product, and corresponds to the customer requirements. Its compilation creates the executable code that will run on the customer's computer. In contrast, scaffolding is used only internally by the development team but does not go to the user. The scaffolding code is analogous to scaffolding that is used in the construction industry: It supports the workers and their tools during the building process and contains ladders or elevators to transport materials to the higher floors, temporary support for beams, platforms for the workers, and so forth. When the construction is done, the scaffolding is torn down and the users get the building without the scaffolding.

The software scaffolding or harness code consists of temporary throwaway parts that contain *test drivers* that control the execution of the tests and *test stubs* that implement a temporary replacement for missing classes and subsystems. It may also contain a simulation of the environment in which the software operates; for example, in programs with a graphical user interface, it may simulate user actions. Control programs are frequently tested with the controlled system being simulated, in order to lower the expenses of the testing and to give testers greater control over the parameters of the controlled system.

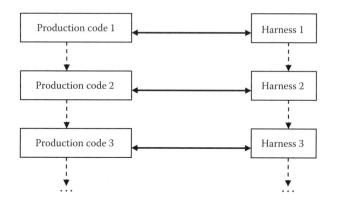

Figure 10.2   Parallel versions of production and harness codes.

The harness and the production code are one system. Each software change modifies not only the production code, but also modifies the harness code. After the concept location, the impact analysis identifies not only the modules of the production code that will change, but also the tests and other harness-code modules that have to be changed. For example, some tests may become obsolete, and these have to be deleted from the harness code, while new tests are introduced. The new tests added during the software change will become a part of the harness code. The prefactoring, actualization, and postfactoring phases update not only the production code, but they update the harness code as well. The parallel evolution of the production code and the harness code is shown in Figure 10.2.

The size of the harness code depends on the application domain and on the expected thoroughness of the software testing. As a rule of thumb, the harness code is on average the same size as the production code.

10.2 Unit Testing

Unit testing is the testing of a specific module of the software; it tests whether these modules correctly fulfill their responsibilities. Unit tests deal with the composite responsibility, or the local responsibility.

10.2.1 Testing Composite Responsibility

Testing of the *composite responsibility* verifies a class together with its supplier slice. The programmers write *test drivers* that substitute for the clients. An example of a test driver is the class TestItem in Figure 10.3; it tests whether class Item together with its supplier class Price fulfill their responsibility. Both classes Item and Price are called the *tested code*.

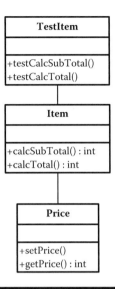

Figure 10.3 Example of a test driver.

Test drivers typically verify whether the tested class fulfills the contract with its clients, particularly whether the postconditions hold if the supplier keeps the preconditions. However, for practical reasons, the drivers rarely can deal with complete preconditions and postconditions, and most commonly, they check the fulfillment of the contract for a specific sampling of input values only.

An example in Figure 10.3 is a part of a point-of-sale system that contains a class that deals with items sold in a store. The following is an example of code of the test driver:

```
class TestItem
  {
  Public:
      Item testItem;
      void testCalcSubTotal()
        {
            assert(testItem.calcSubTotal(2, 3) == 6);
            assert(testItem.calcSubTotal(10, 20) == 200);
        }
      void testCalcTotal()
        {
            assert(testItem.calcTotal(0, 5) == 5);
            assert(testItem.calcTotal(15, 25) == 40);
        }
  };
```

In this example, the `assert` statement is a special statement that is used in the tools for unit testing; it contains a condition that checks whether the contract for a particular value is satisfied. The contract for that value is expressed as a logical statement, in this case an equivalence that checks whether a method returns the correct values. If the condition of the assert statement is not satisfied, the tester is notified that the test failed. If an `assert` statement is not available, it can be simulated by a combination of other statements.

Class `TestItem` consists of two tests, each testing a different method of class `Item`. The method `calcSubTotal` calculates one line of a customer receipt, where for a given number of items and given price the method calculates the subtotal to be paid, which is given by the formula: (price of the item) * (number of items). The corresponding test checks whether the method is doing this correctly for specific values 2 and 3. The method `calcTotal` adds the values of the first and the second parameter; the `assert` statements checks whether the method does that correctly for specific values 15 and 25.

10.2.2 Testing the Local Responsibility

Sometimes the local responsibility of a class needs to be tested. This situation arises when the supplier classes are not available or have not been tested and, therefore, confidence in them is low. In these cases, the user has to provide not only the drivers that substitute for the clients, but also *stubs* that substitute for the suppliers. These stubs are part of the testing harness code together with the drivers. Because the stubs are throwaway code, the programmers usually try to spend less time on their implementation than they would spend on the final supplier classes.

Several stubbing techniques save the programmer's effort. There are stubs with *less effective* but easier to implement algorithms; for example, if the supplier is supposed to sort the data, the stub uses a trivial but inefficient sorting algorithm. As a result, the test becomes less efficient, but since the users are not involved, it does not have great impact.

Another stubbing technique is to use a *limited range* of the contract (precondition) that the stub can handle and do the testing only within this range; this can simplify the code of the stub substantially. For example, if the supplier is supposed to convert the date into a day of the week, the stub may do that only for a selected month, for example, January 2011, and not worry about the quirks of the Gregorian calendar. Of course, this type of stub limits the composite responsibility of the client class also, and therefore, limits the range of the tests.

User intervention is a stubbing technique that interrupts the test and asks the user who is running the test for the correct answer from the stub. This technique is practical only in situations where the stub is executed only a few times during the test, or the stub provides a technique for how the value will be recorded and repeatedly used; otherwise, it becomes tedious. Also, the human user may input incorrect values; hence, this stubbing technique is to a certain degree unreliable.

The most controversial stubs are those with a *replacement contract* that provide a quick but incorrect postcondition. For example, the supplier is asked to convert a date into a day, but the stub always returns "Wednesday" as the answer, so the stub provides an incorrect answer most of the time. Stubs of this type can be written very quickly, but they introduce an intentional bug into the testing process. Testing with this type of stub may still provide valuable results if it is used with caution for some peripheral responsibilities that are not essential for the functioning software, and if the intentional bug that is introduced by this stub has an easy workaround.

10.2.3 Test-Driven Development

One of the promising unit-testing techniques is the *test-driven development* (TDD) that was mentioned in chapter 5 in Figure 5.2. In TDD, the programmers use the change request as the starting point and, based on this, they define a corresponding unit test. After such a test is written, they write or modify the actual code of the relevant unit and immediately test it. If the test fails, they correct the code and then repeat the corrections until the code passes the test.

A benefit of this approach lies in the fact that if there is an ambiguity in the change request, it is discovered early during the test writing. If the programmers cannot decide what the postcondition values should be for certain precondition values, then there is a problem with the requirement. Hence, the ambiguity is discovered early, before the effort is spent on actual code writing. This helps to prevent certain types of bugs that are caused by the ambiguity of the requirements.

Another benefit is that the test focuses the programmers' efforts on the essential code that helps to pass the test, which is also essential for the actualization of the change request. The programmers are sometimes tempted to add elaborate but unnecessary wrinkles to the code that are not only unnecessary, but can become a distraction and a source of bugs. TDD helps to avoid this gold plating.

10.3 Functional Testing

Functional testing verifies the functionality of the whole software that is available to the users. In many ways, it is similar to testing the composite responsibility, where the supplier slice is now the whole program. However, functional testing has to take into account the interface through which the program interacts with the outside world. This interface often has different properties than the rest of the software, and it plays a substantial role in the functional testing.

Programs with a GUI are a very common type of software. These programs are characterized by the fact that the users can select various features from the menus. Programmers do functional testing by executing these features one by one and observing the program behavior. For example, in the point-of-sale applications, there is a feature "print out a sales receipt"; the programmers verify this feature by selecting it from the menu, supplying the data, and observing whether the sales receipt is printed correctly, which means that the feature behaves as specified in the requirements or in a user manual. The complete coverage of all features means that the users test all features that the application offers.

Manual functional testing can become tedious; there are tools that record the events on the interface, and they can be used when automating functional testing. When the programmers test the software for the first time, they do the tests manually with the recording turned on. When they repeat the tests, they replay the recording. Several record/playback tools are currently available.

10.4 Structural Testing

Structural testing bases the testing on the structure of the code. The idea is the following: Since programmers cannot guarantee a complete correctness of the code by testing, they accept a reduced target. They guarantee that a reasonable number of the code units will be executed at least once. This guarantees that at least some of the more obvious bugs are discovered; those are the bugs that are revealed by a single execution of the unit.

An important notion of structural testing is *coverage*, which identifies the units that have been executed at least once and how they relate to each other. The coverage can be done on different granularities. The coarsest granularity that is usually considered is the granularity of the methods. In the example of Figure 10.3, there are the following methods: calcSubTotal(), calcTotal(), getPrice(), setPrice(); complete method coverage guarantees that each of these methods is executed at least once. This may look like a rather crude approach, as it guarantees very little in terms of the program correctness. However, it is still a valuable approach that guarantees the correctness of the software better than an arbitrary selection of tests.

Finer granularities that are used in structural testing include the granularity of statements; *statement coverage* guarantees that every statement of the program is executed at least once. There are many ways that a test suite can cover a statement. A *minimal test suite* covers all statements of the program and does not have any redundant tests, that is, it does not contain any tests that cover only statements that are not already covered by other tests. A minimal test suite is of particular importance because it efficiently accomplishes the coverage goal.

Consider the following code fragment:

```
read (x); read (y);
if x > 0 then
    write ("1");
```

```
else
        write ("2");
end if;
if y > 0 then
        write ("3");
else
        write ("4");
end if;
```

Each test for this code must specify two input values, one for the variable x and one for the variable y. The test suite consisting of a single test {<x=2, y=3>} covers statements write ("1") and write ("3"), but does not cover write ("2") and write ("4"); hence, it does not provide complete coverage. The test suite {<x=2, y=3>, <x=97, y=17>, <x=-1, y=-1>} covers all statements, but it is not minimal; the test {<x=97, y=17>} is redundant because it covers only statements that are already covered by test {<x=2, y=3>}. The test suite {<x=2, y=3>, <x=-1, y=-1>} covers all statements and is minimal.

A minimal test suite that provides complete coverage is ideal, but unfortunately, it is very hard and expensive to implement it in large programs. Very often, the test suites have redundant tests, and they cover only part of the code. The reason why it is hard to do higher coverage is the following: It is very easy to write the first test because no matter what it covers, it increases the test suite coverage. However, as the number of tests grows and the uncovered statements are fewer, it is increasingly hard to aim the tests at these remaining uncovered statements. To create new nonredundant tests takes more and more effort, and at some point, the managers may decide that the increased coverage is not economical. That is why many test suites fall short, sometimes far short, of complete coverage.

10.5 Regression and System Testing

After a change has been made, the programmers must retest the software to reestablish confidence that the former functionalities of the software still work properly. Regression testing attempts to find whether the change inadvertently introduced stray bugs into the intact parts of the software.

Because regression testing verifies the parts that are not supposed to change, tests from the past constitute the bulk of the regression test suite. The suite may consist of tests that use various testing strategies, and it is not uncommon that it combines the structural, unit, and functional testing. The original tests were created when the particular issue was tested the first time. After that, they become a part of the test suite, and they are reused repeatedly whenever regression testing is conducted.

Repeatability of the tests is the problem that the programmers have to address in this context; if a test worked in the past and the tested functionality did not change, the repeated test must return the same result. Repeatability can be a challenge in

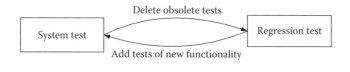

Figure 10.4 System and regression test suites.

certain situations; for example, if a test requires a manual mouse click on a specific point on the screen. Fortunately, there are tools available that allow the recording of the user actions; these actions can be recorded when the test is run for the first time and become part of the test suite. They are repeatedly replayed whenever the regression test suite runs.

There are two closely related test suites: regression and system test suites, as depicted in Figure 10.4. The *system test suite* verifies the whole functionality of software at a particular moment in time, and it is used to validate the new baseline. However, after a change, some tests become obsolete because the corresponding functionality has changed. These tests are deleted, and the resulting test suite is the *regression test suite* for the software after the change. When the tests for the new functionality are added to the test suite, a new system test is created, and it is then ready for the next baseline testing.

As new tests are added, the test suite often grows, and it can become time consuming to rerun it. For large programs, the system testing is often done overnight or over weekends.

10.6 Code Inspection

Code inspection is a totally different approach to software verification than testing. Its basic idea is that somebody else other than the author reads the code and checks its correctness. Code inspection does not require execution of a system, and it can be applied to incomplete code or to other artifacts like models or documentation. Code inspections are based on the idea that software defects are a programmer's mistakes, and that it is easier for other programmers to spot these mistakes than it is for the original programmer.

Habituation

To explain the success of code inspections, we have to understand the problem of *habituation*. Habituation is a term from psychology and neurobiology that explains how people (and animals) become blind to repeatedly experienced stimuli.

If there is a repeated stimulus, the response from the nervous system declines. For example, shortly after putting on clothes, people stop noticing them. People who live next to railroad tracks become habituated to the train noise and sleep soundly through the night, while a visitor who has not habituated repeatedly wakes up with each passing train.

Habituation is nature's coping mechanism. Imagine how overwhelmed our nervous system would be if all stimuli, no matter how repetitive, would be processed with the same intensity. There is so much to distract us: people walking behind classroom windows, the spot on the wall, a forgotten flier on the desk in front of us, and so forth. After the first glance, all these stimuli fade away and we can concentrate on the lecture, thanks to habituation.

However habituation also has a dark side. Some stimuli should not fade away, because they require our persistent attention. An example is traffic signs: Commuters who have traveled a road 100 times habituate and stop noticing the traffic signs. However, if there is a change—for example, a new stop sign in a place where it was not before—habituation can cause a serious accident. The departments of transportation know this, and when they introduce a new stop sign, they usually post one or several warnings that notify the commuters: "Watch out, there will be a new stop sign ahead," hoping that the commuters will notice one of these warnings.

The inability of programmers to find their own software bugs also belongs to this dark side of habituation. After reading their own code several times, programmers no longer read the code with the same intensity, but recall from memory what they think the code contains; hence, some rather obvious errors repeatedly escape their attention. A different reader who does not have the same habituation discovers these errors right away. The programmers can productively reinspect their own code, but only after a passage of time when the habituation has worn off (Thompson, 2001).

Inspections and testing are complementary verification techniques. There are bugs that are easily discovered by testing but are hard to spot by a human. An example is misspellings of long identifiers; they are intercepted early in the testing, during the compiling stage, but they can be very hard for programmers to spot. On the other hand, some bugs occur only in special circumstances, and it is hard to create a targeted test that aims at such circumstances. In this case, human readers have an advantage because, as they read the code, they can assess it from the point of view of these unlikely situations. An example is a potential division by zero in a code statement. Human readers can point out that, under certain circumstances, there is a danger that division by zero will occur and cause program failure. To create a test that causes such a situation can be much more difficult.

Inspections can also check whether different artifacts agree with each other. They can check whether the code implemented in actualization corresponds to the change request, whether the UML model corresponds to the actual code, and so forth. However, inspections cannot check some nonfunctional characteristics such as performance.

Inspections can be successful only if the code reviewer has knowledge of the technologies used in the process, understands the program domain, and understands the specifics of the change request. Code inspections may seem to be an extra cost, but they have proved to be an effective technique that increases the quality of the code.

The inspection process is sometimes formalized in code *walk-throughs*, which are conducted in a very structured way. A walk-through team is made up of at least four members: the author of the inspected code, a moderator, and at least two code reviewers. The walk-through process consists of preparation, where the code or other work products are distributed to the inspection team. For each document, one participant inspects the document thoroughly. Then there is the meeting in which all team members participate. The whole group walks through the document under direction of the reviewer, who notes the errors, omissions, and inconsistencies in the code; the other members of the team add their own observations. The moderator chairs the meeting and notes the discovered errors. In the end, the moderator produces a report from the walk-through session that contains recommendations that list the documents that need corrections and the documents that have to be completely reworked.

Summary

Software verification increases the quality of software by finding and removing bugs from the code. The two most common and complementary techniques of verification are testing and inspection.

Testing executes the program or its parts and assesses whether the program behaves correctly. Structural testing monitors execution of code units, most commonly the statements and methods. Unit testing selects a specific unit of the code, usually a class or a method, and tests its composite responsibility with the help of specially written drivers. Sometimes it tests its local responsibility with the help of both drivers and stubs that substitute for the supplier units. Test-driven development is a technique where the tests are written first, and the code is written after that and tested. Functional testing executes the software as a whole as it appears to the user. Regression testing reestablishes confidence in the parts of software that have not been touched by the change, and system tests verify a new baseline that includes both old and new code.

Software inspection is a process wherein programmers other than the author read the code and point out the bugs; the programmers approach the code from a fresh perspective and are able to spot bugs that escape the attention of the original authors.

Further Reading and Topics

Software verification is a key software engineering issue, and an enormous amount of research and practical work has been done and published in this field. There are specialized books and numerous papers that deal with it in a more thorough manner. Chapter 13 describes testing as the main task of a specialized group of developers, who are called testers; for them, a more thorough treatment of this topic is necessary. To answer that need, specialized courses on verification often appear in curriculums. Examples of textbooks that cover testing in a more thorough manner are those by Jorgensen (2008), Binder (1999), and many others.

In related literature, structural testing is often called white-box testing, while functional testing is often called black-box testing. The halting problem that is the theoretical basis for the incompleteness of all testing strategies is explored in the theoretical literature, for example, by Hopcroft, Motwani, and Ullman (1979).

The strategies for test selection of both functional and unit testing, including boundary-value testing and equivalence-class testing, are presented in a book by Jorgensen (2008). Unit testing and the tools that support it are described in a book by Hamill (2004). Test-driven development is explored in a book by Beck (2003). Several tools that support testing of GUIs through the record/playback strategy are described by Ruiz and Price (2007).

Unit testing is usually done bottom-up: The first units (classes) that are tested are the classes that have no suppliers. Once they are tested, their clients are tested, then the clients of the clients, and so forth, until the whole software is tested. A topological sort on the class-dependency diagram establishes the order in which the unit tests are conducted. However, this simple strategy does not work when there are loops in the dependency graph. These loops have to be disconnected, and the classes that lost their suppliers due to this disconnection have to be tested with the use of stubs (see chapter 14 and also a paper by Kung, Gao, and Hsia [1995]).

Structural testing and testing coverage is explored in great detail in a book by Ammann and Offutt (2008). Automatic test generation that aims to produce pre-defined coverage is discussed by Korel (1990).

Regression testing is done frequently and, therefore, an important issue is the reduction of the time that regression tests need to run. Various techniques that explore the regression-test creation and reduction are explored in a paper by Rothermel, Untch, Chu, and Harrold (2001). Among them are *firewalls* that limit the regression tests to the neighbors of the changed classes, with the idea that most of the regression bugs introduced by a change are forgotten change propagations (White, Jaber, Robinson, & Rajlich, 2008).

A thorough description of code inspections is presented by Fagan (1999). An important issue is the estimation of the defects that are left in the code, because it is an indicator of the quality of the code. A statistical technique called capture-recapture that uses inspection data was developed for that purpose (Humphrey, 1999; Biffl, 2002). The resulting indicator of the software quality is called *defect density* or *fault density*, and it is estimated that solid software of today contains 2.0 residual defects per 1,000 lines of code. The cutting edge of what can be achieved is 0.1 defects per 1,000 lines of code, but there is a trade-off between defect density and software cost. Some avionics software, where human life is at stake, aims at that high standard while accepting the extra cost that the additional testing and additional inspections require. The history of modifications and past faults also serves as a predictor of the faults left in the code (Ostrand, Weyuker, & Bell, 2005).

The change propagates not only through the production code, but it also propagates to the harness code, and in particular to the tests contained in the harness code. The tests are tied to the production code through dependencies, and there-fore, each change that affects a part of the production code propagates through these dependencies to the harness code and identifies the tests that are no longer valid (Ren, Shah, Tip, Ryder, & Chesley, 2004).

Exercises

10.1 After completing 100% statement coverage, is software without a bug? Give a simple example to validate your answer.

10.2 What is unit testing and why is it used?

10.3 What is the difference between inspection and testing?
  a. Give example of a bug that is easily found by testing
  b. Give example of a bug that is hard to find by testing
  c. Give example of a bug that is easily found by inspection
  d. Give example of a bug that is hard to find by inspection

10.4 What is regression testing? What does regression testing prevent?

10.5 Design a minimal test suite that cover all the statements of the following function:

```cpp
#include <iostream>
using namespace std;
char* f(int number){
   if (number>=0){
          switch (number){
                  case 0: return "yellow";
                  case 1: return "red";
                  case 2: return "green";
                  default: return "no color";
          }
   }
   else
     cout<<"error: the number has to be positive";
}
```

10.6 For the following program, design a minimal test suite:

```java
public static void main(String args[]) {
    int i,j;
    int k = 0;
    i = Integer.parseInt(args[0]);
    j = Integer.parseInt(args[1]);
    if (i>30) {
          if (i<=60 &&j<=150)
                k=1;
          else if (i<=90 &&j<=150)
                k=2;
          else
                k=3;
    }
    if (i==j &&i<=30)
         k=4;
    System.out.println(k);
}
```

10.7 Explain the difference between unit and functional testing.

10.8 In test-driven development, a test is written first and then the code to pass it. Given the following test, write a method that passes the test.

```
public class TestGrade {
  Grade testGrade;
  public void testGetFinalGrade() {
        assert(testGrade.getFinalGrade(70) == "Pass");
        assert(testGrade.getFinalGrade(69) == "Fail");
  };
```

10.9 Expand the test in exercise 10.8 to include grades A to F using the following grade scale:

Letter Grade	Minimum percentage
A	90
B	80
C	70
D	60
F	< 60

10.10 The following class Item needs to be tested:

```
public class Item{
   Price p = new Price();
           public Item(int priceOfItem){
                   p.setPrice(priceOfItem);
           }
   public double calcSubTotal(int numItems){
return numItems * p.getPrice();
}
public double calcTotal(double subTotal, double tax){
   return subtotal + tax;
}
 };
```

However, the class Price is not available. Write a stub of class Price for testing.

10.11 Explain the inspection process.

10.12 Inspect the following code and identify bugs in it.

```
public double calculatePercentage(int x, int y){
   if(x == 0)
           return 0;
   else
           return x/y;
}
```

References

Ammann, P., & Offutt, J. (2008). *Introduction to software testing*. Cambridge, U.K.: Cambridge University Press.

Beck, K. (2003). *Test-driven development: By example*. Boston, MA: Addison-Wesley Professional.

Biffl, S. (2002). Using inspection data for defect estimation. *Software IEEE, 17*(6), 36–43.

Binder, R. (1999). *Testing object-oriented systems: Models, patterns, and tools*. Boston, MA: Addison-Wesley Professional.

Fagan, M. E. (1999). Design and code inspections to reduce errors in program development. *IBM Systems Journal, 38*, 258–287.

Hamill, P. (2004). *Unit test frameworks*. Sebastopol, CA: O'Reilly Media.

Hopcroft, J. E., Motwani, R., & Ullman, J. D. (1979). *Introduction to automata theory, languages, and computation* (Vol. 3). Reading, MA: Addison-Wesley.

Humphrey, W. S. (1999). *Introduction to the team software process*. Boston, MA: Addison-Wesley Professional.

Jorgensen, P. (2008). *Software testing: A craftsman's approach* (3rd ed.). Boca Raton, FL: Auerbach Publications, Taylor & Francis Group.

Korel, B. (1990). Automated software test data generation. *IEEE Transactions on Software Engineering, 16*, 870–879.

Kung, D. C., Gao, J., & Hsia, P. (1995). Class firewall, test order, and regression testing of OO programs. *Journal of Object-Oriented Programming, 8*(2), 51–65.

Ostrand, T. J., Weyuker, E. J., & Bell, R. M. (2005). Predicting the location and number of faults in large software systems. *IEEE Transactions on Software Engineering, 31*, 340–355.

Ren, X., Shah, F., Tip, F., Ryder, B. G., & Chesley, O. (2004). Chianti: A tool for change impact analysis of Java programs. *ACM SIGPLAN Notices, 39*, 432–448.

Rothermel, G., Untch, R. H., Chu, C., & Harrold, M. J. (2001). Prioritizing test cases for regression testing. *IEEE Transactions on Software Engineering, 27*, 929–948.

Ruiz, A., & Price, Y. W. (2007). Test-driven GUI development with TestNG and Abbot. *IEEE Software, 24*(3), 51–57.

Thompson, R. (2001). Habituation. In *International encyclopedia of the social and behavioral sciences*. (N. J. Smelser & P. B. Baltes, Eds.). Oxford, U.K.: Pergamon.

White, L., Jaber, K., Robinson, B., & Rajlich, V. (2008). Extended firewall for regression testing: An experience report. *Journal of Software Maintenance and Evolution: Research and Practice, 20*, 419–433.

Chapter 11

Conclusion of Software Change

Objectives

The last phase of software change is a phase where the programmers integrate the modified code into the baseline, prepare software for future changes, and may release the new version to the users. After you have read this chapter, you will know:

- Build of the new baseline
- Preparation of the software for future changes
- Release of the new version

***

After the previous phases of the software change have been completed, conclusion is the last phase, as depicted in Figure 11.1. In this phase, programmers commit the updated code to the version control system. As we discussed in chapter 3, conflicts may arise with teammates' parallel updates, and resolving these conflicts is a part of this phase. After the changes have been committed and conflicts have been resolved, a new baseline is created in a process that is called the *build*.

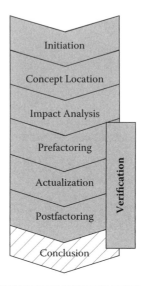

Figure 11.1   Conclusion phase of software change.

11.1 Build Process and New Baseline

The new baseline differs from the old one by modifications in several files. The build process first recompiles the modified files and then links all files into a new executable. Verification follows; this verification guarantees that the new baseline is as bug free as possible and that it represents a progress of the project, not a regress. The verification is often done by system testing, and it can take a significant amount of time and significant computer resources, depending on the size of the project. For many projects it is done overnight or over the weekend. Often, a specialized testing team conducts this baseline testing.

To do a build that includes testing of the new baseline, the programming team typically has a deadline by which programmers have to commit their changes; this is the time when the build starts. If some programmers miss that deadline, they have to submit their changes for the next build. However, in that case, they have to guarantee that their changes comply with the new baseline. That means that a missed build is not just a postponement of the commit, but there is additional work involved. If the files that the programmers worked on extensively change in the new baseline, it can be significant additional work.

If programmers commit faulty code and the bugs are discovered during the baseline testing, the testing team has to respond. If the bugs are minor, the testing team can still certify the updated code as the new baseline and add the correction of these bugs into the product backlog, with the idea that they will be fixed as a part of future changes. If the bugs are more serious but they are discovered early in the testing process, the testing team can selectively reject the commits that caused the bugs and create the new baseline without them. The team also can ask the programmers who committed faulty code to fix the faults.

However, in some instances, all the work done on the new baseline has to be rejected, and no new baseline is created. In the language of the programmers, this is called a broken baseline or a failed build. If that happens, the programmers will return to the old baseline, and all work that was done to update it is either invalidated or postponed. On large projects, this may represent a significant financial loss. There is pressure to disregard project faults and accept the baseline with minor defects as a successful build; therefore, each project has a standard that determines which defects are showstoppers that require a broken build to be declared. Obviously, the projects that do not compile or do not link, and hence, cannot even run, belong to that category.

Usually, the testing team is able to identify which files caused the broken baseline and the programmers who committed them. Many teams have a penalty for breaking the build, and certainly the reputation of the programmers who broke the build suffers.

Software verification is part of the build; it is most commonly done by system testing. The frequency and extent of the build verification depends on the size of the program and the expected quality of the software. To postpone the build for too long means that there could be a large accumulation of bugs or conflicts that makes the build more difficult and less likely to succeed. An analogy of a build is kitchen cleaning: If cleaning of the kitchen is postponed too long, the accumulation of dirty dishes becomes too big, and the task of cleaning becomes intimidating. The programmers who face this big task caused by a delayed build are tempted to postpone it even further. The best policy is to schedule a build in advance, and then to stick to the schedule.

Daily overnight builds became a standard of medium-sized projects. The resulting new baseline is the starting point for the next round of software changes.

Daily Builds at Microsoft

The Microsoft process of program development is characterized by many developers who work on large software projects, and they work on their individual software changes in parallel. They synchronize their results through daily builds. The daily build starts at a specific time in the evening and runs overnight. If the build is successful, a new baseline is available the next morning, when the programmers show up for work.

If the programmers want to have their work included as a part of the build, they have to commit before the deadline when the build starts. If they miss the deadline, they have to work toward the next deadline, but there will be a different baseline by then, and they have to update their files, and sometimes they even have to redo their work in the context of the new baseline. They are expected to commit every few days. Every build first recompiles changed files and then links the entire system into a new executable file. That is followed by a system test that tests this new baseline.

The complete build can be an extensive process. An example is Microsoft Windows NT 3.0, which consists of 5.6 million lines of code. A complete build took up to 19 hours, and hence, it could not be done overnight (Zachary, 2009). To speed up the process, a greatly reduced system test called a *smoke test* has been developed. According to the Microsoft website, "The term smoke testing originated in the hardware industry. The term derived from this practice: After a piece of hardware or a hardware component was changed or repaired, the equipment was simply powered up. If there was no smoke, the component passed the "test" (Microsoft, 2005). A smoke test exercises the entire system but uses only a limited number of very basic tests; it is the first indication whether the baseline works or whether something is fundamentally wrong. A smoke test rarely runs for longer than one hour. While the smoke test is done frequently, a more thorough system test is conducted at larger time intervals.

Of course, broken builds do occasionally happen, and Microsoft immediately identifies a culprit code and the culprit programmer who created that code. For Windows NT, where many programmers participated and the cost of a broken build was large, the programmers had beepers, and if the broken build was caused by their code, they would be mercilessly dragged out of the bed in the middle of the night and asked to fix their code on the spot.

The software process used at Microsoft guarantees that the code files that the individual programmers work on do not deviate from each other too much. Daily baseline testing, even the minimal smoke testing, indicates that the code is not decaying. Daily build also gives the programmers experience with the entire system, establishes the individual programmer reputation, and improves the morale (McCarthy & McCarthy, 2006). Because of these documented advantages, the daily build was adopted by many successful software development processes across the whole software industry, and they form the foundation of the processes explained in the later chapters of this book.

11.2 Preparing for Future Changes

Once the software change is finished, the preparations for future changes start. The change request that was just implemented is labeled "inactive" or deleted from the backlog and the new requirements that arrived are added. The product backlog is reanalyzed and reprioritized because the past software changes make some future changes easier and others harder; some requirements become more urgent while others become less critical; and new knowledge gained during the change gives a better insight into the value or difficulty of future changes.

Throughout the software change, the programmers work very hard to comprehend the changing software, and some authors claim that this comprehension constitutes more than half of their total effort (Corbi, 1989). There is a danger that this arduously gained comprehension will soon be forgotten and that all the effort that went into it will be lost if it is not properly recorded. A single programmer's resignation can have serious consequences because the comprehension—effectively half the work he or she has done—departs as well. The project team then must rebuild the knowledge of the parts that only the departing programmer comprehended, often at a considerable expense. Even if all programmers stay with the project, over time they forget the infrequently visited parts of the software. Software change conclusion is an opportunity to record the newly gained comprehension before it is lost.

The vehicle for recording this comprehension is *external documentation*. The external documentation is a set of special documents that describe the software, but are separate from the source code. Because the external documentation is separate from the code, it can be updated without a need to recompile the code. *Annotations* describe the functioning of the different parts of the software. The information that particularly needs to be recorded are the contracts between the clients and suppliers, coordinations among the modules of the software, explanations of the cryptic parts of the code, or the nature of the algorithms that the code implements.

11.3 New Release

Establishing a baseline is an internal matter of the project, and its purpose is to synchronize the programmers' work and assess the quality of the code. From time to time, the programmers do an even more thorough verification and then release the baseline code to the users as a new version. Substantial extra work is always required for a release; therefore, the frequency of the releases is both a technical and a business decision.

It has become customary to have less frequent major releases and more frequent minor releases. Major releases are the releases where the functionality of the software is substantially changed, while minor releases deal only with small updates or bug fixes. A common practice is to designate major releases with the number before the decimal point, while the minor releases are designated by the numbers after the decimal point. For example, there may be an application AwesomeApp 4.2, where the number 4 is the number of the major release, while 2 is the number of the minor release that updates major release 4. This process was summarized in chapter 2 as the "versioned model of software life span." It has become customary to download and install major releases, while minor releases are often delivered as patches that are incorporated into the users' program.

In situations where there is only one user or few users who fund the project, these users can exercise their large clout, and they may influence the decision of when software is released. They typically conduct a test that determines whether the software is release worthy. The task they conduct for that purpose is *acceptance testing*. It is functional testing that thoroughly tests various software functionalities. If the users are satisfied, the software is approved for release; otherwise, the programmers have to do additional work and fix all of the users' objections.

As explained in chapter 10 on software verification, the verification—whether by testing or by inspections—cannot guarantee a complete correctness of the software. In fact, it is very common that the early releases are burdened by bugs and that only later in the software evolution do programmers find and fix them. The users of the software can help to find these bugs because they use it in ways that the original programmers often do not expect.

The large releases of software with large user communities are done in several steps that are commonly called *alpha release*, *beta release*, and *general release*. The alpha release is usually done in-house, and it means that the software is subjected to a thorough functional testing, often by a different team than the team of developers. As the defects are discovered, the developer team fixes them while the testing team continues the testing.

In the beta release, select outside users are involved; sometimes these users are called beta testers. Very often these users are selected because of their loyalty and technical prowess. They understand the tentative nature of the program verification, report the bugs they find, and suggest software improvements. There may be a special contract between software developers and beta testers that contains a reduced software price (or may even pay for their service), nondisclosure agreements, and so forth.

Finally, when bugs reported from the alpha and beta releases are fixed, there is an unrestricted general release where the typical customers receive the product. The reports from these users serve to prepare new small releases.

User manuals and *help systems* are typically prepared as a part of a release. They help the customers to use the system, and they have to be regularly updated to reflect the latest changes.

Summary

Software change conclusion builds a new software baseline; this new baseline is the starting point for future changes. The build process involves an extensive testing by system test. Selected baselines are released to the users as new versions of the software. Major versions are distributed as downloads of the software, while minor versions are frequently distributed as patches. Preparation for future changes includes updates of the product backlog or updates of the external documentation. Software change conclusion is the last phase of the software change and the last chapter of this section of the book.

Further Reading and Topics

Some authors recommend frequent builds several times a day to avoid the need to integrate too many changes at once. The advantage is that the smaller changes that each build handles lead to an improved likelihood that the build will be successful, and the cost of broken builds is smaller. However this strategy is viable only in smaller projects where the build takes less time (Duvall, Matyas, & Glover, 2007).

The previous chapters emphasized the need for verification of all software modifications, throughout the whole software change process. Despite all efforts, and as a consequence of the incompleteness of all available verification techniques, software changes still introduce bugs into the code. The work that studies these bugs is surveyed by Kim, Whitehead, and Zhang (2008).

The popular tool Javadoc extracts annotations from the comments in the code (Oracle, 2011). Incremental redocumentation is a process that opportunistically adds further information to the annotations. Whenever programmers make a change and obtain comprehension of a specific file or class, they record that comprehension in the relevant annotation. Over time, the documentation of the program accumulates, and it is mostly concentrated in places with a high frequency of visits, which are the places that need the documentation the most (Rostkowycz, Rajlich, & Marcus, 2004).

An overwhelming number of the patches are incorporated into the code while the program is not running. In contrast, some programs cannot be stopped, and the changes require patching the program while it is running. In these situations, the new binary code of the patches has been created in the traditional way, but it is integrated into the running system by *runtime activation*, which requires special strategies (Hicks & Nettles, 2005).

There may be additional activities of change conclusion that depend on the specific software process that is employed in the project. These activities are described in future chapters in the context of the specific processes.

Exercises

11.1   What is a broken baseline? How can it be avoided?

11.2   What happens if a programmer misses a deadline for build?

11.3   What is a common meaning of numbers 4 and 2 from the name of the application "AwesomeApp 4.2"?

11.4   What is the difference between alpha and beta releases? What makes these two releases different from general releases?

11.5   Why is baseline system testing not sufficient for the release to general customers?

11.6   List three reasons a nightly build is important.

11.7   Why should a project have a standard that determines when a broken build should be declared?

11.8   What is the advantage of running a smoke test instead of just relying on the system test?

References

Corbi, T. A. (1989). Program understanding: Challenge for the 1990s. *IBM Systems Journal, 28*, 294–306.

Duvall, P., Matyas, S., & Glover, A. 2007. *Continuous integration: Improving software quality and reducing risk*. Upper Saddle River, NJ: Addison-Wesley.

Hicks, M., & Nettles, S. (2005). Dynamic software updating. *ACM Transactions on Programming Languages and Systems (TOPLAS), 27*, 1049–1096.

Kim, S., Whitehead, E. J., & Zhang, Y. (2008). Classifying software changes: Clean or buggy? *IEEE Transactions on Software Engineering, 34*, 181–196.

McCarthy, J., & McCarthy, M. (2006). *Dynamics of software development*. Bellevue, WA: Microsoft Press.

Microsoft. (2005). *Guidelines for smoke testing.* Retrieved on June 21, 2011, from http://msdn.microsoft.com/en-us/library/ms182613(VS.80).aspx

Oracle. (2011). *Javadoc tool.* Retrieved on June 21, 2011, from http://www.oracle.com/technetwork/java/javase/documentation/index-jsp-135444.html

Rostkowycz, A. J., Rajlich, V., & Marcus, A. (2004). A case study on the long-term effects of software redocumentation. In *Proceedings of 20th IEEE International Conference on Software Maintenance* (pp. 92–102). Washington, DC: IEEE Computer Society Press.

Zachary, P. G. (2009). *Showstopper! The breakneck race to create Windows NT and the next generation at Microsoft.* New York, NY: Free Press.

SOFTWARE PROCESSES

Contents

This part of the book presents the most common software processes. It explains what a software process is and what the forms are (model, enactment, performance, and plan). Then it deals with the iterative process of a solo programmer (SIP), the team agile iterative process (AIP), the directed iterative process (DIP), and the centralized iterative process (CIP); these processes are primarily applicable to the stages of software evolution and servicing, but they also apply to initial implementation and reengineering. This part then covers initial development and the final stages of software life span, and hence it presents an overview of processes applicable to all stages of software life span.

Chapter 12

Introduction to Software Processes

Objectives

The software engineering discipline studies successful projects of the past and uses this experience as a recommendation for future projects. An accumulated experience with software processes is the core of software engineering. The iterative processes of software evolution and servicing play a prominent role, and one of them—the solo iterative process (SIP)—is explained in this chapter.

After you have read this chapter, you will know:

- The granularities and forms of software processes
- The solo iterative process (SIP)
- The two main work products and three main loops of SIP
- The enactment and measures of SIP
- Planning in SIP

***

At the core of the study of processes is the belief that a good process leads to good product and vice versa. This belief is shared by all engineering disciplines, including software engineering. To discover good processes, software engineers study both successful and unsuccessful past projects and try to identify both the good insights that led to successes and the mistakes that led to failures. There is a large variety of software processes that were tried in the past. To orient ourselves in these processes, we start with the characteristics that allow us to classify them.

12.1 Characteristics of Software Processes

A process is a routine that converts one thing into another or modifies something. For example, there are chemical processes that mix components and produce compounds, or an administrative process that starts with an appearance in a government office and results in a driver's license, or the process of a loan modification that starts with filling an application and results in changed terms of the loan, and so forth.

Software processes are specialized processes that develop or modify software. There are many software processes that have been employed in the past, and this chapter starts with their classification according to their basic characteristics: process granularity, form, stage they are employed in, and team organization.

12.1.1 Granularity

Coarse granularity processes deal with long periods of time, and fine granularity processes deal with short time intervals. Theoretically speaking, the software lifespan models of chapter 2 are very coarse software processes that consist of stages. Stages are also processes of somewhat finer granularity (see Table 12.1), where the granularity decreases from top to bottom.

Most of what software engineers usually call *processes* fits within a single stage or into a few neighboring stages. This book follows this common practice and uses the generic word *process* for the processes that fit within a single stage of the life span or into neighboring stages. The processes, in this narrow sense of the word, consist of tasks that in turn consist of phases or subtasks. For example, software change is a task of the software evolution processes, and it contains the phases (subtasks) of concept location, impact analysis, actualization, and so forth. Phases are further divided into steps or actions. Table 12.1 summarizes this terminology.

Table 12.1   Granularities of Software Processes

Granularity	Example
life span	staged, V-model
Stage	evolution, servicing
Process	SIP, AIP, DIP, CIP
task	software change, build
phase, subtask	concept location, actualization
action, step	inspection of a class

12.1.2 Forms of the Process

Another important characteristic is the *form* of the software process. The process can be in the form of a *process model* that describes the tasks, their relations, their results, and the stakeholders who participate in them. The process model is a blueprint of how to conduct a process and, as all models, it presents an abstraction and simplification of reality.

The process can also be in the form of *enactment*, which is the actual process that is happening in a project. The enactment consists of the real tasks and produces real results. As each project has its own peculiarities, there are inevitable deviations and exceptions from the process model. They should be minor and infrequent; massive deviations and exceptions indicate that there is something wrong with the process model.

Process *performance* is the set of measurements that an observer of an enacted process collects. The tasks of the process are measured for their duration, their cost, and other measures. There are also measurements related to the characteristics of the work products produced by the process, including their size, quality, and so forth. Other measurements may address the characteristics of the stakeholders, including the productivity, work quality, frequency of interactions, and so forth.

A process *plan* summarizes expected future performance and required resources for a given process. It may include the projected time needed to complete future tasks, the required number of team members, the expected quality of the results, and so forth.

12.1.3 Stage and Team Organization

An important characteristic is the stage the processes work in. The stages of evolution and servicing require *iterative processes* that are characterized by repeated changes to existing software. Software evolution and servicing command the largest amount of a software engineer's time; therefore, these processes are the first ones that we are addressing in this and in the next chapter. They are followed by noniterative processes of initial development (chapter 14) and final stages of software life span (chapter 15), although some tasks of these processes can be also done iteratively.

The rest of this chapter describes the iterative process of a solo programmer, and the next chapter describes the iterative processes employed by a team.

12.2 Solo Iterative Process (SIP)

All iterative software processes repeatedly modify software and are particularly suitable for the stages of software evolution and servicing. The solo iterative process (SIP) is characterized by a single programmer working alone. Despite its simplicity,

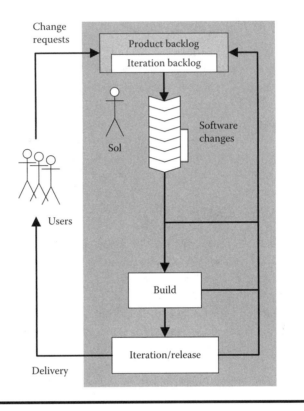

Figure 12.1 SIP model.

SIP shares some characteristics with the team iterative processes, and hence, it is a suitable introduction into the topics of the software processes.

When solo programmers work on their projects, a fundamental question arises: Why should they worry about a process and software engineering at all? In chapter 1, we talked about the original ad hoc processes that characterized the early software projects; they often worked and produced valuable software for their time. Why not let the solo programmers of today do the same, to react flexibly and creatively to the various challenges they are facing?

The short answer to that question is that even the solo programmers have to meet their obligations, fulfill their promises, and pay their bills. They need to know where they stand and be able to plan the future; they need to *manage* their own resources. SIP is a software process that single programmers use while working alone on a software project.

The SIP model is shown in Figure 12.1. For easier reading, the solo programmer who is the hero of this process is named "Sol"; please note that, although rare, the name can be either male or female, a first name, or a nickname. In Figure 12.1, Sol does all tasks that lie within the shaded rectangle; the other stakeholders are the users of Sol's product. Two work products play a prominent role in SIP and other iterative processes: the product backlog and the code.

Sol receives the requirements from the users, records them in the product backlog, analyzes them, and prioritizes them, as was explained in chapter 5. Sol then selects the highest priority requirements from the product backlog and creates the iteration backlog that consists of all the requirements that will be implemented in the next iteration. The iteration in SIP often coincides with a new version release, and the iteration backlog is a collection of the requirements that will be implemented in this next version. The iteration/release loop is the outer loop of the SIP process.

From the iteration backlog, Sol selects a specific change request and implements the corresponding software change, going through its various phases that were described in the previous part of the book (see the schematics in Figure 12.1). Then Sol updates the product backlog by closing or deleting the change request that has been implemented. After that, Sol selects the next change request from the product backlog. These tasks are presented by the inner loop of the SIP model.

At regular intervals, Sol builds a new baseline to monitor more thoroughly the progress of the project. This is the middle loop of the SIP model.

More elaborate versions of SIP deal with additional work products like the documentation, models, user manuals, and so forth. Sol updates these other work products as additional tasks within the three iterative loops of SIP.

12.3 Enacting and Measuring SIP

Sol enacts the SIP model on a specific software project. While enacting the process, Sol works on the tasks and work products that the SIP model specifies. As an example, suppose Sol works on a point-of-sale application. The upper part of Table 12.2 contains a short fragment of the log of enacted SIP that records the tasks and subtasks that Sol performed, while the lower part contains the explanation of the log acronyms.

In the first subtask, Sol selects the change request "Add cashier session" from the product backlog. During the next subtask, concept location, Sol determines that the relevant concept is located in class `CashierRecord`. Impact analysis follows and identifies four classes that need to change. The refactoring is next, and it extracts class `Session`.

At this point, Sol decides to make an exception to the SIP model and works on the task "Download and install new version of Bugzilla." After that, Sol returns back to the next task of the SIP model and actualizes a new version of the class `Session`. Then Sol builds a baseline. While doing the system test for the baseline, Sol finds two bugs and decides to add them to the backlog rather than fixing them immediately. The process enactment then continues with additional tasks that do not appear in the log fragment in Table 12.2.

Table 12.2 SIP Enactment

	Task	Comments
1	Ini	add cashier session
2	CL	`CashierRecord`
3	IA	4 classes
4	Ref	extract class `Session`
5	Ex	install new version of Bugzilla
6	Act	class `Session`
7	Bas	add two regression faults to the backlog
8		. . .
	Code	**Meaning**
	Pri	backlog prioritization
	Div	dividing the change into smaller parts
	Ini	software change initiation
	CL	concept location
	IA	impact analysis
	Ref	refactoring and testing
	Act	actualization and testing
	Test	other testing
	Bas	baseline build
	Rel	release
	Ex	exceptional task or phase

The full log of enacted SIP may span weeks, months, and even years. Table 12.2 monitors the process on the granularity of phases, and this is the recommended granularity. However on some projects, that granularity seems to be too detailed, and Sol monitors the use of time on the coarser granularity of tasks, which makes the logs shorter and less tedious, but sometimes leads to a loss of important information.

12.3.1 Time

The single most important resource of the SIP is Sol's time, and measuring the use of time is the foundation for Sol's planning. Time tracking has been discussed in many contexts, particularly in the context of *time management*. It is an accounting system for time, telling Sol how time was spent in the past. The raw time data for SIP are collected in an expanded log of Table 12.3. It is an expansion of the upper part of Table 12.2, and each row of the log records the start, end, and interruptions for each task. The last column contains the size of code that Sol dealt with while working on the tasks, and it is explained in the next subsection.

The time log contains raw data that have to be processed. There is a difference between the total time and the clean time that is obvious to every observer of the game of American football. Each game consists of four 15-minute quarters, but interruptions do not count toward these 15 minutes. Hence, 15 minutes is the clean time of each quarter, while total time includes all interruptions and can take considerably longer. In the log fragment of Table 12.3, there are two columns for a number of interruptions and for their summary time in minutes. Clean time is then given by the formula

$$\text{Clean time} = \text{end time} - \text{start time} - \text{time of interruptions}$$

Table 12.3   Time Log

	Process Enactment					Interrupt		
	Task	Comments	Date	Start	End	#	Time	Size
1	Ini	add cashier session	4/21	8:32	8:39	1	2	
2	CL	CashierRecord		8:42	8:52			340
3	IA	4 classes		8:52	9:23	2	12	420
4	Ref	extract class Session		9:27	10:46	3	25	36
5	Ex	install new version of Bugzilla		10:51	11:42	2	6	
6	Act	Class Session		1:23	2:17			98
7	Bas	add two regression faults to the backlog		2:22	3:12	3	12	12,000
8		. . .						

Sol uses the log data to extract answers to questions of the following type: What is the weekly summary of clean time on the project? What is the average time for concept location? As the time goes on, is the phase of concept location becoming faster or slower? Over the last month, how much time was spent in the exceptional tasks that are not parts of the SIP model? Is there a task or step of the SIP model that was not done in a week or in a month? The answer to all these and similar questions can be extracted from the log, and they give Sol a picture of the project progress.

12.3.2 Code Size

The complexity of the tasks is often related to the size of the code they deal with. The most common measure for program size is the number of lines of source code, abbreviated "LOC." For larger programs, the size may be expressed in thousands of lines of code "kLOC" or even millions of lines of code "MLOC." However, it has to be understood that this measure is very inaccurate, and there is a dispute as to how the lines should be counted. The recommended measure counts only "lines with something other than comments and whitespace (tabs and spaces)" (Wheeler, 2002). Even then, different programming or coding styles can lead to different code sizes. Also, the same problem solved in different programming languages can lead to a substantially different number of lines.

Despite these problems, LOC became the most commonly used measure of program size, perhaps because there are easily available tools to compute it, and the other measures are not much better. Because of the inaccuracy involved, only the most significant digit or most significant two digits are meaningful, and the actual measures produced by the tool should be rounded to these one or two digits; we talk about programs of the size 900 LOC, 23 kLOC, 3.4 MLOC, and so forth.

Sol wants to record the size of the code that is inspected, written, or tested in the tasks of the enacted process. The rightmost column of Table 12.3 contains these data. Tasks 1 and 5 do not deal with the code, so no size is recorded. For subtasks 2, concept location, and 3, impact analysis, Sol records the size of the inspected code. For subtasks 4, refactoring, and 6, actualization, Sol records the lines of the code modified or written from scratch. In subtask 7, baseline, Sol records the total size of the baseline code. The size of Sol's code changes over time, and during software evolution, it usually increases as the evolution adds new functionality.

12.3.3 Code Defects

As with any other product, software quality is a large concern. An important measure of software quality is the number of defects (bugs) that are left in the code. Defects are the properties of software that cause software to behave differently than expected; examples of defects are incorrect computations, premature terminations, and so forth. The defects lower the quality of software.

Table 12.4   Defect Log

	Defect Found					Origin		
	Date	Time	Task	Location	Description	Date	Task	Fixed
1	11/4	9:00	CL	`Cashier.get()`	For I = 0, loop does not terminate	3/12	Act	12/8
2	11/4	2:32	Bas	--	The pop-up window for 3rd cashier does not appear	?		11/25
3	11/4	3:02	Bas	`Price.get()`	Price = 0 raises exceptions	4/21	Ref	
4				. . .				

Defects in the code can be found by testing and by inspections, as explained in chapter 10. Sol keeps a defect log that monitors the known defects in the code. Defects can be discovered during testing or during inspections. Sol's inspections are less effective than inspections by another programmer because of habituation, but after a certain amount of time, Sol views the code from a fresh angle and discovers defects. An example of a defect log is in Table 12.4.

In the log in Table 12.4, defects are listed in the order they are discovered; the task during which they have been discovered is listed as well. If the location of the defect is known, it is listed in the next column; the column after that lists a brief description of the bug. Sol tries to determine the origin of the defect and estimates both the date and the tasks that caused the defect. If Sol is unable to determine the origin, the two columns are left blank. Finally the last column contains the date on which the defect was fixed.

The defect log can be mined for the answers to the following questions: What are the tasks most likely to introduce a defect? What is the average time from introduction of a bug to its discovery and fix? How many known but unfixed defects are in the software on any particular date?

12.4 Planning in SIP

Sol collects the process data in order to plan. Planning is a prediction of the future, and if Sol says that the next version of the program will be released in March, Sol is making a prediction. As with every prediction, there are uncertainties and risks involved; the customers are more satisfied if Sol makes accurate predictions.

Measuring the past may seem to be less important than correctly planning the future, but it is well known that data about the past are good predictors about the future. In fact, the future cannot be predicted with any level of certainty without knowing the past. Recording the past and planning for the future are closely related.

The unique and unprecedented tasks are very hard to plan. It is much easier to plan for repetitions of past tasks, assuming that the planned tasks are similar to the past tasks. In SIP, the repetitive tasks are the tasks in the three loops of SIP, and to make them more predictable, they should be made more alike.

Repetition and Planning

There is an old adage, "Repetition is the mother of skill." For repetitive tasks, Sol learns how to do them well. When cooking an omelet each morning, Sol learns what the temperature should be, how long it takes, how much cooking oil is required, how to avoid getting burned in the process, and so forth. That helps not only to produce a good omelet, but also to plan the breakfast for tomorrow. For example, if cooking and eating breakfast took Sol 30 minutes each day during the past week, it is reasonably safe to predict that tomorrow it will also take 30 minutes; this figure can be used when planning for tomorrow.

However, there is a risk in planning even repetitive tasks. What if Sol makes a mistake, runs out of food, and has to run to a nearby grocery store? The time planned for breakfast will grow! If Sol deviates from the routine and tries to cook a new kind of dish never tried before, the risk is even larger.

Understanding the risks and uncertainty is one of the main issues in planning. A time-honored technique of controlling risk is to emphasize the repetitive nature of the process and try to make the process as repetitive as possible.

12.4.1 Planning the Software Changes

The strategy that Sol uses in the planning of the changes is an *analogy* between the past tasks and the future tasks. If a future task is similar to a past task, Sol assumes that the effort needed to implement it is similar. Accuracy of planning improves with time, when a larger log is available, because it becomes more likely that Sol will find a more accurate analogy present in the log. At the beginning, the planning is based on less data, and hence, it is more of a guess, but as time goes on, the analogies become more and more fitting and the planning becomes more and more accurate.

Planning of the early phases of SIP may be based on the experience gained from other projects or on the experience of other programmers, but these other projects and other programmers may possess very different characteristics, and hence, the analogy is weak and estimates are very inaccurate. Of course, some variables change as the process continues: The size of the code, the quality of the code, Sol's knowledge of the code and of the domain problem, and so forth. When estimating the future tasks, Sol must take into the account these changing characteristics also.

The accuracy of planning future tasks is improved by *decomposition*. The task of software change is decomposed into phases, as explained in chapter 5. While planning, Sol decomposes future software changes into phases, and for each phase, Sol finds in the log the phases that are the most similar to the planned phase. Sol estimates the time for each future phase based on the analogy with these past data, knowing that all estimates of this kind are burdened by inevitable errors. Then Sol adds these estimates and produces the total for the whole change. In this total, the errors hopefully compensate each other: The overestimates of some phases compensate for the underestimates of other phases, and the resulting total for the whole change has a higher accuracy.

A part of planning software change is the prediction of software quality and introduced bugs. The defect log serves here to indicate by analogy how many bugs will be introduced by the future changes, how long it will take to fix them, and how much effort that is going to take. If too many bugs are allowed to accumulate, the quality of the code deteriorates, and the pace of the work on the project may slow down.

12.4.2 Task Determination

The effort required for each task should be within a narrow range, so that tasks can be properly planned and executed. If they fall within that range, their planning can be based on past experience, and the new experience from them can serve as guidance for the future task. A typical recommended upper range for tasks is a few (for example, two) days of work; all larger tasks should be decomposed into smaller ones. During planning, Sol divides all larger changes into smaller subtasks. These extra-large changes that need decomposition are sometimes called *epics*.

The division of the epics into tasks (sometimes called *tasking*) should be done in such a way that the resulting tasks are well defined. One tasking strategy *separates multiple concepts*. Some requirements deal with multiple concepts that can be separated into tasks, where each task deals with a different concept.

As an example, suppose that the change request is "Customers can download and then cash sales coupons." This is a large change request (epics). Sol estimates that its implementation would be out of range of a typical task and therefore, divides it into smaller tasks. The concepts that can be used to separate the tasks are "download," which deals with the Internet, and "cashing," which deals with the process of a sale in the store. The two smaller tasks then are:

1. Build an Internet website from which customers can download coupons
2. Update customer payment to include cashing coupons

These smaller tasks now fall within the customary range, and Sol replaces the original change request in the product backlog with these two tasks.

In another strategy, the tasks deal with the same concept, but they represent an *increasing complexity* of the concept's extension. An example is the point-of-sale application in chapter 18, which supports a small store. The requirement can be separated into tasks, where the first task implements a store that has only one cashier, sells one item of a fixed price, and uses only cash. The following tasks increase complexity and add multiple items, fluctuating prices, multiple cashiers, methods of payment other than cash, and so forth.

12.4.3 Planning the Baselines and Releases

The baselines and builds are internal matters of the project. The best strategy is to schedule them at regular intervals, for example, every day at the end of the shift, or perhaps every other day. It is not advisable to postpone the baseline creation, because the longer the postponement, the more unsolved problems accumulate, and they can become overwhelming.

Releases are a part of the outer loop of the SIP model. They present Sol's accomplishments to the world, and hence, they are no longer an internal matter, like baselines and individual software changes are. In planning of releases, Sol has to take into account business considerations. Very often, Sol promises a release with a certain new functionality on a certain date, and the thrust of Sol's planning is to make sure that this promise is realistic. Sol then monitors whether, with the passage of time, the "facts on the ground" still indicate that the promise remains realistic.

Table 12.5 is an example of a *release backlog table* that Sol uses in planning the releases. The rows of the table represent the requirements iteration backlog that Sol wants to introduce into the point-of-sale program in the next release. They are prioritized in descending order, with the most important requirement on line 1.

The column on the right is a plan at the beginning of the effort, after 0 hours were spent on the effort, and it contains estimates in hours of work for each requirement. Sol arrived at these estimates by decomposition and analogy, as presented in section 12.4.1, and rounds the resulting numbers to full hours. Sol estimates that the total effort of introducing these 12 features is 330 working hours, shown at the bottom of the right-hand column.

After 100 hours of the work, Sol returns to the planning and creates another column in the table, column labeled "100" in the top row (see Table 12.6). At this point, Sol is done with features 1, 2, and 3. However some of the original estimates turned out to be inaccurate, and Sol replaces them with real data: Requirements 2 and 3 took longer than originally thought, and Sol highlights the updated data in gray. In the table, Sol separates the real data from the estimates by a thick line to the left and bottom of the real data. With the additional knowledge now available, Sol corrects the estimates for features 7 and 9, also highlighted in gray. After this new planning, 340 more hours of work remain to fulfill what was promised, and the total effort is increased to 440 hours, indicating that there will be a delay (slip) in the release date. The remaining effort and total effort needed to reach the goal are in the bottom two lines.

Sol also returns to planning after 285 and 405 hours were spent on the project, respectively, and adds two additional columns to the table. The data in Table 12.7 are of two kinds: The data representing the real effort on requirements already

Table 12.5 Release Backlog Table

Plan After X Hours of Work	0
1: initial	10
2: inventory	30
3: multiple prices	30
4: promo prices	30
5: cashier login	20
6: multiple cashiers	30
7: cashier sessions	35
8: detailed sale	30
9: multiple line items	35
10: payment	20
11: credit payment	40
12: check payment	20
remaining effort	330
total effort needed to reach the goal	330

implemented are above the thick line, while the updated estimates for the remaining requirements are below that line. The table indicates that the project acquired additional delays highlighted in gray.

After 405 hours of effort, Sol is already late against the original estimate and must make a decision: Either stop now and release the software without requirements 11 and 12, or cause an additional delay and complete all the requirements of the original iteration backlog. This is a business decision, and it involves carefully weighing the pros and cons.

Table 12.7 presents the first alternative where Sol decides to complete the promised backlog, at the expense of further delay. The last column of Table 12.7 contains the final data for the process that took 475 hours total.

Table 12.8 presents the other alternative where Sol decided to deliver the next version after 405 hours of work and drop requirements 11 and 12 from the original plan, in order to avoid further delays. Requirements 11 and 12 will return back into the product backlog and Sol will consider them for the next version.

The release backlog table and its updates compare the original plan against the actual progress and give an early warning if delays may have occurred. The rows labeled "remaining effort" are highlighted in the tables, and they present in simple

Table 12.6   Updated Release Backlog Table After 100 Hours of Effort

Plan After X Hours of Work	0	100
1: initial	10	10
2: inventory	30	50
3: multiple prices	30	40
4: promo prices	30	30
5: cashier login	20	20
6: multiple cashiers	30	30
7: cashier sessions	35	80
8: detailed sale	30	30
9: multiple line items	35	70
10: payment	20	20
11: credit payment	40	40
12: check payment	20	20
remaining effort	330	340
total effort needed to reach the goal	330	440

terms Sol's progress as compared to the plan. Sol pays particular attention to these data, as they summarize in simple terms the progress and the setbacks.

Summary

Software processes describe stakeholders, tasks, and work products within a single or a few neighboring stages of software life span. They are presented in the form of the process model that describes idealized principles of the process, or the process enactment that describes the reality of a specific project, or the process performance that collects process data, or the process plan that uses these data to predict the future course of the project.

The solo iterative process (SIP) describes the process of a single programmer; it deals mainly with two work products: the product backlog, and the code of the software. There is a single programmer who carries out the tasks of the process, and there are users who receive new versions of the software and produce requirements for future functionality. The process contains three nested loops: In the outer loop

Table 12.7   Final Release Backlog Table With Delayed Completion of the Entire Feature Set

Plan After X Hours of Work	0	100	285	405	475
1: initial	10	10	10	10	10
2: inventory	30	50	50	50	50
3: multiple prices	30	40	40	40	40
4: promo prices	30	30	30	30	30
5: cashier login	20	20	20	20	20
6: multiple cashiers	30	30	55	55	55
7: cashier sessions	35	80	80	80	80
8: detailed sale	30	30	30	30	30
9: multiple line items	35	70	70	70	70
10: payment	20	20	20	20	20
11: credit payment	40	40	40	50	50
12: check payment	20	20	20	20	20
remaining effort	330	340	180	70	0
total effort needed to reach the goal	330	440	465	475	475

called iteration, the programmer selects the highest priority requirements and turns them into the iteration backlog. Once implemented, they will become a part of the new software version that will be delivered to the users. In the inner loop, the programmer takes the change requests from the iteration backlog and implements them in the code. In the middle loop, the programmer builds a new baseline and runs a system test.

The programmer collects the data in logs that include a time log and defect log, and uses them in estimating future tasks, baselines, and releases. The planning of tasks is based on decomposition and analogy with previous similar tasks. The release backlog tables are based on estimating individual tasks, and they monitor how close the programmer is to finishing all the tasks for the release.

Further Reading and Topics

Software processes are a large field; one of the pioneering papers was written by Osterweil (1987). An interplay of the processes and the technology that supports

Table 12.8 Final Release Backlog Table With Incomplete Feature Set

Plan After X Hours of Work	0	100	285	405
1: initial	10	10	10	10
2: inventory	30	50	50	50
3: multiple prices	30	40	40	40
4: promo prices	30	30	30	30
5: cashier login	20	20	20	20
6: multiple cashiers	30	30	55	55
7: cashier sessions	35	80	80	80
8: detailed sale	30	30	30	30
9: multiple line items	35	70	70	70
10: payment	20	20	20	20
11: credit payment	40	40	40	50
12: check payment	20	20	20	20
remaining effort	330	340	180	70
total effort needed to reach the goal	330	440	465	475

them is discussed by Finkelstein, Kramer, and Nuseibeh (1994). A detailed description of the process measurements employed by an individual programmer is presented by Humphrey (1997).

In the current state of the art, the performance of the software process in one project cannot be mechanically used in planning another one. This is the issue of the external validity of the process measurements, and it is discussed by Fuggetta (2000) and other authors. The independent variables of software processes are still not properly understood, and additional research is necessary before the experience from one project can be confidently used in another project.

Within the same project, external validity is less of a problem, as most of the independent variables remain the same, and the data collected in the past serve as a good predictor for planning future tasks. This technique has been called "yesterday's weather" (Cohn & Martin, 2005), based on the observation that, in many geographic locations, the best prediction for today's weather is to assume that it will be the same as yesterday's weather.

The collection, processing, and use of time logs is discussed by Humphrey (1997). Several tools supporting time logs are available from the open-source community or from the vendors.

The code size is discussed by Wheeler (2002), and "source line of code" (SLOC) in that paper is equivalent to what is called "line of code" (LOC) in this book. An alternative measure of code size is *function points* (Garmus & Herron, 2001).

The remaining effort to reach an iteration goal is discussed by Schwaber and Beedle (2001), and it is presented as a release backlog table in this book. An example of the development of a small application using SIP is presented in chapter 18.

Exercises

12.1　Explain the granularity of processes and give examples of various granularities.

12.2　What are the four forms of the software process? How are they related to each other?

12.3　In Awesome Software Company (ASC), developers are rewarded based on their productivity as measured by LOC/day.
　　a. What are the advantages and disadvantages of such a criterion?
　　b. One developer, Bob, decides to increase his productivity by repeating the same lines of code. What are the effects of such a practice during software evolution?
　　c. After a while, the manager detects a higher defect density in the code written by Bob. What type of verification should the manager use to detect the problems introduced by Bob?

12.4　How is process enactment different from the process model? Can there be different enactments of the same process model?

12.5　Explain the three loops of the SIP model and how are they related.

12.6　Why do programmers keep a log of their time spent on the project? What entries do programmers record in the log?

12.7　How is the size of the code measured? How accurate is the measure?

12.8　What is a defect log? Why is it important to keep it?

12.9　What are the options when the release backlog shows that the original deadline cannot be met?

12.10　How would you modify the release backlog if, during the process, it becomes obvious that an additional task is required?

References

Cohn, M., & Martin, R. C. (2005). *Agile estimating and planning*. Englewood Cliffs, NJ: Prentice Hall.

Finkelstein, A., Kramer, J., & Nuseibeh, B. (1994). *Software process modelling and technology*. New York, NY: John Wiley & Sons.

Fuggetta, A. (2000). Software process: A roadmap. In *Proceedings of the Conference on the Future of Software Engineering* (pp. 25–34.). New York, NY: ACM.

Garmus, D., & Herron, D. (2001). *Function point analysis: Measurement practices for successful software projects*. Reading, MA: Addison-Wesley.

Humphrey, W. S. (1997). *Introduction to the personal software process*. Reading, MA: Addison-Wesley.

Osterweil, L. (1987). Software processes are software too. In *Proceedings of International Conference on Software Engineering* (pp. 2–13). Washington, DC: IEEE Computer Society Press.

Schwaber, K., & Beedle, M. (2001). *Agile software development with Scrum*. Upper Saddle River, NJ: Prentice Hall.

Wheeler, D. A. (2002). *More than a gigabuck: Estimating GNU/Linux's size*. Retrieved on June 30, 2011, from http://www.dwheeler.com/sloc/redhat71-v1/redhat71sloc.html

Chapter 13

Team Iterative Processes

Objectives

Most software projects require a larger effort than what a solitary programmer can handle; therefore, programmers often have to organize themselves into teams. This chapter describes the most common team organizations and processes. After you read this chapter, you will know:

- The agile iterative process (AIP)
- The iteration and daily loop of AIP
- The directed iterative process (DIP)
- The difference between developers and testers in DIP
- The centralized iterative process (CIP)
- The project circumstances that require CIP and the role of architects, code owners, and quality managers in CIP

***

Software teams work on large software projects and most often deal with iterative processes of software evolution or servicing. The iterative nature of these tasks favors organizing the workers into teams. The most common variants of the team organization and their corresponding iterative software processes are explained in this chapter.

The directed teams and centralized teams entrust project monitoring, planning, and key project decisions to the managers. In contrast to that, agile teams base their work and their planning on a consensus among the programmers and limit the role of the managers.

13.1 Agile Iterative Process (AIP)

The stakeholders of AIP are the programmers, managers, and users. The *programming team* in AIP typically consists of 5–10 people, and they arrive at decisions mostly by consensus. To make that consensus easier to reach, agile teams avoid specialization. All programmers have universal skills, and they are capable of doing any programming task; that greatly simplifies the assignment of tasks to individual team members. A model of the agile iterative process (AIP) is depicted in Figure 13.1, and the tasks that are done by the programmers are within the shaded rectangle.

In AIP, the *product manager* supervises the business decisions, is responsible for the profitability of the product, and controls the product backlog and the prioritization of the requirements. The product manager also accepts or rejects the results of the programmers' work and decides when and how the product is released to users.

The *process manager* is responsible for enacting the AIP and for removing the impediments. The impediments may include hardware problems, network problems, the need for training, the need to present and defend the project to the top managers, and so forth. The process manager ensures that the team is fully functional and productive and shields it from external interferences. However, the assignment of tasks to individual team members and monitoring the progress of

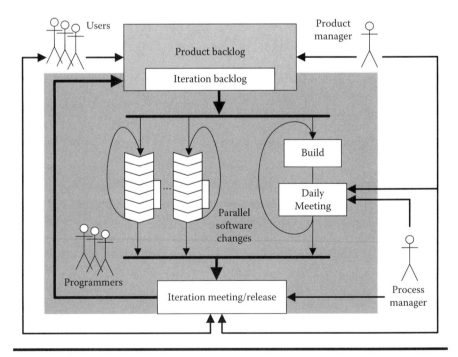

Figure 13.1   AIP model.

the project is not done by the process manager; this responsibility is entrusted to the team members and the consensus within the team.

The AIP model in Figure 13.1 contains an iteration loop (emphasized in bold) that is explained in detail later. Nested within it are parallel *software change loops* that represent the individual programmers who work on software changes in parallel, using the techniques that were explained in the second part of this book. Whenever they finish a change, they commit the resulting code to the repository and start another change. If there are conflicts among their commits, they resolve them through the consensus. There is also a parallel daily loop that consists of a build process and a daily meeting.

13.1.1 Daily Loop

The daily loop in AIP includes the tasks of the *build* and the *daily meeting*. The build process prepares a new baseline, most often overnight, as discussed in chapter 11.

The daily meeting takes place after the build, and the whole programming team participates. During the daily meeting, the programmers discuss the results of the last build. They also explain to their teammates what they have accomplished since the last meeting, the progress of the tasks they are currently working on, and what the plans are for the next day. They may clarify ambiguities in the change requests, discuss the quality of code, identify the need for code refactoring, and so forth.

They also discuss the problems at hand, for example, conflicts between commits, problems that baseline testing revealed, hardware problems, problems that surfaced during their work on the tasks, or similar problems. The meetings bring out into the open the daily challenges that the programmers experience. After the daily meeting, the programmers resume their individual work.

The daily meetings are short; the recommended duration is 15 minutes. They build the consensus that the team needs to function. To accomplish that, they have to be frank, polite, and to the point.

The process and product managers participate in the daily meetings in a limited way. The product manager helps resolve issues that are related to the business side of the project, including ambiguities in the change requests. The process manager makes sure that the daily meeting is short and professional, but allows the team to set its own priorities and build a consensus. In exceptional situations, the process manager steps in when the team is unable to resolve a serious problem on its own.

13.1.2 Iteration Planning

The iteration is the bold loop of the AIP model (see Figure 13.1). It covers a time period of one to four weeks, with the most common duration being two weeks. It contains the *iteration meeting*, where all stakeholders participate. The meeting has two parts: The first part reviews the previous iteration, and the second part plans the next iteration.

Let's start with this second part of the meeting, the *iteration planning*. Planning the next iteration is done based on the experience from previous iterations. The participants in the planning process take into account the product backlog, team capabilities, changing business conditions, the stability or volatility of the technology used in the project, and so forth. Based on these factors, they establish the goals of the next iteration.

As a start, the programmers know the length of the iteration expressed as the number of work hours that are planned for the iteration, denoted L, and the number of programmers, N, that will participate. They estimate the team *iteration capacity* as $C = L*N$.

From the product backlog, which contains all of the requirements for future product functionality, the participants select a subset called the *iteration backlog*, in a similar way as in SIP (solo iterative process). Those are the requirements that will be implemented in the next iteration. For that, the programmers use the requirements prioritization and estimated effort for the individual requirements. They arrive at the estimated effort for each requirement by using decomposition and analogy, as in SIP: They look for analogous tasks that were done in past iterations and, based on the relevant data, they estimate the future necessary effort. Then they select the highest priority tasks until they fill the iteration capacity, and thus they create the iteration backlog. The sum of all the task estimates should be approximately the iteration capacity.

13.1.3 Iteration Process

Once the iteration backlog is defined, the programming team starts its *iteration work*: The individual programmers pick their tasks from the iteration backlog based on their priority, and then work on them in parallel. They also produce daily baselines and participate in daily meetings. A characteristic feature of AIP is that the team works autonomously with minimal direction from the managers, and organizes its work through a consensus that is reached by programmer interactions during the iteration meetings, the daily meetings, and other communications among the team members. This consensus allows the team to react to various situations that may arise. The process manager makes sure that this process continues smoothly and interferes with it only in emergencies.

A successful iteration implements all the requirements of the iteration backlog; however, sometimes if there is a slip in the schedule, only a subset is implemented. In the rare situation when the iteration backlog turns out to be easier than planned, the team may implement additional requirements that go beyond the iteration backlog. A characteristic of AIP is that the time for the iteration is rigid; the iteration meeting is set in advance, and implementing a subset of the iteration backlog is the only option if the schedule slips. Postponing the iteration meeting because of the schedule slip is not an option. Only in unforeseen emergencies can the iteration end prematurely, for example, if there is a sudden dramatic change in the business priorities of the company.

Individual programmers in the AIP are encouraged to keep individual time logs that indicate the time it takes to do the tasks or phases. The team as a whole keeps the defect log. Also, the team as a whole keeps an iteration backlog table that is identical to the release backlog table of SIP. However, a difference is that the assessments of the iteration progress are done daily during the daily meeting where the latest data are presented. Useful tools are iteration backlog charts that plot the remaining effort; they are easy to grasp, easily visible by the whole group, and they handily contrast the iteration plan with reality. Figures 13.2 and 13.3 provide examples of the iteration backlog charts.

Figure 13.2 contains the ideal iteration backlog chart. The days of the iteration are plotted on the horizontal axis (it is a 10-day iteration), and the effort remaining to complete the iteration is plotted on the vertical axis. On day 0, before the iteration starts, the remaining effort is equal to the iteration capacity; in this case it is equal to 800 hours. In the perfect world of this chart, each day brings the goal closer exactly as estimated; by the middle of the iteration on day 5, the remaining effort is 400 hours, and at the end of iteration on day 10, the remaining effort is exactly 0.

A more realistic example of actual remaining effort is in the chart of Figure 13.3. It differs from the ideal by imperfect estimates and also by unexpected problems that surface during the iteration. The iteration backlog chart starts like the ideal chart, with the iteration capacity equal to 800 on day 0, but then it deviates from it. Already during the second day, after the inaccurate estimates have been corrected and unexpected events have been absorbed, the iteration goal is now estimated to be further away than the estimate on day 0. Similar ups and downs appear on the

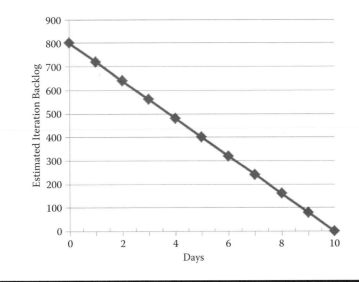

Figure 13.2   Ideal iteration backlog chart.

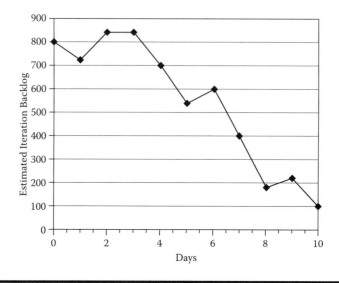

Figure 13.3   Actual iteration backlog chart.

remaining days of the iteration, and the iteration ends on day 10 with the original goal not being reached—there are 100 hours of estimated work remaining.

Agile Manifesto

There are a variety of agile processes, and they differ from each other in certain recommended practices. The best-known characterization of all agile processes is contained in the Agile Manifesto, which was authored by 17 leading software developers who met in 2001 at Snowboard Ski Lodge in the Rocky Mountains. Later it was signed by numerous others (Agile Alliance, 2001). While being revolutionary in the context of the year 2001, it became the mainstream of thinking that guides today's software processes, which is a testament to the rapid change of software engineering views during the last decade.

The core of the Agile Manifesto is summarized in the values presented in Table 13.1. Each line contains the desired goal in boldfaced text and a criticism of the prevailing practice of software engineering in the year 2001 in lightfaced text. The first line emphasizes individuals and interactions that build a consensus among the project stakeholders, and that is the primary characteristic of the agile approach. The reference to the processes in the lightfaced text of the first line should be read as "rigid and arbitrary processes and tools" that were imposed on the programmers by management, often based on unproven theories—a very common practice in the historical context of 2001.

Table 13.1   Agile Manifesto Values

Individuals and interactions over processes and tools
Working software over comprehensive documentation
Customer collaboration over contract negotiation
Responding to change over following a plan

The second line addresses another issue in the historical context of 2001, where overemphasis on secondary work products like documentation or models sometimes overshadowed the work on software code. The managers of that time sometimes took working software for granted, and focused excessively on these secondary work products. This second line redirects the attention back to the work product that matters most—the software code.

The third line addresses a consequence of the waterfall life cycle: The assumption was that the whole software life span can be planned with reasonable certainty, similar to the construction of a suburban house. This approach assumed that the plan could be the basis for a contract between the customers and the developers that specified all functionality delivered at a specific time. Of course, this view did not take into account the volatility of requirements, volatility of technology, and volatility of knowledge, which made these plans grossly inaccurate. Note that in many professions, the contract between customers and suppliers is based on the idea of a *retainer*, rather than on reaching specific goals by a specific date. A medical doctor is paid by effort, rather than being contracted for a specific outcome, and the same is true of lawyers. This third line of the manifesto recognizes the futility of the outcome-based contract, and it is a step in the direction of programmers working on the basis of a retainer, rather than a fixed outcome and date.

The last value—responding to change—is common to all processes of software evolution, and it is the fundamental characteristic of all iterative processes that are covered in this book, including SIP from the previous chapter, and AIP, DIP, and CIP of this chapter.

13.1.4 Iteration Review

The iteration ends with an *iteration review*, which is a part of the iteration meeting, and allows the programmers and the managers to evaluate the just-finished iteration; the iteration review is scheduled as the first part of the iteration meeting. Presentations and hands-on demonstrations of the latest version of the software are the main part of the review. The stakeholders assess the current state of the product and identify any discrepancies between the expectations and the reality of the project. This assessment becomes a part of the planning for the next iteration.

The participants may also discuss the *release* of the next version to the users. Iterations should produce software that is ready for release, and the iteration review assesses both technical and business aspects and decides whether to actually release the software to the users, or whether it is better to wait for a future iteration.

13.2 Directed Iterative Process (DIP)

The directed iterative process (DIP) is a process where the decisions, planning, and task assignments are done by the process managers. Because the managers handle the decisions and there is no need to seek a consensus, the DIP process does not contain regular meetings. DIP also scales to large-size teams and allows specialization. Some projects employ hundreds of programmers who may work in different geographical locations under a hierarchy of managers. A model of the DIP process is presented in Figure 13.4.

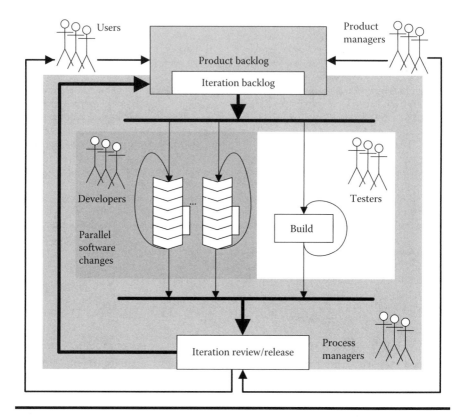

Figure 13.4   DIP model.

13.2.1 DIP Stakeholders

DIP allows programmers to specialize. A common division of labor in the programming team is the division between developers and testers, as depicted in Figure 13.4. The *developers* work on software changes, while the *testers* monitor the quality of the code and produce the baseline at regular intervals, usually on a daily basis. Testers also maintain the system test suite, delete obsolete tests, and create new tests for new code. The division of labor between the developers and testers is desirable not only because each group needs different skills, but also to avoid a potential conflict of interest. The developers may be tempted to gloss over problems in their own code and may try to conceal their own coding shortcomings. The independent testers do not have this temptation, and their verdict about the quality of the code is more credible than that of the developers.

The role of the *product managers* is similar to their role in AIP; they understand the software and its position in the market. They collect requirements and maintain the product backlog, including the prioritization of tasks. They monitor the status of the tasks and the status of the code, and decide when and how to release new versions of the code to the users. In large projects, there can be several product managers, each dealing with a specific issue of product quality or its position in the market.

The *process managers* enact, monitor, and plan DIP. As part of enactment, they issue directives to the developers and testers and tell them which tasks to do. They protect the productivity and morale of the team and step in whenever morale or productivity is under threat that may come from external or internal sources. An example of an internal threat is an individual who fails to cooperate with other programmers; cooperation among the programmers is an essential ingredient of team morale, and a repeated failure to cooperate is an issue that the process managers must resolve. External threats include unreasonable demands from higher level managers or powerful users, inadequate resources, and so forth.

13.2.2 DIP Process

The bold loop in Figure 13.4 is the *iteration loop*. It starts with the product and process managers jointly defining the iteration backlog, which contains requirements that will be implemented in the next iteration. Then there are parallel repeated software changes and daily builds; the iteration ends with an iteration review that may recommend software release.

In the *software change loop*, the managers select tasks from the product backlog and assign them to the developers. Developers then work on these changes in parallel, implement the corresponding changes, and commit the updated code and other work products to the repository.

The *build loop* is the responsibility of the testers. At a certain specified time interval, most often daily, the testers run system tests on the code and establish a new baseline that becomes the starting point for the next changes.

Process managers enact DIP and set up the monitoring and planning. They monitor the size and quality of the code and the individual programmers' performance. They also plan and monitor the iteration loop. The plan for the iteration backlog is similar to the one in SIP and AIP, and the analogy of the planned tasks with the past tasks serves as the basis for the planning. For monitoring, they may also use iteration backlog charts like the one in AIP.

However, because of software essential difficulties, there is a constant danger that managers will lose grasp of the issues that the programmers are facing; therefore, the developers and testers have to provide the managers with an accurate and timely feedback that serves as the basis for management decisions. Poor quality of communication between programmers and managers may lead to a loss of important information and negatively impact the work of the whole team.

The iteration ends with an iteration review, where the current state of the project is presented to upper management, investors, users, and other stakeholders. If the results of the review are favorable, the project may be released to the users. The typical length of iterations in DIP is longer than in AIP and ranges from one to six months.

13.3 Centralized Iterative Process (CIP)

AIP and DIP processes are based on the assumption that the quality of most of the commits that the programmers produce is acceptable. Symbolically, this is depicted in Figure 13.5, which plots the quality of commits on the horizontal scale, from lowest on the left to the highest on the right, and on the vertical scale is the number of the commits. The figure assumes something close to a normal distribution of quality.

The unacceptable commits are shaded in gray, and Figure 13.5 shows the project, where the instances of the low-quality commits are rare. If an unacceptable commit happens, the mechanisms of the respective processes are sufficient to deal with the situation.

Figure 13.6 presents a different situation, where unacceptable commits are frequent, and therefore, the process has to have a mechanism to filter them out. In this situation, *code guardians* decide whether a commit meets the standard that is required by the project and reject failing commits. The process is called a *centralized iterative process* (CIP) and is presented in Figure 13.7.

CIP is used in several different situations. One is when the developer teams consist of programmers with widely different skills. An example is an open source community that consists of volunteers. Another example is an extra large and geographically distributed project that has many participating programmers who do not know each other. There are academic projects that have students with different skills and a wide range of motivations. All these projects employ CIP as their process.

In other projects, the expected software quality is exceedingly high, above the skills of most programmers. An example of that is avionics software, where human life is at risk and bugs have to be avoided at any cost. In these situations, the developers are no longer allowed to commit their code at their discretion, and each commit has to pass rigorous checks by guardians before it is allowed to become part of the version control system repository.

The *code guardians* specialize in different aspects of code quality. They are architects, quality managers, code owners, and so forth. The guardians evaluate the programmers' commits and have the right to accept or reject them, as depicted in Figure 13.7.

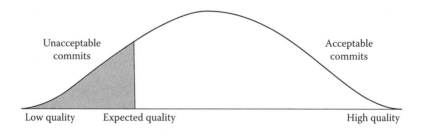

Figure 13.5   Quality of commits in AIP and DIP.

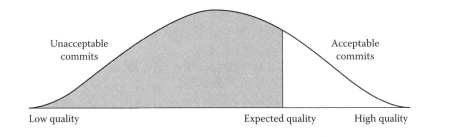

Figure 13.6   Quality of commits in CIP.

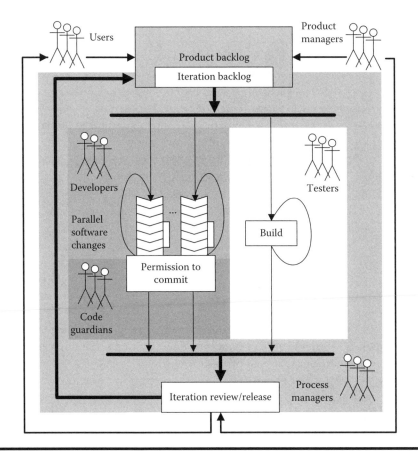

Figure 13.7   CIP model with code guardians.

Chapter 4 briefly described software architectures as prescriptive models. Architectures have to be preserved during evolution and, therefore, they consist of a set of rules that the programmers must observe. An example is the rule that only a few selected classes can access the database; all other classes must request the help of these privileged classes if they want access. The reason is to keep the overall structure simple, and if there is ever a need to make changes in the database interface, the change propagation of such a change is limited to the classes that have database access. Software *architects* are guardians of these rules.

Quality managers are specialists whose role is to protect the quality of software and prevent introduction of faults. They check developers' commits through further inspections or tests before they allow them to become a part of the repository.

Code owners are usually senior programmers who possess specific knowledge of a specific part of the code. They are guardians of quality and style of that part of the code, and if developers try to commit a change to that part, they have to get the owner's permission. Code ownership is frequently used in open-source software, but can be used in other contexts as well. There can be several code owners, each owning a part of the code.

There are many specialized tasks that the software project requires, and in large teams that use DIP or CIP, these tasks are sometimes done by specialists. There may be *requirements engineers* whose responsibility is to elicit, analyze, and prioritize the requirements. The *manual writers* produce user manuals and *documentation writers* produce documentation. Sometimes their background is in communication or English, rather than programming. There could be *network and operating system specialists*. In extra-large systems, there even can be *concept locators* whose sole responsibility is the concept-location phase of a change (S. Eick, personal communication, 1998). This specialization increases the effectiveness of the work on the tasks, while at the same time it may complicate the communication within the team; it is the task of the managers to decide whether this tradeoff contributes to the success of the team.

Summary

Software teams are organized in several different ways and use several different process models. The agile iterative process (AIP) relies on a consensus among the programmers and limits the role of the managers. AIP is a suitable process for smaller teams where the complexity of the tasks is high, and therefore, a consensus is a better way to arrive at decisions than a manager's directive. The iteration of AIP typically takes one to four weeks, and it contains an iteration meeting where the stakeholders of the project meet, assess the current state of the project, and assess whether to release the current version of the software or to wait for a future iteration. The stakeholders also plan the next iteration, and from the product backlog, they select the iteration backlog, which contains the changes that will be implemented in the next iteration.

In the directed iterative process (DIP), managers control the process enactment and make the key process decisions. DIP scales to large-size software and large-size projects. It is particularly suitable for situations where a management directive works better than a consensus; examples are large teams, geographically distributed teams, and teams with many specialized roles. The programming team of DIP typically consists of developers who develop the code, and testers who maintain the test suite and build the baseline. The centralized iterative process (CIP) is suitable for teams with a wide variability of skills or teams with unusually high expectations of quality. CIP has code guardians that inspect developers' commits and accept or reject them, and hence, they guard the quality of the code in the version control repository. Among them, architects guarantee that the program architecture will be preserved through the evolution; code owners guarantee the quality of the commits in the part of the code they own; and quality managers guarantee the general quality of the commits.

Further Reading and Topics

There are many variants of directed processes that are described in the literature. Among them is the *team software process* (TSP) (Humphrey, 1999). TSP pays particular attention to managers and their roles. The book lists several specialized management roles, each with different responsibilities. These refined roles include a development manager who leads the development and testing of the product, a planning manager who guides team planning and monitoring, a quality manager who tracks the quality of the code, and many others.

TSP also collects some process measures that are a result of industry-wide surveys, for example, defects inserted per hour (Humphrey, 1999). However, the applicability of these measures to a specific project that deals with a specific problem domain and a software team with specific skills is still is a matter of debate.

The *rational unified process* (RUP) is an iterative process where iterations have the following potentially overlapping phases: inception, elaboration, construction, and transition (Kruchten, 2004; Jacobson & Bylund, 2000). The management issues of RUP are discussed by Bittner and Spence (2006).

The *open-source process* has been extensively used and studied. Because this process typically deals with a large community of developers, code ownership is an important issue (Bowman, Holt, & Brewster, 1999).

Geographically distributed teams are increasingly frequent in software development. The teams are located in several locations within the same country or even overseas. The advantage of such an arrangement is that the teams pool resources that are not available in a single location. However, the physical distance also brings a special set of challenges (Herbsleb & Mockus, 2003).

A *clean-room* software process tries to prevent software defects, while other processes concentrate on discovery and removal of existing defects. The clean-room process relies heavily on the use of software inspections and on formal methods (Prowell, Trammell, Linger, & Poore, 1999).

The *classroom iterative process* is a reduced version of DIP, where the role of program manager, process manager, and testers is merged into a single role of a supervisor. This simplified process is appropriate for classroom introduction to software engineering (Petrenko, Poshyvanyk, Rajlich, & Buchta, 2007).

An *agile process* exists in many variants. Among them, *scrum* is a widely used agile process of today (Schwaber & Beedle, 2001). The name "scrum" originates from rugby, where players decide on a strategy of how to play the next phase of the game (Takeuchi & Nonaka, 1986) while standing in a close circle, and that is a metaphor for daily meetings and iteration meetings.

Lean software construction is inspired by just-in-time manufacturing, and it tries to eliminate all unnecessary overhead from the software processes. Everything that does not add value to the customer is suspect and a candidate for elimination (Poppendieck & Poppendieck, 2003).

Extreme programming (XP) is a variant of the agile processes, and it contains 12 practices (Beck, 2000; Jeffries, Anderson, & Hendrickson, 2000). Some of these practices overlap with the practices explained in the context of SIP and AIP, but other practices are unique to XP and often are carried to the extreme; that fact gave the name to this process. These practices are:

The planning game. XP recommends a thorough planning of the iterations along the lines that were described in the context of SIP and AIP. The planning game includes prioritization of the change requests (user stories in XP language), estimates of the effort it takes to implement them, selection of the user stories for the next iteration backlog, and assignment of the tasks to the programmers in the team.

Simple design. Simple design fulfills the business requirements with the fewest possible classes and methods. It is biased toward currently implemented user stories and it does not contain provisions for the future. Because of volatility, the future is considered uncertain, and to provide elaborate preparations for future changes that may never be needed is considered a waste of resources.

Small releases. The goal of small releases is to put the system into production as soon as possible so that programmers receive feedback from customers as fast as possible. The most valuable features from the point of view of the customers should be delivered first.

Metaphor. There should be a simple and easy-to-understand metaphor that describes the overall idea of the software so that the programmers do not drown in its complexity. Examples of simple metaphors are an ATM machine, the contract between a client and a supplier, purchasing an item or a set of items from a store including a shopping cart and checkout, and similar metaphors.

Pair programming. XP recommends that all programming be done in pairs. The pair constantly communicates about the task at hand; one person types at the keyboard ("driver") and the other person looks at the screen and comments ("navigator"); the navigator has an opportunity to think about broader issues that include improvements, test cases, and so forth. This work in pairs is in fact a continuous code inspection; every piece of code that is committed has been seen by at least two people and higher quality code is the result.

The pairs regularly change, and this presents an opportunity to exchange knowledge of the code and the project during the discussions within the pairs. If a more senior team member is teamed up with a junior member, it provides an opportunity to train the junior member of the team. On the other hand, there is a need for the pair to function, and both paired programmers must exhibit characteristics and behaviors that make this possible.

Immediate testing. XP recommends immediate update of the test suite as a part of each change and to do a full battery of system tests that include unit tests and functional tests. Unit testing is done continuously, and all unit tests have to pass every time; if they do not, an immediate remedial action has to be taken. Functional tests are also run regularly, and they also have to pass every time.

Immediate refactoring. Refactoring is used in XP whenever the code structure deviates from the ideal; refactoring was discussed in chapter 9.

Collective ownership. Every member of the XP team owns the code of the whole system; there are no specialized owners of any specific parts. Each team member can change or improve any part of the system at any time, without seeking anybody's permission.

Continuous integration. XP recommends creating a new baseline after a few hours of development. This lessens the problem of broken baselines, because the amount of effort that a broken baseline destroys is smaller. XP requires that all problems that led to a broken baseline be immediately resolved.

On-site customer. XP recommends that a real customer be a part of the team and be actually located in the same physical space as the rest of the team. The on-site customer presents and defends customer needs and concerns that the programmers are often unaware of. The customer also clarifies the ambiguities and omissions in the requirements and sets the priorities.

Coding standards. The collective code ownership requires that the team adopts a unified coding standard that will make the comprehension of other peoples' code easier.

40-hour week. Programming is hard work, and programmers need to rest and have time to attend to their personal matters. Excessive hours on a regular basis are counterproductive and only lead to a drop in productivity.

Exercises

13.1 In AIP, who decides what changes will be implemented in the next iteration?

13.2 Who meets in the iteration meeting and what do they decide?

13.3 Consider an AIP iteration that is scheduled to take 10 days, but on day 5 the programmers realize they won't be able to finish the backlog until day 11. Should they extend the iteration, or should they return the unfinished changes to the product backlog? Why?

13.4 What is the advantage of separating programmers into developers and testers?

13.5 How do product managers control the product development?

13.6 In CIP, why is it necessary to sometimes reject developers' commits?

13.7 Create an iteration backlog chart for each day based on Table 13.2.

13.8 In DIP, who is responsible for the build loop?

13.9 Why are code owners important in open-source software projects?

13.10 Is "extreme programming" a variation on AIP or DIP?

13.11 How does the process manager's role differ from AIP to DIP?

13.12 Assign each aspect to one or more of the following: AIP, DIP, or CIP.
   a. Consensus
   b. Programmers and testers
   c. Daily loop
   d. Product backlog
   e. Iteration loop
   f. Product and process manager
   g. Parallel software changes
   h. Code owners or architects
   i. Iteration review

13.13 State three of the values expressed in the Agile Manifesto.

Table 13.2   Estimated Remaining Effort

Day	Remaining Effort
1	600
2	650
3	500
4	250
5	320
6	120

References

Agile Alliance. (2001). *Manifesto for agile software development.* Retrieved on June 23, 2011, from http://agilemanifesto.org/

Beck, K. (2000). *Extreme programming explained.* Reading, MA: Addison-Wesley.

Bittner, K., & Spence, I. (2006). *Managing iterative software development projects.* Boston, MA: Addison-Wesley Professional.

Bowman, I. T., Holt, R. C., & Brewster, N. V. (1999). Linux as a case study: Its extracted software architecture. In *Proceedings of the International Conference on Software Engineering (ICSE)* (pp. 555–563). New York, NY: ACM.

Herbsleb, J. D., & Mockus, A. (2003). An empirical study of speed and communication in globally distributed software development. *IEEE Transactions on Software Engineering, 29,* 481–494.

Humphrey, W. S. (1999). *Introduction to the team software process.* Boston, MA: Addison-Wesley Professional.

Jacobson, I., & Bylund, S. (2000). *The road to the unified software development process.* Cambridge, U.K.: Cambridge University Press.

Jeffries, R. E., Anderson, A., & Hendrickson, C. (2000). *Extreme programming installed.* Boston, MA: Addison-Wesley Longman.

Kruchten, P. (2004). *The rational unified process: An introduction.* Boston, MA: Addison-Wesley Professional.

Petrenko, M., Poshyvanyk, D., Rajlich, V., & Buchta, J. (2007). Teaching software evolution in open source. *Computer, 40*(11), 25–31.

Poppendieck, M., & Poppendieck, T. (2003). *Lean software development: An agile toolkit.* Boston, MA: Addison-Wesley Professional.

Prowell, S. J., Trammell, C. J., Linger, R. C., & Poore, J. H. (1999). *Cleanroom software engineering: Technology and process.* Boston, MA: Addison-Wesley Professional.

Schwaber, K., & Beedle, M. (2001). *Agile software development with Scrum.* Upper Saddle River, NJ: Prentice Hall.

Takeuchi, H., & Nonaka, I. (1986). The new new product development game. *Harvard Business Review, 64*(1), 137–146.

Chapter 14

Initial Development

Objectives

In this chapter, you will learn about the initial development of completely new software from scratch. After you have read this chapter, you will know:

- The software plan and its role in initial development
- The elicitation and analysis of the initial product backlog
- The design of the classes and their dependencies
- CRC cards
- Bottom-up implementation of the first version

***

Starting a project from scratch is not as common as it was in the past, but when it occurs, it presents unique opportunities and challenges. During initial development, the project stakeholders make fundamental decisions, and the consequences of these decisions will be present in the software throughout its entire life span. The tasks of the initial development are the creation of a software plan, then creation of the initial product backlog, initial design, and finally implementation of the first version (see Figure 14.1). The process resembles a miniature waterfall with the difference that it runs only for a relatively short and predetermined time.

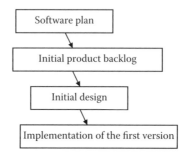

Figure 14.1   Tasks of the initial development.

14.1 Software Plan

The first task of initial development is to create the software plan that summarizes the goals and circumstances of the project. At the beginning of the project, there is usually a good deal of flexibility; however, wise choices must be made, as they are difficult to reverse later. The software plan identifies the important issues so that informed decisions can be made. The project's stakeholders review this document and reach an agreement so that surprises and disappointments are minimized. The document contains both the data and the narrative. It is a brief document of about 10 pages, and it allows the managers to make an informed fundamental decision: to go ahead with the project or not.

The emphasis of the software plan is on brevity and unambiguous communication. This section presents the recommended outline of the software plan.

14.1.1 Overview

The overview gives a brief introduction to the plan. It explains the *purpose* of the project and lists the reasons to embark on it. It also briefly explains the project *objectives* and the expected results of the project. It explains the *scope* of the project: what is to be covered and what is to be left out.

The subsection titled *assumptions* lists the assumptions that the project plan writers made, like the availability of resources, situation of the market, and so forth. The *constraints* subsection explains the project boundaries, like the limitations of the available resources, deadlines to be met, and so forth. The section on *deliverables* explains what work products will be delivered early in the project and when.

The subsection on the *evolution* and *range* of the software plan briefly explains how far into the future the current plan reaches; the plan typically covers the stage of initial development and early iterations of software evolution, but the accumulations of uncertainties due to volatility limit the range of the plan. This subsection of the software plan acknowledges this mounting uncertainty and the limits of the plan. It also states whether the software plan is to be revised, and when.

The subsection titled *summaries* overviews the rest of the software plan for quick reading. In particular, a brief summary of the process, organization, and management are contained in this subsection.

14.1.2 Reference Materials

This part of the plan lists all references where readers can find additional information related to the project. This may include references to similar past or current projects, references to books about the process to be employed by the project, articles that describe the domain and the algorithms, websites dealing with the technologies to be used, and so forth.

14.1.3 Definitions and Acronyms

This part is a vocabulary of the terms and acronyms used in the software plan and in the project. Each project has its own specialized vocabulary, and this vocabulary is explained here. This section should make the rest of the project plan understandable to a reader who does not have the specialized project expertise.

14.1.4 Process

This part describes in greater detail the project process. It describes the scope of the initial development and the subsequent early evolution. It describes the specific methods to be used in the project, the testing plan, and the work products. It summarizes the techniques to be used to ensure the quality of the product, including the testing and code inspections. There may be additional aspects of the process like the security, data conversions, installations, and specifics of the process enactment.

14.1.5 Organization

This part explains the roles of the various actors and specialists that the project requires. It explains how the project participants are going to be organized into teams, departments, divisions, and so forth; how these units are going to be managed; and how they are going to interact with each other and with other external units. If there are subcontractors involved who produce certain work products for the project, this section describes their role.

14.1.6 Technologies

This part of the plan describes the required project technologies that include the programming languages and their environments, libraries and frameworks, version control system, hardware for the project, and so forth. There may be a need to purchase equipment or software tools, and time for training of team members.

14.1.7 Management

This part also explains how the progress of the project is going to be monitored. This includes mechanisms for monitoring requirements volatility, adherence to the planned schedule and budget, code quality control, project risks, and so forth. The management plan also defines the metrics to be used for monitoring, how the results of monitoring are to be reported, and how corrective actions are going to be taken.

14.1.8 Cost

Estimated project cost is an important part of the data on which the managers base their decisions. The cost estimate uses an analogy with other similar projects and acknowledges the level of uncertainty in this estimate. It also states how this estimate is going to be adjusted based on the data that will become available as the project progresses.

14.2 Initial Product Backlog

Once the project plan is finished and approved by the managers, the product development can start. However, at this point, the product backlog is empty and the first task is to elicit the initial requirements.

14.2.1 Requirements Elicitation

The unusual aspect of initial development is that there is no product, and therefore, there are no product users who can volunteer their views and help to formulate the requirements. The potential future users usually consider the project to be abstract, and they see the benefits to be far in the future. Some highly motivated potential users may be enticed to collaborate in creating a vision for this future product, but experience has shown that participation of users at this stage is lukewarm, and various techniques must be used to entice them to participate.

The first step in requirements elicitation is to identify whom to ask, that is, to identify the stakeholders. The stakeholders are recruited from the ranks of the future users, current or future project staff, current or future project managers, veterans from similar past projects, experts on the project domain, and so forth. The more of these groups and subgroups are reached during requirements elicitation, the more representative the product backlog will be.

Because the stakeholders are reluctant to participate in requirements elicitation in this early part of the project, the software engineers have to employ various specialized techniques and methods. One of the prominent techniques for initial requirements elicitation is *prototyping*, which was discussed in chapter 2. The prototype is a quick implementation of the basic functionalities of the new software with an emphasis on the user interface, and the purpose is to demonstrate to future users the look and feel of the future system. The users can get hands-on experience with this prototype, and that prompts them to require improvements or new features. These new requirements become a part of the product backlog.

14.2.2 Scope of the Initial Development

Once the raw initial requirements have been elicited, the next step is to analyze them following a process similar to the one described in chapter 5. The next step selects the *initial backlog*, a subset of the product backlog that will be implemented during initial development.

Initial development should give quick feedback about the feasibility of the project to all stakeholders, and this consideration determines which requirements will make it into the initial backlog. The project risks and the process needs both play a prominent role in the prioritization, and to address them, initial development often tries to include requirements that use all tiers and all technologies of the project, for example, the database, graphical user interface (GUI), client-server support, and so forth.

The need to provide a thorough assessment of risks and process needs conflicts with the need to provide quick feedback to the stakeholders. Timely feedback requires minimal initial development that avoids the problems that plagued the waterfall. As in many engineering situations, a suitable compromise must be found. The programmers should weigh all requirements proposed for the initial backlog and make sure that they really have to be there. In particular, all requirements that impact the users in novel ways should be postponed into evolution, so that they can be withdrawn if they turn out to have undesired effects.

If the size of the initial backlog is kept small, initial development is fast, the project stakeholders receive timely feedback, and the volatility that accumulates in the meantime does not get out of hand. The evolution that starts afterwards can handle all the requirements that were left out.

Requirements Creep

Requirements creep is a common thing in our lives. When shopping for a car, it is tempting to look at cars that are slightly bigger and have a few more features than the car that we originally budgeted. In a restaurant, it is tempting to order an especially tasty dessert after a hearty meal, and so forth.

The same thing can happen in software projects: When doing initial development, why not add a couple of features? Or opt for a bolder and more comprehensive feature? Or try a brand new idea? This is called requirements creep, and it is one of the reasons for project failures. One extra feature here, another one there, and soon one of them becomes the proverbial straw that broke the camel's back. Requirements creep represents a serious project risk, and it was an endemic problem in the context of waterfall projects.

Software evolution guards against requirements creep, because iterations have a limited duration, and only a limited number of requirements make it into an iteration based on hardnosed prioritization. If a faulty requirement still creeps in, the version that implements it can be withdrawn and replaced by an earlier version.

However, initial development does not have this option to revert to an earlier version. At the same time, the system still has very tentative contours; therefore, some ill-thought-out goals can creep into the project plan or into the initial backlog. Unrealistic expectations in the project plan may make the managers feel that they have been deceived. Untried, excessively ambitious, or unnecessary requirements in the initial backlog can be very hard or impossible to undo, and they often lead to serious operational problems and to project cancellations.

One example among many is the London Ambulance System that was used briefly in the early 1990s and whose operation was blamed for 20 unnecessary deaths. The commission that conducted inquiry into this failure concluded that there were numerous errors during the planning and initial requirements phase, and stated: "There is little doubt that the full requirements specification is an ambitious document. As pointed out earlier its intended functionality was greater than was available from any existing system" (Communications Directorate, 1993).

An example of an ill-thought-out requirement that crept in was the brand new strategy of selecting who was going to respond to a call. The system allocated the nearest free ambulance to respond to a call, which sounds very reasonable. However the London metropolitan area is very large, and with each call, some ambulances drifted farther and farther away from their home base, finally reaching areas of London they were not familiar with. Apparently, at that point, they often got lost and sometimes even had to ask pedestrians for directions! Thus this new and untried requirement of allocating the nearest ambulance, although it looked reasonable at first, had serious practical consequences that were unacceptable, and the inclusion of this untried practice in the system belongs to the category of requirements creep.

The lesson learned is that such novel requirements should not creep into the initial backlog but, instead, they should be postponed into evolution so that the version that implements them can be withdrawn if there are unforeseen negative consequences. The programmers working on initial development should be aware of these pitfalls and exercise great caution. The initial development should address only a very select set of fundamental issues, and the rest should be postponed into evolution.

14.3 Design

Design is the next task of initial development. It produces a model of the future first version of software, and the main issue that the designers address is the decomposition of the software into its parts. The design gives the programmers a glimpse into the implementation problems and their solutions while the investment into the software is still small, and hence, exploring several alternatives is not prohibitively expensive.

The design identifies the classes, their relations, and responsibilities. Unified Modeling Language (UML) class diagrams are often used as a notation in which the model is expressed. Besides that, the class-responsibility collaboration (CRC) cards that are described in section 14.3.5 are a frequently used alternative, but numerous other notations also have been proposed and used.

The design is usually divided into phases that follow a certain *methodology*. A large number of software design methodologies have been proposed, and this section presents a methodology that starts with extraction of significant concepts (ESC) that was used in the context of concept location in chapter 6, and it is used here with a slight modification. ESC identifies the classes of the future program, and it is followed by identification of the class responsibilities and class relations. Either CRC cards or UML class diagrams are often used to record the progress of the design task, but other notations may be used as well.

14.3.1 Finding the Classes by ESC

The first phase is to find the classes of the future system, and this is done by a slightly modified ESC that consists of the following steps:

- Extract the set of concepts used in the initial backlog.
- Delete the *irrelevant concepts* that are intended for communication with the programmers and do not deal with the program.
- Delete *external concepts* that lie outside the scope of the initial development.
- The remaining concepts are *relevant concepts*. Divide them into *significant* concepts that deserve to be implemented as a class, and *trivial* concepts that do not require a full class implementation.
- If necessary, change the names of the concepts into identifiers that are suitable to be used in the code.

14.3.2 Assigning the Responsibilities

In the next step of the design, each class is assigned responsibilities. Each trivial concept is assigned to the most closely related class as its responsibility. After that is done, the other responsibilities are the actions that are taken by the program algorithms, for example, "compare two names" that may be required by a search algorithm. The designers estimate what actions the program algorithms need, and then assign them as responsibilities to the appropriate classes.

14.3.3 Finding Class Relations

Some of the classes may handle too many responsibilities and need help. In that case, they contract with other classes that assume some of these responsibilities.

This is how dependencies among the classes are established. Coordinations among the classes are also established in this step.

14.3.4 Inspecting and Refactoring the Design

The design at this stage is inspected and improved by refactoring, which may introduce additional classes, responsibilities, and interactions. If the responsibilities of any of the classes lead to a class that is too large, or if a class assumes a range of responsibilities that have very little in common, the programmers create new supplier classes and move some of the responsibilities to these suppliers. For example, if there is a class Student that contains the student's personal data like date of birth and address, together with the student's transcript, the personal data are refactored into a newly formed class Person.

The same refactoring operations can be done with the design as they are done with the code, but design refactoring is much easier than code refactoring because the design does not contain the details that the code does. Because of that, it is recommended that all obvious refactoring be done during the design rather than implementation.

14.3.5 CRC Cards

In the context of the methodology outlined here, some people have found *CRC cards* to be a useful tool for recording various steps of the design. Class-responsibility collaboration (CRC) cards are small cards, 3 × 5 in. or 4 × 6 in. in size, and each of them is used for one class. Each CRC card has three compartments: class name, responsibilities, and cooperations (see Figure 14.2). The small size of the cards is intentional; we do not want to overload the classes with too many responsibilities or cooperations.

The software designers create a card for each class and fill out the name of the class, assign class responsibilities, and list all cooperations the class is involved in.

Class name: Inventory	
Responsibilities:	**Cooperations:**
Order items	Item

Figure 14.2   CRC card.

The design consists of a stack of CRC cards. It can be readily updated, as cards are easily added, removed, or replaced.

The design is a model of the future code and, like all models, it is an abstraction that lacks many details, and these details have to be filled in during the next task of implementation. Often there are deficiencies in the design, and the implementation must correct them, sometimes at the cost of great amount of rework.

14.3.6 Design of Phone Directory

This example illustrates the design of a small program. The initial backlog of this example is the following: A person's telephone number is found by searching a directory, which contains records of several persons. The user enters names, and the program returns the respective phone numbers. The session is terminated by entering the string xxx.

The same initial backlog with the relevant concepts in italics is the following: A *person's telephone number* is found by *searching* a *directory*, which contains *records* of several persons. The *user enters names*, and the program *returns the respective phone numbers*. The session is *terminated by entering the string xxx*.

The next step is in Table 14.1. In the left column are the concept names as they appear in the initial backlog; all of them are relevant. In the right column are the corresponding identifiers to be used in the CRC cards and the code. Among them, the significant concepts are highlighted in bold, and they will be the future classes.

The next step uses the CRC cards of Figure 14.3. Each class has its own CRC card with the name of the class on the top. The trivial concepts are assigned as

Table 14.1 Relevant Concepts and Significant Concepts

Concept Name in Backlog	*Concept Name in Code*
A person's telephone number	PhoneNumber
Searching	Search
Directory	**Directory**
Record	**Record**
User	**UserInterface**
Enters	EnterName
Name	**Name**
Return the phone numbers	returnPhone
Terminated by entering string xxx	terminate

Class name: Directory	
Responsibilities: search list addRecord deleteRecord	**Cooperations:** Record Name

Class name: UserInterface	
Responsibilities: main	**Cooperations:** Directory Record Name

Class name: Record	
Responsibilities: phoneNumber returnPhone putRecord	**Cooperations:** Name

Class name: Name	
Responsibilities: enterName terminate nameString compare	**Cooperations:**

Figure 14.3 CRC cards of Phone Directory.

responsibilities of the most relevant classes and entered into the left compartment of the CRC cards. The cooperations among the classes are then listed in the right-hand compartment. The designers also select the algorithms and data structures and, based on them, they add additional responsibilities to the bottom of the left-hand compartment.

The stack of four CRC cards representing the completed design of the program is shown in Figure 14.3. The stack can be converted into a UML class diagram of Figure 14.4. However, before that, all cooperations have to be converted into class associations. In Figure 14.4, all are converted into the part-of relations.

14.4 Implementation

After the design has been completed, the next task is the implementation of the first version of the software. The implementation contains two concurrent activities: writing the code and testing it. The programmers either write the code of the classes first and then they write test drivers for the unit tests, or they write the test drivers first and then the corresponding code. The most common implementation strategy is the bottom-up strategy, where the programmers write and verify the suppliers first, and then they write and verify the clients.

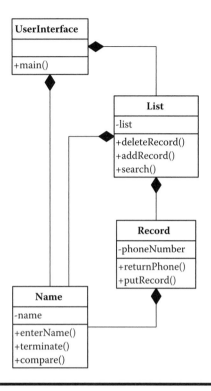

Figure 14.4   UML class diagram of Phone Directory.

14.4.1 Bottom-Up Implementation

Bottom-up implementation is a process that is driven by the desire to minimize the number of testing stubs for unit tests, because they represent an extra expense and delay in the project. The programmers are guided by the dependency graph. First they implement the bottom classes that do not have any suppliers, and then they implement their clients, the clients of the clients, and so forth. In the dependency graphs without cycles, all suppliers can be written before the clients, so there is no need for writing any stubs.

Figure 14.5 contains the dependency graph that corresponds to the UML class diagram of Figure 14.4 and CRC cards of Figure 14.3. The bottom-up implementation sequence that this dependency graph allows is Name, Record, List, UserInterface. In this particular case, this is the only bottom-up implementation sequence, but more complex dependency graphs may allow multiple bottom-up implementation sequences.

Cycles in the dependency graph present a problem to this process. If they are small, the whole cycle can be handled in one step of the bottom-up implementation. If the cycles are large and cannot be credibly verified in one step, the cycles have to be disconnected and a stub has to be written for one class in the cycle.

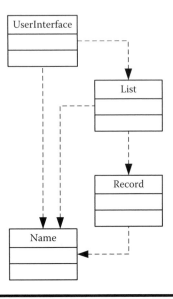

Figure 14.5 Dependency graph of Phone Directory.

The programmers inspect the design of all classes and decide which class can be replaced by a stub at the least cost, and then write the stub for that class. That disconnects the cycle, and the bottom-up process can be applied.

Figure 14.6 presents an example of a dependency graph with a cycle, where classes B, C, and D form a cycle. After the programmers inspected the design, they concluded that the easiest stub to write would be the stub for class B. The modified dependency graph with the stub appears in Figure 14.7. The sequence of class implementation then is: StubB, D, C, B, A.

If it were class C in Figure 14.6 that had the easiest stub to write, then the modified dependency graph with the stub for class C would be as presented in Figure 14.8. One of the sequences of class implementation then is: StubC, B, D, C, A.

When all classes of the program have been written and tested, the final part of bottom-up development is functional testing of the completed version of software.

The process of bottom-up implementation can be viewed as consisting of repeated software changes that are, in this particular context, greatly simplified and consist only of actualization, conclusion, and verification phases, where actualization consists only of creation of new client classes. The bottom-up process follows the design document and, in theory, there is no need for other phases of software change like code refactoring or change propagation. However, as mentioned before, design documents often have various deficiencies that are discovered during the

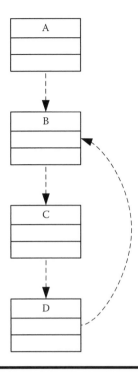

Figure 14.6 Dependency graph with a cycle.

implementation, and the introduction of new classes also requires refactoring and change propagation.

During the bottom-up development, the baseline of the project may consist of several disconnected supplier slices. They are integrated into greater and greater slices by the actualizations of new clients, and finally the whole program is integrated into one.

14.4.2 Code Generation from Design

There is substantial overlap between the information that is contained in the design documents and the corresponding code. The class names, class members, class associations—all of these things are a part of the design and can be directly copied into the code. There are tools that process this design information and generate *code skeletons*. Of course, these skeletons do not contain all the necessary code; there are missing parts that need to be filled in, in particular the bodies of the methods. The code generated from the design is like a blank form, where certain parts are already there but other parts have to be filled in. These code skeletons can save the programmers a substantial amount of work.

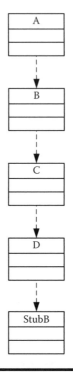

Figure 14.7   Modified dependency graph with stub for class B.

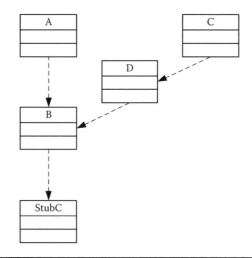

Figure 14.8   Modified dependency graph with stub for class C.

14.5 Team Organizations for Initial Development

The tasks of initial development have a very dissimilar character, and different skills are required for the project plan, initial requirements, design, and implementation. On large projects, different teams with different qualifications may participate in these separate tasks. However, often a single team goes through all the tasks of initial development and obtains help from different consultants who are experts in specific tasks. The initial development is often used to recruit people into the team, because few people are needed for the early tasks, but the need for additional people grows in later tasks, particularly during the implementation; after that, the team is ready for evolution.

Implementation of the first version can be done iteratively in the tailored processes of SIP (solo iterative process), AIP (agile iterative process), DIP (directed iterative process), and CIP (centralized iterative process). The main difference with the original processes is that the iteration backlog consists of the classes of the design rather than the requirements. The programmers pick these classes from the iteration backlog one by one and implement them using a simplified process of software change, until the whole initial version is implemented. For that, they most often follow the bottom-up strategy that was outlined in the previous section.

14.5.1 Transfer from Initial Development to Evolution

Initial development ends with the first version of the software, which serves as a baseline for subsequent evolution. The stakeholders have to decide whether this version is ready for release, or whether the first release should be postponed until the conclusion of one or several evolutionary iterations. The subsequent evolution fills in the missing requirements that the initial development was unable to implement, and also reacts to the volatility that has accumulated during the initial development.

To get evolution off the ground, the evolution processes need an updated product backlog and, therefore, the last part of the implementation is to update the backlog. The programmers delete or inactivate all the requirements that have been successfully implemented, and add new requirements that surfaced during the initial development.

In rare circumstances, the product backlog is empty after the initial development, or contains only minor corrective changes. This happens when the software is small or oriented toward an unusually stable domain, like a washing machine control program. In that case, the software life span in fact follows the waterfall model, and there is no evolution. Instead, the next stage is one of the final stages of software life span: the servicing, phaseout, or shutdown.

Summary

Initial development starts a new project from scratch. The project plan provides documentation for the managerial decision of whether to go ahead with the project or not. If the managerial decision is positive, the requirements elicitation elicits the initial requirements and selects the initial backlog for the implementation. The design produces the classes, their responsibilities, and cooperations. CRC cards or UML class diagrams are common notations that record the design. The implementation produces the first version of software. The bottom-up implementation process minimizes the need for stubs during unit testing. The whole process of initial development runs for a limited time, implements only the most important requirements, and addresses the most important project risks.

Further Reading and Topics

An IEEE document (IEEE, 1998) defines a suggested format of a software plan in more detail.

Software design is one of the most developed subfields of software engineering, and there are numerous books and articles dealing with it. See, for example, the work of Booch (1991) and Coad and Yourdon (1991). A survey of design techniques appears in a book by Budgen (2003). CRC methodology and CRC cards are explained in detail by Bellin and Simone (1997). The short overview of the software design in this chapter only briefly outlines this large subfield. To illustrate how large it is, the query "software design" in Google Scholar (2011) produced more than 300,000 hits!

Bottom-up implementation is favored by the current strongly typed languages that require definitions of entities before their use, and hence, they require a definition of the suppliers before the clients. It is also favored by the current testing technologies, in particular technologies that favor unit testing of the whole supplier slice (Hamill, 2004).

However, there are also processes of top-down implementation that are a mirror image of the bottom-up, because they implement and verify clients before developing the suppliers. The verification of the clients in this context is often done by inspections that do not need the stubs, or by unit testing with the help of stubs. This process starts with the top modules that support interaction with the users. Their behavior reflects the requirements and, therefore, starting the development with them ensures that the requirements will not be missed or deformed by the process (Rajlich, 1985, 1994).

A combined development that has advantages of both top-down and bottom-up is present in *V-development* (not to be confused with the V-model of software life span!). In the first phase, it implements the software modules top-down and verifies them by inspections; inspections do not need stubs and can be applied to incomplete code. When the bottom modules are reached, the process reverses direction; the testing phase starts and then moves bottom-up from the suppliers toward the clients.

Code generators convert the design into a skeleton of the code, and numerous tools have been developed for that purpose. (See, for example, Budinsky, Gross, Steinberg, & Ellersick, 2009).

Software design is the process that offers an opportunity to identify code reuse. To write and verify the code is a slow process, and software reuse of ready-made code can greatly speed it up and improve productivity. The reuse can use products that are specifically prepared for reuse, or it can be opportunistic, where code from old projects is used in new ones. Issues of software reuse are summarized by Frakes and Kang (2005).

Exercises

14.1 How does initial development differ from the waterfall?

14.2 What are the tasks of initial development?

14.3 What is the purpose of the software plan?

14.4 List five sections of the software plan.

14.5 Why do initial requirements have to be elicited? What does *elicitation* mean?

14.6 What is the difference between the product backlog and initial backlog?

14.7 What are the criteria for the selection of the initial backlog?

14.8 Create a product backlog for a small software that controls a washing machine.

14.9 For the product backlog created in the previous question, create a design using CRC cards.

14.10 How does a design that uses CRC cards differ from a design that uses UML class diagrams?

14.11 What do you have to do to convert CRC cards into a UML class diagram?

14.12 Write an example of a code skeleton that is generated from a class diagram that contains two classes. Describe by comments a code that is missing in the skeletons and will have to be written by programmers.

References

Bellin, D., & Simone, S. S. (1997). *The CRC card book*. Reading, MA: Addison-Wesley.

Booch, G. (1991). *Object-oriented modeling and design with applications*. San Francisco, CA: Benjamin/Cummings Publishing.

Budgen, D. (2003). *Software design*. Reading, MA: Addison-Wesley.

Budinsky F., Gross, T. J., Steinberg, D., & Ellersick, R. (2009). *Eclipse modelling framework* (2nd ed.). Upper Saddle River, NJ: Addison-Wesley.

Coad, P., & Yourdon, E. (1991). *Object-oriented design*. Englewood Cliffs, NJ: Yourdon Press.

Communications Directorate, South West Thames Regional Health Authority. (1993). *Report of the inquiry into the London Ambulance Service.* Retrieved on June 24, 2011, from http://www.cs.ucl.ac.uk/staff/a.finkelstein/las/lascase0.9.pdf

Frakes, W. B., & Kang, K. (2005). Software reuse research: Status and future. *IEEE Transactions on Software Engineering, 31*, 529–536.

Google Scholar. (2011). Search term "software design." Retrieved on June 24, 2011, from http://scholar.google.com/scholar?hl=en&q=%22software+design%22&btnG=Search &as_sdt=0%2C23&as_ylo=&as_vis=0

Hamill, P. (2004). *Unit test frameworks.* Sebastopol, CA: O'Reilly.

IEEE. (1998). *IEEE standard for software, project management plans* (IEEE Std. 1058-1998). Washington, DC: IEEE Computer Society Press.

Rajlich, V. (1985). Paradigms for design and implementation in ADA. *Communications of the ACM, 28*, 718–727.

———. (1994). Decomposition/generalization methodology for object-oriented programming. *Journal of Systems and Software, 24*(2), 181–186.

Chapter 15

Final Stages

Objectives

As software technology has matured, more and more software systems are reaching the final stages of the software life span. After you have read this chapter, you will know:

- The reasons why software evolution ends
- The servicing stage and its difference from evolution
- The techniques of software change that are acceptable during servicing but not during evolution
- The phaseout stage, when servicing is discontinued
- The activities of closedown
- The heterogeneous systems and iterative reengineering

***

The past emphasis of software engineering has been on the early stages of the software life span, and the initial development has gained particular attention. This is not surprising because software technology still has a relatively short history, and starting new projects has been the dominant activity in the past. However, an increasing number of software projects now reach the final stages, and therefore, they are an important software engineering topic as well. These final stages have already been introduced in chapter 2, but this chapter presents a more complete exposition. The stages are servicing, phaseout, and closedown, as presented in the lower right part of Figure 15.1.

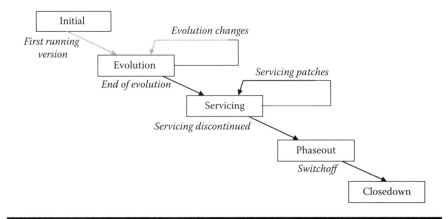

Figure 15.1   Final stages of software life span.

15.1 End of Software Evolution

Software evolution is a software engineer's response to the volatility of the requirements, volatility of stakeholder knowledge, or volatility of technology. Software evolution ends for several different reasons: stabilization, decay, cultural change, or business decision.

15.1.1 Software Stabilization

One of the reasons for software evolution is the volatility of stakeholder knowledge. As the stakeholders explore the problem that software solves, they learn more about it. Very often, they do it by trial and error, where they try certain ideas. If the ideas work, they keep them, and if they do not work, they reject them. In the situations where the software domain is stable and the technology is stable as well, stakeholder learning is the sole cause of the evolution. Once the problem is sufficiently explored and the correct solutions are found, the software project reaches a point of stability where further substantial changes are unnecessary. This is called *stabilization* of software.

Stabilization of software frequently occurs in real-time systems that control a specific mechanism, for example, a car ignition. The domain of the software is a particular car engine. Once the engine is produced and used, it does not change, and therefore, the domain is stable. The only reason for evolution is the volatility of stakeholder knowledge, where the stakeholders are learning how to control this specific engine ignition. Once the stakeholders complete their learning and find the solution, there is no reason for further evolution.

15.1.2 Code Decay

Code decay is another reason for the end of evolution. Although software is not material and is not subject to wear and tear, its structure decays under the impact of software changes. The symptoms of code decay are increased difficulty of making software changes and decreasing change quality, particularly an increase in the presence of bugs introduced by the changes. The decaying software can have confusing contracts between software suppliers and clients, unexpected coordination among the classes, illogical identifiers or comments, concept extensions delocalized into several classes, and so forth. Code decay is the result of accumulated problems that postfactoring did not resolve in a timely fashion.

Concept location in decayed code may become very hard. If the code does not have meaningful identifiers or comments, the grep search utility does not work. If there are no clean and understandable contracts, the dependency search does not work either. A decayed structure of software may complicate unit testing or code inspection and, as a result, the changes become increasingly difficult and risky. The software becomes increasingly unpredictable, costly to evolve, and costly to debug. It may reach the point where further evolution is beyond the capabilities of the programming team, and this pushes the software into the servicing stage.

Insufficient knowledge is one of the reasons for code decay. To understand a software system, software engineers must understand the domain of the application, the architecture, the algorithms, the data structures, and the concept extensions in the code. They must understand all code strengths and weaknesses. If that knowledge is not available, the new code that they produce does not mesh with the old code, and software changes aggravate code decay. Even refactoring requires a thorough knowledge of software, and without it, it is no longer possible, and the system further decays.

The programmers may record part of the knowledge in the program documentation, but usually this knowledge is of such size and complexity that a complete recording is not available. Everything that is not recorded persists in the form of tacit individual or group knowledge. This tacit knowledge is constantly at risk of being lost or forgotten. Changes in the code make this knowledge obsolete, and software engineers may forget some of the knowledge over time. In addition, the software engineers who leave the project take their knowledge with them, and if they do not transfer this knowledge to other members of the team, that knowledge is lost, and this can also trigger code decay.

As the symptoms of decay proliferate, the code becomes more and more complicated, and the knowledge that is necessary for further evolution actually increases. When the gap between the knowledge of the team and the growing complexity of software becomes too large, the software evolvability is lost and, whether by accident or by design, the system slips into servicing.

15.1.3 Cultural Change

A special instance of loss of knowledge is cultural change. Software engineering has more than half a century of history, and there are programs still in use that were created a half century ago. These programs were created in a time of completely different properties of hardware: Computers were slower and had much less memory, often requiring elaborate algorithms to swap information into and out of the memory. Moreover, the programmers used different programming techniques, wrote in obsolete languages and for obsolete operating systems, and held different opinions about what constitutes a good structure of software. The recently developed object-oriented techniques were unknown at that time.

The programmers who created these programs are no longer available, and the current programmers who try to change these old programs face a double problem: Not only do they have to recover the knowledge that is necessary for that specific program, but they also have to recover the culture within which these programs were created. Without that, they may be unable to make the changes in the program.

15.1.4 Business Decision

Evolution of software may also end for business reasons. Any product can lose its usefulness through either "physical obsolescence," when it tears or wears down, or "moral obsolescence," when it is still functioning but is no longer needed. Software is not physical; therefore, it does not wear or tear, but it can become obsolete when it loses its usefulness. When that happens, managers decide to stop software evolution.

Another business reason is based on the fact that software evolution is expensive, and it typically requires the effort of the best personnel. The situation may arise that the company no longer wishes to spend the resources on further evolution and the managers stop it, even if the technical properties of the program still allow it.

15.2 Servicing

After the evolution ends, software enters the servicing stage. The purpose of the servicing is to protect the residual value of software. The threats to that value can come from bugs that surface during the use, or from changes in the domain or technology to which the software must adapt; the servicing is dominated by adaptive and corrective changes.

Because the resulting structure of the code is no longer a matter of concern, servicing frequently uses actualization techniques that would be inadmissible during evolution. A prominent technique of this kind is the use of *wrappers*, as represented in Figure 15.2.

Wrappers, as the word implies, do not change the code that has a deficient functionality. Instead, they wrap it in additional code that transforms the new precondition into the old one, then executes the old code, and finally transforms the old postcondition into the new one. The wrapped code remains undisturbed, does not need to be understood by programmers, and does not need to be verified. The size of the wrapped code can range from a single method to the whole program.

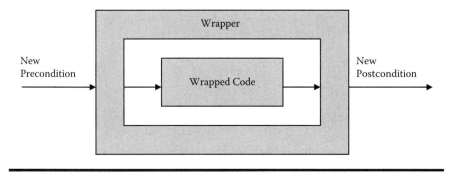

Figure 15.2   Wrappers.

Wrapping seriously deteriorates the structure of the program. Within the wrapped part of software, the contracts between suppliers and clients become illogical, and the concept extensions become delocalized between the old code and the new wrapper. These conditions make future changes more difficult. For that reason, this technique is not recommended during the stage of evolution; however, it may become tolerable when the software nears the end of its life span.

Wrapper for Y2K

In the context of Y2K that was discussed in chapter 5, the life span of many programs was extended by the use of a wrapper that shifted the two-digit original "window" of January 1, 1900–December 31, 1999, to a new window, for example, January 1, 1930–December 31, 2029. That extended the useful life of the software into the future and reinterpreted the codes of unused years January 1, 1900–December 31, 1929, as codes of future years January 1, 2000–December 1, 2029. For programs wrapped in this way, the new window will ultimately run out again, but the hope is that by that time, new programs that correctly handle the date will replace them.

The correct change does not use the wrapper but addresses the problem head-on and extends the code for the year to four digits. The programs changed that way do not have an early expiration date, and they can operate until December 31, 9999.

When comparing the stage of servicing to the stage of evolution, there are similarities: Both stages consist of repeated software changes, and the changes have similar phases. Because of that, the processes SIP (solo iterative process), AIP (agile iterative process), DIP (directed iterative process), and CIP (centralized iterative process) are also applicable to servicing.

However, there are also important differences. Because servicing is not interested in increasing the value of software, the only considerations are correctness and the cost of the changes. There is no longer any need to preserve the code properties that allow large future changes. Therefore, the structure of the code is no longer a concern, and the software changes skip the phase of postfactoring, including the associated costs. However, regression tests are even more prominent in servicing than they are during evolution; the preservation of the old functionality that the users rely on is of the highest importance. Because of these differences, certain teams specialize in servicing, and they take over when software moves into the servicing stage.

15.3 Phaseout and Closedown

The phaseout is the next stage of the software life span. It is characterized by the absence of new updates to the software. The customers use *workarounds* when they encounter defects. The owners of the software may still provide help to the users, and part of that help includes bulletins that describe recommended workarounds. An example is a workaround for a security risk for an application that was issued by Microsoft (2011).

The boundary between servicing and phaseout does not need to be abrupt; management may gradually withdraw support from the software and limit servicing to the highest-priority bugs or adaptations, while issuing bulletins on how to work around the less important issues. Management also can intensify or restart the servicing and put additional resources into it if the business situation changes and a need for more intensive servicing becomes apparent.

Closedown is the end of the software life span. The reasons for closedown vary: The work done by the system may no longer be needed; or new and better software has appeared and replaced the old one; or the software was already in the stage of phaseout, but a new serious problem appeared and pushed the software over into closedown. We have already seen an example of that: The Y2K problem was the reason why approximately 20% of the software applications worldwide were closed down at the end of the 20th century (Kappelman, 2000).

Several actions must precede closedown. There may be persistent data that needs to be preserved: student transcripts, some customer records, birth certificates, and so forth. The closedown then contains a phase where the old data are migrated to the new system, and that may involve data conversion; the quality and integrity of this conversion must be evaluated before the old system is shut down.

If new software is replacing the old software, there may be a need to retrain users in the use of the replacement system. Sometimes contracts define the legal responsibilities of the individual stakeholders when the software shuts down.

15.4 Reengineering

Section 15.1.2 described the transition from software evolution to servicing. It can occur as stealthy code decay that leads to the loss of software structure or loss of software knowledge and results in the loss of software evolvability. If code decays, but the expectations for the system are still high and users still request new functionalities, then management has the following options:

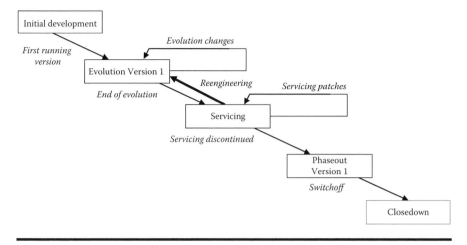

Figure 15.3   Reengineering in software life-span model.

■ Maintain the increasingly unsatisfactory status quo
■ Transfer the work to the servicing stage and refuse the change requests that cannot be honored
■ Rejuvenate the system by reengineering

Reengineering reverses the code decay, but there is a large asymmetry involved: While the code decay happens spontaneously and sometimes even unnoticed, reengineering can be an arduous process. Hence, the transition from evolution to servicing is a very significant episode that substantially lessens the value of software, and the reversal can be very expensive. The modified life-span model that includes reengineering is depicted in Figure 15.3.

Reengineering does not change the functionality of software; it only changes the structure and, therefore, it is similar to refactoring. However, while refactoring aims at small and localized code improvements—for example, changing a name of an identifier or extracting a function, as discussed in chapter 9—reengineering typically reorganizes and rewrites the decayed code of the whole system or substantial parts of it.

The first phase of a reengineering task is called *reverse engineering*, where the programmers analyze the old code and extract the relevant information from it. In the next phase, the programmers analyze this information, delete what became obsolete or unnecessary, and create the new design. Finally, they use this new design to implement the code; this last phase is called *forward engineering*.

In Figure 15.4, the horizontal axis represents time and the vertical axis represents the level of abstraction. The code has a low level of abstraction, while the extracted information and new design are abstract. The process of reengineering visits all four quadrants of Figure 15.4.

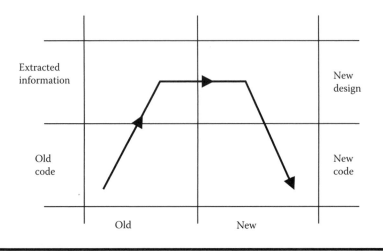

Figure 15.4   Scheme of the reengineering.

15.4.1 Whole-Scale Reengineering

The process of reengineering can be a *whole-scale* process (the model is depicted in Figure 15.5), and it is similar to that of the initial development as presented in chapter 14. The first task is the creation of a plan that estimates the duration and the cost of the reengineering effort. Next, the knowledge from the old code is extracted. Then the design phase follows and, finally, the new code is implemented according to this design.

However, the whole-scale reengineering effort has problems that resemble the problems of the waterfall. For large software, a whole-scale reengineering can be a difficult, expensive, and unpredictable undertaking. During the reengineering process, the requirements volatility continues and may lead to a growing difference between the reengineered software and the users' expectations. To prevent that, the project owners have to evolve two projects in parallel: the old one that is currently

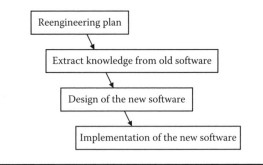

Figure 15.5   Whole-scale reengineering.

in use, and the new one that is being prepared for the future. If they do not properly evolve the new system, it may end up being obsolete before being released.

The risk is magnified by the fact that, during the reengineering, the tolerance of the users toward any inadvertent alteration is low. The users are accustomed to the old software and are very sensitive to any disruption of their routine. Their tolerance of alterations in that routine is usually much smaller than the tolerance of the users of brand-new systems. They typically expect exactly the same functionality from the new project and do not tolerate any deviations. To develop a system that has an identical functionality as the old one may be hard to accomplish, and this fact presents a significant risk for a whole-scale reengineering effort.

15.4.2 Iterative Reengineering and Heterogeneous Systems

Iterative reengineering is a process that avoids the problems of whole-scale reengineering. It blends software evolution and reengineering into a single iterative process that can use the SIP, AIP, DIP, or CIP process model. The blended process deals with heterogeneous systems.

The assumption behind the previous chapters was that the software systems are *homogeneous*, that is, all modules are in the same stage of the software life span. *Heterogeneous systems* are systems whose code consists of some modules that are evolvable, other decayed modules that cannot be evolved, or stabilized modules that do not need to be evolved. An example of heterogeneous software is given in Figure 15.6, which presents evolvable software modules as white rectangles, stabilized modules as black rectangles, and decayed modules as gray rectangles.

The iterative reengineering interleaves reengineering tasks and regular evolution tasks. The evolutionary tasks follow the process of chapters 5–11, and the phases of concept location and impact analysis identify the affected modules. Table 15.1 summarizes what to do with the changes that impact modules in various stages of life span. The changes that involve only evolvable modules or small changes that involve stabilized modules present no problem. Large changes to stabilized modules are not supposed to happen; perhaps when such a change request appears, it may be an indication that the module is not truly stabilized. Servicing changes that involve decayed modules may involve wrapping and, hence, again they can be scheduled without a problem. However, the large changes that require evolution of decayed modules cannot be done and have to wait until after the programmers reengineer these decayed modules.

To minimize user disruption, the programmers reengineer the old system one task at a time, based on the project priorities. If the result of the reengineering task is unsatisfactory, the programmers can always return to the earlier version, and this lessens the reengineering risk. This approach also minimizes the disruption of the users' routine, and the results of the reengineering are immediate, concrete, and limited in scope. Justification and budgeting of iterative reengineering is

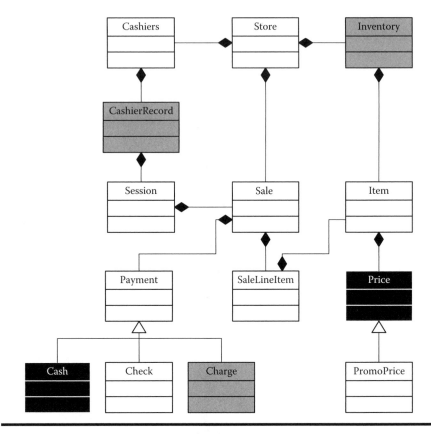

Figure 15.6 Heterogeneous software.

easier because the expenses of the individual reengineering tasks are limited, and immediate feedback on the success of the process is available.

If the old code is only partially decayed, forward engineering can preserve the healthy part of the old code and reimplement only the decayed part, and that may speed up the reengineering. *Redevelopment* is the most radical reengineering where none of the code of the decayed program is usable. However, even in that case, the functional tests or select unit tests still should be used because they validate that the functionality of the new code does not depart from the old one.

The other aspect of the code that needs to be preserved is the knowledge accumulated in the code. As the evolution of the software progresses, often the knowledge

Table 15.1 Changes in Heterogeneous Software

	Evolvable	*Stabilized*	*Decayed*
Small change to the functionality	do	do	wrap
Large change to the functionality	do		postpone

of the domain accumulates in the code and is not recorded anywhere else: It is not recorded in any books, reports, or documentation. This knowledge must not be lost during the redevelopment because it represents a large business value. An example of such knowledge is the knowledge of how to calculate insurance premiums: The premiums are dependent on a particular state and are impacted by the laws of the state, court decisions, demographics, ZIP codes, and many other factors. The formula to calculate this premium is based on accumulated experience over a long period of time, and the same formula must be used in the new code after redevelopment; otherwise, important business value is lost.

Incremental reengineering is a preferable process, but it works only in the situations where the old and new modules can communicate with each other and run as a single executable software. This is guaranteed when the old and new modules use the same technology, including the same hardware, language, and compiler, but it can be a problem when this condition is not satisfied.

Summary

Software evolution ends through software stabilization, when there is no longer any volatility, or through code decay, when the complexity of the code outruns the cognitive capabilities of the programming team, or through a business decision, when investment into further evolution is no longer economically viable. After software evolution ends, the next stage is servicing, where the programmers do only minor corrective or adaptive changes. Servicing sometimes uses techniques that would be unacceptable during the evolution, like wrapping. When servicing stops, software enters the stage of phaseout and, finally, closedown. Reengineering is a process that returns software from the final stages back to evolution. It consists of three steps: reverse engineering, where relevant information is extracted from the old code; new design, where this information is used to determine new classes and their relations; and forward engineering that implements the new classes. The recommended process of reengineering is the iterative process, where the reengineering tasks are interleaved with servicing or evolutionary changes. The software that iterative reengineering deals with is heterogeneous software, where some modules are evolvable, while others are decayed or stabilized and cannot be involved in evolutionary changes.

Further Reading and Topics

A symptom that the software evolution is nearing its end is the declining rate of system growth. It was documented for some software systems by Paulson, Succi, and Eberlein (2004). Code decay was documented by Eick, Graves, Karr, Marron, and Mockus (2001). However, it is possible—with extraordinary effort—to evolve even decayed code; some of the encountered situations and their solutions are discussed by Feathers (2005). Legacy code is a term that describes the decayed code (Feathers, 2005).

Software maintenance is an older term and a synonym for software servicing. However, note that in the old waterfall model, the term *maintenance* was used as an umbrella term for all stages of the life span that follow the initial development and, hence, it may include evolution, servicing, phaseout, and closedown. Since evolution, servicing, and the remaining stages are so different in many of their characteristics, the old observations that apply to software maintenance should be used with caution.

A different team than the original development team often does software servicing in order to cut down on costs. However, there is a sensitive issue of handover when the development team transfers the project to the servicing team. The goal is to hand over not only the code, but also the necessary knowledge (Pigoski, 1996).

The length of the life span of software in Japan was surveyed by Tamai and Torimitsu (1992). Several software domains were included in the survey, including manufacturing, financial services, construction, media, and so forth. For software larger than 1 million lines of code, the average life span was found to be 12.2 years, with a standard deviation of 4.2 years; there was a larger variation in the life span of smaller software. The reasons for the closedown were found to be the following: Hardware or system change was the reason in 18% of the cases; new technology was the reason in 23.7% of the cases; the need to satisfy new user requirements was the cause in 32.8% of the cases; and deterioration of software maintainability caused the remaining 25.4% of the cases.

Reengineering in the presence of different technologies is described by Olsem (1998). The publication describes the process of reengineering that replaces an old technology with a new one in an iterative fashion, and gateways are used as wrappers that support coexistence of the modules that use different technologies in the same system. Reengineering in the presence of a knowledge in the code that is not recorded elsewhere and must be extracted and preserved is described by Kozaczynski and Wilde (1992).

Selected tasks of iterative reengineering are described by Demeyer, Ducasse, and Nierstrasz (2003). A redevelopment of a highly decayed code that also is implemented in an obsolete language and obsolete programming culture is described by Rajlich, Wilde, Buckellew, and Page (2001). A survey of reverse-engineering techniques is presented by Müller et al. (2000).

Exercises

15.1 What are the main differences between software evolution and servicing?

15.2 Name two causes of code decay.

15.3 During servicing, what phase of software change is skipped? Why?

15.4 Suppose that you have a method in the code that calculates a day for a given date within year 2011, and it has a day and a month as parameters. How would you wrap this method so that it calculates a correct day for the year 2012?

15.5 How does phaseout differ from servicing?

15.6 What is code stabilization and what is its cause?

15.7 What is the difference between homogeneous and heterogeneous software?

15.8 In a process that mixes reengineering with evolution, how are the reengineering priorities determined?

15.9 If a module was in the decayed state, what techniques could be used to modify its contract with its clients?

15.10 What must programmers preserve during the closedown phase?

15.11 What is the difference between reverse engineering and reengineering?

References

Demeyer, S., Ducasse, S., & Nierstrasz, O. M. (2003). *Object-oriented reengineering patterns*. Waltham, MA: Morgan Kaufmann.

Eick, S. G., Graves, T. L., Karr, A. F., Marron, J. S., & Mockus, A. (2001). Does code decay? Assessing evidence from change management data. *IEEE Transactions on Software Engineering (TSE), 27*(1), 1–12.

Feathers, M. (2005). *Working effectively with legacy code*. Boston, MA: Prentice Hall Professional.

Kappelman, L. A. (2000). Some strategic Y2K blessings. *IEEE Software, 17*(2), 42–46.

Kozaczynski, W., & Wilde, N. (1992). On the re-engineering of transaction systems. *J. Software Maintenance, 4*(3), 143–162.

Microsoft. (2011). *Microsoft security advisory: Vulnerability in Microsoft DirectShow could allow remote code execution*. Retrieved on June 23, 2011, from http://support.microsoft.com/kb/971778

Müller, H. A., Jahnke, J. H., Smith, D. B., Storey, M. A., Tilley, S. R., & Wong, K. (2000). Reverse engineering: A roadmap. In *Proceedings of the Conference on the Future of Software Engineering* (pp. 47–60). New York, NY: ACM.

Olsem, M. R. (1998). An incremental approach to software systems reengineering. *Journal of Software Maintenance, 10*(3), 181–202.

Paulson, J. W., Succi, G., & Eberlein, A. (2004). An empirical study of open-source and closed-source software products. *IEEE Transactions on Software Engineering, 30*, 246–256.

Pigoski, T. M. (1996). *Practical software maintenance: Best practices for managing your software investment*. New York, NY: John Wiley & Sons.

Rajlich, V., Wilde, N., Buckellew, M., & Page, H. (2001). Software cultures and evolution. *Computer, 34*(9), 24–28.

Tamai, T., & Torimitsu, Y. (1992). Software lifetime and its evolution process over generations. In *Proceedings of IEEE International Conference on Software Maintenance* (pp. 63–69). Washington, DC: IEEE Computer Society Press.

CONCLUSION IV

Contents

The concluding part of the book contains a chapter on the related topics that people working on software projects frequently encounter. The book concludes with a chapter that presents an example of a software change, and a chapter that presents an example of the solo iterative process (SIP).

Chapter 16

Related Topics

Objectives

Software engineers, in their education and in their software projects, frequently deal with topics that are a part of other academic disciplines. After you have read this chapter, you will know the roles of these related topics:

- Other computing disciplines
- Professional ethics, with a particular emphasis on confidentiality and privacy
- Software management
- Ergonomics (human factors)

***

This book presents a core part of the knowledge that software engineers need to be successful in their projects and their careers. There are additional related fields and overlapping disciplines whose knowledge they also need. This chapter contains a brief overview of some of them and points to further reading where the reader can gain a deeper knowledge of these related fields.

16.1 Other Computing Disciplines

Software engineering belongs to a family of computing disciplines that deal with computer-related topics from different points of view. Each of these disciplines has a different emphasis and overlaps with software engineering in a different way. The divisions among the disciplines are often a matter of historical accident. From the point of view of the current software projects and programmer needs, they may have lost their justification. Nevertheless, they still exist and divide the field of computing into separate disciplines. The curricula for software engineering education reflect these divisions (ACM, 2006).

In chapter 3, we encountered technologies that software engineers need to know, but that are traditionally considered separate academic topics with their own courses, textbooks, journals, and conferences. Besides them, there are additional computing disciplines that lie outside traditional software engineering limits, and this section gives a brief survey.

16.1.1 Computer Engineering

Computer engineering concentrates on computer hardware and computer-controlled equipment. The specific topics of computer engineering include circuits, digital logic, operating systems, digital signal processing, distributed systems, embedded systems, and so forth. Embedded systems are a topic that deals with the development of devices that contain embedded hardware and software. Examples of such devices are washing machines that contain control chips and their programs, cars that have numerous chips that control ignition and other functions, cell phones, medical tools and machines, and many other devices.

There is a substantial overlap between software engineering and computer engineering: Software engineers need to know the properties of the hardware and the control software while developing applications, and computer engineers need to know the principles of software engineering while developing control software. Software engineers often work together with computer engineers in the same teams. Although the development of embedded systems requires knowledge of software engineering principles, it has a distinct flavor. It solves a distinct set of problems and utilizes distinct software models and technologies (Barr & Massa, 2006; Gupta, 1995).

16.1.2 Computer Science

Computer science emphasizes the theoretical and scientific aspects of computing. The subfields of computer science are algorithms, computability, intelligent systems, bioinformatics, and so forth. Many subjects of computer science are abstract, and they are independent of technologies or software engineering processes and paradigms. The theory of algorithms is an example of that independence (Cormen, Leiserson, Rivest, & Stein, 2009).

Historically, computer science is the oldest computing discipline, and for that reason, it often serves as an umbrella that contains other computing disciplines. For example, in many academic programs, software engineering is a part of computer science, rather than the other way around.

16.1.3 Information Systems

The information systems discipline developed in business schools, and it deals with business software. The subfields of emphasis are databases, computer networks, and web programming. There are also specialized subfields like health information systems (Checkland & Holwell, 1998).

16.2 Professional Ethics

As software assumes a more central role for the functioning of society, it is more and more important that it contribute to society's well-being rather than becoming a growing threat. Software engineers are at the center of this significant social development, and they should understand the big picture and be well versed in ethical issues.

The concern about software threats is well founded, as illustrated by a long litany of computer woes (Neumann, 1995). Because of the essential difficulties of software that were discussed in chapter 1, society is often hindered when dealing with these issues, and a large responsibility falls on the shoulders of software engineers, who have to be sensitive to the public interest. Computer crime is perhaps the most serious of the ethical failures.

16.2.1 Computer Crime

Many computer crimes are variants of theft or vandalism. For example, in the year 2005, "British police made a number of arrests in the case of a plan to steal huge sums of money from accounts at the British office of the Sumitomo Mitsui Bank by transferring it into their accounts in various countries. Their basic trick was to plant software on the bank's computers that exposed login names and passwords to them" (Neumann, 2009).

Computer crime is the topic of the growing field of computer forensics (Carrier, 2005). This discipline deals with gathering evidence for criminal convictions, and it lies in an intersection between software engineering and criminal justice. Software engineers may be called to help with gathering this evidence, or to testify, or to provide necessary expertise, and should be prepared to fill this role.

16.2.2 Computer Ethical Codes

Despite the novelty of software, the responsibility of software engineers is the classical responsibility of one person to another that has been present in human society through the ages. Software engineers make choices, and these choices affect the lives of others, positively or negatively. These issues have been studied by the discipline of ethics. Natural law is the conceptual ethical framework that can serve as the foundation of conduct in novel situations (Finnis, 1983).

While natural law is generic, professional groups often feel that they need to develop specific guidelines. The classical professional code of conduct in the field of medicine is the Hippocratic oath (NIH, 2002); the modern oaths of medical doctors stem from it.

Similarly, like the medical community, professional societies of software engineers have developed ethics codes that codify the conduct of software engineers. For example, see *Software Engineering Code of Ethics and Professional Practice* (ACM, 1999). There is a short and long version of the document; the short version states the following:

> Software engineers shall commit themselves to making the analysis, specification, design, development, testing and maintenance of software a beneficial and respected profession. In accordance with their commitment to the health, safety and welfare of the public, software engineers shall adhere to the following eight principles:
>
> 1. *Public.* Software engineers shall act consistently with the public interest.
> 2. *Client and employer.* Software engineers shall act in a manner that is in the best interests of their client and employer consistent with the public interest.
> 3. *Product.* Software engineers shall ensure that their products and related modifications meet the highest professional standards possible.
> 4. *Judgment.* Software engineers shall maintain integrity and independence in their professional judgment.
> 5. *Management.* Software engineering managers and leaders shall subscribe to and promote an ethical approach to the management of software development and maintenance.
> 6. *Profession.* Software engineers shall advance the integrity and reputation of the profession consistent with the public interest.
> 7. *Colleagues.* Software engineers shall be fair to and supportive of their colleagues.
> 8. *Self.* Software engineers shall participate in lifelong learning regarding the practice of their profession and shall promote an ethical approach to the practice of the profession.

16.2.3 Information Diversion and Misuse

The novel capabilities of computers amplify numerous ethical issues, and one especially troubling ethical issue is the diversion and misuse of information. Computers have the capability to collect information on an unprecedented scale and to process this huge amount of information through data-mining algorithms. It is easily foreseeable that the results of that process may end up in the wrong hands, and the society that would allow this exploitation of information would find its freedom under serious attack. To have a Big Brother who knows more about you than you yourself, or to have private snooping agencies with some petty agendas focused on your every move, is unfortunately within technological reach.

Privacy and confidentiality rights are an important wall that can stave off this nightmare, and software engineers should tirelessly work to protect confidentiality rights. It is important to know that confidentiality rights are rooted in natural law (Fagothey, 1967). In the medical field, the Hippocratic oath contains the clause: "Whatever I see or hear in the lives of my patients, whether in connection with my professional practice or not, which ought not to be spoken of outside, I will keep secret, as considering all such things to be private" (NIH, 2002).

To protect their confidentiality, individuals must have the right to give or withdraw consent to use information about them. They must retain the right to know the collected information, correct it, and even to withdraw it from the database, the same way that customers can withdraw their name and phone number from the phone book. Software engineers are key players in all these situations, and they hold an important aspect of our freedom in their hands. They should be vigilant about this threat and monitor how their projects observe confidentiality.

Note that some of the most popular applications routinely collect user data to enhance the customer's experience. However, software engineers should be vigilant to prevent diversion of these data toward purposes that might be unethical. The ethical and social issues of software engineering are discussed in greater detail in a book by Kizza (2002).

16.3 Software Management

Chapters 13, 14, and 15 dealt with the software team processes, and these teams require management to guarantee smooth functioning. Software engineers must understand the team management issues so that they can effectively contribute to the team effort.

The management discipline studies how to manage teams and resources and how to guarantee a successful outcome of projects. Typically, business schools teach this discipline. Generic management skills include operations management, business law, human resources management, accounting and finance, marketing and sales, economics, quantitative analysis, business policy and strategy, and so forth (Gomez-Mejia, Balkin, & Cardy, 2008).

Besides these generic management skills, software managers require specialized skills that are necessary for the direction of software projects. Chapter 13 divided the management tasks into process management and product management. The process management is inward looking, concerned with the internal matters of process, people, and resources, while product management is outward looking, concerned with the world outside that includes product position in the market and product reputation.

Medium-size teams follow this division, and they have two specialized managers: one being the process manager and the other being the product manager (sometimes called product owner). In small teams, a single manager often fills both roles, while large teams may have a whole hierarchy of managers, where each manager deals with a specialized task (Humphrey, 1999).

16.3.1 Process Management

Process management deals with issues of the process in all its forms, including the process model, enactment, measurement, and plan. It also deals with the issue of resource allocation so that the project can progress unhindered, including personnel, equipment, space, supplies, and so forth.

One of the considerations of the process managers is the quality and predictability of their processes. The previous chapters describe ideal processes, but the reality sometimes falls short of the ideal. To compare their processes, communities have developed standards against which the processes can be measured (Jalote, 2000; ISO, 2008). There are national and international organizations that certify the degree to which the companies comply with the standard; customers frequently require this certification; it confirms a sound production process that will result in a high-quality product.

16.3.2 Product Management

While process management deals mainly with the issues of the process and the team, product management is concerned with the product and its position and reputation in the market. The issues that the product managers deal with are the scope of the product, its readiness for the release, its cost and profitability, prioritization of the individual requirements from the point of view of the users, and so forth.

Quality management is an especially important product management task (Kan, 2002). Product managers have the right to reject low-quality commits or entire low-quality baselines or versions if they decide that the quality would be injurious to the reputation of the product. Product managers closely collaborate with the sales department and monitor relations with the users.

16.4 Software Ergonomics

The field of ergonomics (also called human factors) studies the interactions among people and systems (Salvendy, 2006). Ergonomics is a broad field and deals with all kinds of human-related issues, such as the optimal height of chairs, and it overlaps with software engineering in several aspects. The relevant part of ergonomics deals with the interaction of programmers and users with the programs.

Cognitive issues are of particular importance to software engineers. The software systems are often complex, and software engineers must try to make them easy to deal with. Human cognitive characteristics are a specific topic that is related to this issue (Posner, 1993).

Software typically can be used in several different ways, and it is helpful to aggregate users into groups based on their goals and habits; these groups are called *marketing personas* (Pruitt & Adlin, 2006). For example, a chess-playing program can have many types of users. One group of users includes the players who use the program to get suggestions for their next move, another group uses it to analyze a complete past chess game to see where they made a mistake, while instructors use it to teach novices about the basics of the chess, and so forth. These are marketing personas, and each marketing persona places different demands on software. To facilitate communication, software engineers sometimes give these personas names, like Edward, Inventor, Student, Beginner, and so forth.

Usability is a term that describes how well software (and other systems) serve their users. Software engineers can test the usability of their systems, and techniques of this testing are described in the literature (Rubin & Chisnell, 2008).

Four Personas Using Institutional Repository in Colorado

The Institutional Repository (IR) is a centralized archive that collects the results of the intellectual work of university faculty and students. It includes experimental data, reports, teaching materials, and so forth. It is a publication venue of a new type. It complements the more rigorous, but also narrower, venues of scholarly publications like journals, conference proceedings, and books.

The University of Colorado is one of the universities that has implemented IR. They conducted a survey of the IR users and analyzed their responses, a process that led to the discovery of four personas (Maness, Miaskiewicz, & Sumner, 2008). To facilitate the communication about them, they gave the personas fake names, and even fake photographs and fake resumes. They are:

> *Professor Charles Williams* teaches humanities and has been at the university for more than 30 years. He uses the IR it to share teaching materials with his students and colleagues. However, he is not a "techie" and is concerned with technical difficulties of using the IR.
>
> *Rahul Singh* is a graduate student who spends most of his time in the lab. He uses the IR to identify collaborators, promote his research, and interact with the world outside the lab.
>
> *Professor Anne Chao* is very active and, besides the IR, she has her own website and a blog where she publishes her views. She also very actively publishes in the traditional venues like conferences and journals.
>
> *Julia Fisher* is starting her graduate studies. She is very active in various social events both on and off campus. Her source of professional information and scholarly references is almost exclusively Internet, and the IR is a part of her strategy for obtaining relevant information and publishing her early results.

Each of the four personas places a different set of demands on the IR and its interface. If the IR is to fulfill its mission, it must provide a support for all four personas; otherwise, it would miss an important segment of the user community.

16.5 Software Engineering Research

Software engineering is a rapidly developing discipline, and new research ideas and new approaches appear frequently. Several journals and conferences present these new developments and allow software engineers to keep up with these changes. The following is a partial list of journals and conferences that present the new results of the research:

> *Transactions on Software Engineering* (IEEE)
> *Transactions on Software Engineering and Methodology* (ACM)
> *Software* (IEEE)
> *Computer* (IEEE)
> *Communications of ACM*
> *Proceedings of International Conference on Software Engineering* (ICSE, ACM/IEEE)
> *Proceedings of International Conference on Software Maintenance* (ICSM, IEEE)
> *Journal of Software Maintenance and Evolution* (Wiley)
> *Software: Practice and Experience* (Wiley)

Summary

Disciplines other than software engineering teach additional skills and insights that software engineers need in their projects and careers. These other disciplines include other computing disciplines, professional ethics, management, and ergonomics.

Exercises

16.1 Can software engineers ignore other disciplines and concentrate only on their own specialty of software engineering?

16.2 How do software engineering and computer engineering overlap?

16.3 How do software engineering and computer science differ?

16.4 This book emphasizes object-oriented technology. What other technologies do software engineers need to know?

16.5 Why is information diversion a serious social problem?

16.6 How does computer crime affect software engineers, even if they are not direct victims?

16.7 Why do you think the writers of the *Software Engineering Code of Ethics and Professional Practice* made the first rule about the public and the second about the client and employer?

16.8 Governments, businesses, and organizations have collected information about people for a very long time. Why is it more likely to be misused with computers?

16.9 What skills besides programming skills are necessary to become effective in software management?

16.10 Could good software ergonomics be considered an ethical concern?

References

ACM. (1999). *Software engineering code of ethics and professional practice*. ACM/IEEE-CS Joint Task Force on Software Engineering Ethics and Professional Practices. Retrieved on July 3, 2011, from http://www.acm.org/about/se-code

———. (2006). *Computing curricula 2005: The overview report*. ACM/AIS/IEEE-CS Joint Task Force for Computing Curricula. Retrieved on July 3, 2011, from http://www.acm.org/education/curric_vols/CC2005-March06Final.pdf

Barr, M., & Massa, A. (2006). *Programming embedded systems: With C and GNU development tools*. Sebastopol, CA: O'Reilly Media.

Carrier, B. (2005). *File system forensic analysis* (1st ed.). Reading, MA: Addison-Wesley Professional.

Checkland, P., & Holwell, S. (1998). *Information, systems, and information systems: Making sense of the field*. Chichester, U.K.: John Wiley & Sons.

Cormen, T. H., Leiserson, C., Rivest, R., & Stein, C. (2009). *Introduction to algorithms* (3rd ed.). Cambridge, MA: MIT Press.

Fagothey, A. (1967). *Right and reason: Ethics in theory and practice* (4th ed.). St. Louis, MO: Mosby.

Finnis, J. (1983). *Fundamentals of ethics* (1st ed.). Washington, DC: Georgetown University Press.

Gomez-Mejia, L. R., Balkin, D. B., & Cardy, R. L. (2008). *Management: People, performance, change* (3rd ed.). New York, NY: McGraw-Hill.

Gupta, R. K. (1995). *Co-synthesis of hardware and software for digital embedded systems*. New York, NY: Springer.

Humphrey, W. S. (1999). *Introduction to the team software process*. Boston, MA: Addison-Wesley Professional.

ISO. (2008). *ISO 9000 essentials*. International Organization for Standardization. Retrieved on July 3, 2011, from http://www.iso.org/iso/iso_catalogue/management_and_leadership_standards/quality_management/iso_9000_essentials.htm

Jalote, P. (2000). *CMM in practice*. Reading, MA: Addison-Wesley.

Kan, S. H. (2002). *Metrics and models in software quality engineering*. Boston, MA: Addison-Wesley Longman.

Kizza, J. M. (2002). *Ethical and social issues in the information age* (2nd ed.). New York, NY: Springer-Verlag.

Maness, J. M., Miaskiewicz, T., & Sumner, T. (2008). *Using personas to understand the needs and goals of institutional repository users*. Retrieved on July 3, 2011, from http://dlib.org/dlib/september08/maness/09maness.html

Neumann, P. G. (1995). *Computer-related risks*. Reading, MA: Addison-Wesley.

———. (2009). Risks to the public. *SIGSOFT Software Engineering Notes, 31*(6), 21–37.

NIH. (2002). *Hippocratic oath*. National Institutes of Health. Retrieved on July 3, 2011, from http://www.nlm.nih.gov/hmd/greek/greek_oath.html

Posner, M. I. (1993). *Foundations of cognitive science*. Cambridge, MA: MIT Press.

Pruitt, J., & Adlin, T. (2006). *The persona lifecycle: Keeping people in mind throughout product design*. Boston, MA: Elsevier.

Rubin, J., & Chisnell, D. (2008). *Handbook of usability testing: How to plan, design and conduct effective tests*. Indianapolis, IN: Wiley.

Salvendy, G. (2006). *Handbook of human factors and ergonomics*. New York, NY: Wiley.

Chapter 17

Example of Software Change

Objectives

This chapter illustrates the phases of a software change that are parts of the process explained in the second part of this book (chapters 5–11). While reading this chapter, you will see an example of a complete software change that consists of the following phases:

- Finding the significant concepts of the change request
- Concept location by dependency search
- Impact analysis
- Actualization by creation of a new component
- Testing the changed code

***

The Drawlets application is a framework that supports drawing figures, including lines, rectangles, rounded rectangles, triangles, polygons, ellipses, text boxes, and so forth. The figures have several attributes, such as size, location, color of the contour, and color of the filling. In this example, the framework is hosted by an application called SimpleApplet that displays the drawing canvas in a web browser window. The toolbar buttons activate drawing tools that create or modify the figures. Figure 17.1 shows the SimpleApplet canvas with a selection of different figures. SimpleApplet has more than 130 classes and 40,000 lines of code.

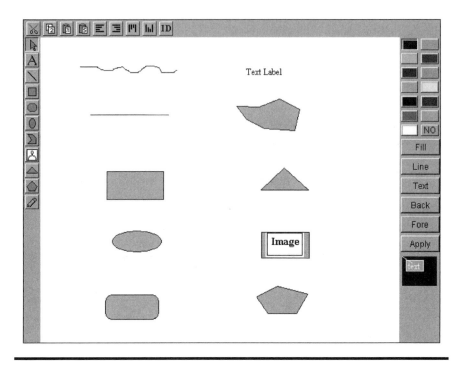

Figure 17.1 SimpleApplet canvas and tool buttons. From Rajlich, V., & Gosavi, P. (2004). Incremental change in object-oriented programming. *IEEE Software, 21,* 62–69. Copyright 1998 Elsevier. Reprinted with permission.

The change request is: "Implement an owner for each figure. An owner is the user who put the figure onto the canvas, and only the owner should be allowed to modify it. At the beginning of a session, the users input their ID and password, and they are the owners of all figures that were created during the session."

17.1 Concept Location

The change request with the concept names in italics is: "*Implement* an *owner* for each *figure*. An owner is the *user* who put the figure onto the *canvas*, and only the owner should be *allowed* to *modify* it. At the *beginning* of a *session*, the users *input* their *IDs* and *passwords*, and they are the owners of all figures that were *created* during the session." Table 17.1 contains these concepts and their classification.

After filtering out irrelevant and external concepts, the programmers are left with relevant concepts and have to decide which ones are significant. The programmers noted that each session has one and only one canvas. They concluded that session properties and canvas properties belong to the same group, and only one of these two concepts needs to be selected as significant and located in the code. Of

Table 17.1 Concepts and Their Classification

	Irrelevant	External	Significant
implement	x		
owner		x	
figure			**x**
user		x	
canvas			**x**
allowed	x		
modify	x		
beginning	x		
session			
input	x		
ID		x	
password		x	
created	x		

the two, the programmers selected "canvas" because it is certain that the extension "canvas" is present in the code, while the extension "session" is less likely to be present. Once the concept "canvas" is located, the "session owner" will be implemented there. The "figure owner" belongs to the group of the basic figure properties, and that is another location that must also be found in the code.

Among the concept-location techniques, a grep search is less convenient in this particular case because of the uncertainty of what specific identifiers are used in the code and in what context they are they used. A dependency search is more likely to be successful, and therefore, it is used in this example.

Figure 17.2 contains a UML class diagram of the top classes of the SimpleApplet and traces the steps that were taken during the concept location. The programmers first visited the top class `SimpleApplet`. The supplier slice of this class is the entire program, and therefore, this is a suitable location to start the search. The concepts "canvas properties" and "figure properties" are not found in this top class; therefore, the programmers searched for them among the suppliers `StylePalette`, `Toolbar`, and `ToolPalette`, but none of them contain these concepts in their extended responsibility. Therefore, the concepts must be located in the supplier slice of `DrawingCanvas`.

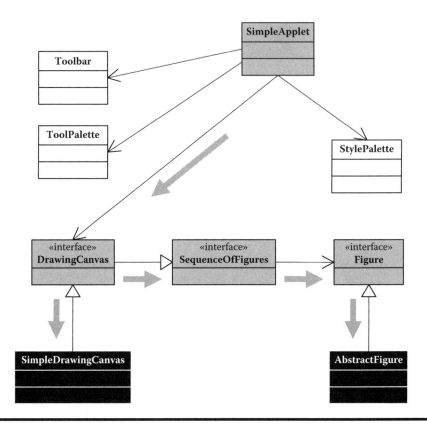

Figure 17.2   Concept location. From Rajlich, V., & Gosavi, P. (2004). Incremental change in object-oriented programming. *IEEE Software, 21,* **62–69. Copyright 1998 Elsevier. Reprinted with permission.**

DrawingCanvas is an interface, and its supplier class SimpleDrawing Canvas implements all responsibilities. There is one and only one instance of SimpleDrawingCanvas for each session of Drawlets; hence, both the canvas attributes and session attributes are concentrated in this class, and it is the logical location of the implicit concept "session owner."

The programmers then searched for the location of Figure properties, visiting again SimpleApplet and DrawingCanvas. The interface DrawingCanvas contains many figures, and the properties of these figures are therefore, a part of its extended responsibility. This part of the responsibility is contracted to SequenceOfFigures, then to Figure, and finally to the class AbstractFigure. The class AbstractFigure holds the basic figure properties, and the programmers concluded that the concept of "figure owner" also should be located in this class.

Once the location of the concepts "session owner" and "figure owner" were found, concept location was completed. The programmers were then ready to begin impact analysis.

17.2 Impact Analysis

Impact analysis starts with the initial impact set that consists of classes SimpleDrawingCanvas and AbstractFigure; both classes of this initial impact set are the locations of the significant concepts. To discover the estimated impact set, we have to follow the interactions of these classes.

SimpleDrawingCanvas interacts with 23 classes; the inspection of these classes determined that only DrawingCanvas was impacted by the change. The class AbstractFigure interacts with 26 classes; of them, classes Figure, AbstractShape, and TextLabel were impacted.

In the next steps, programmers inspected the classes that interact with these impacted classes. If the inspection revealed that they were either impacted or propagating the change, their neighbors were inspected also. The result of this iterative process is the estimated impact set that is represented by classes marked by gray in Figure 17.3.

17.3 Actualization

The concept "owner" was implemented in the new class OwnerIdentity that holds the owner ID and a password, and supports a dialog box that lets users change the current session owner. Another class OwnerListener is a supplier to the class OwnerIdentity, and it notifies the program when the user clicks on a button in this box.

The newly created class OwnerIdentity and its supplier OwnerListener were incorporated into the old code by creating an instance of OwnerIdentity in both AbstractFigure and SimpleDrawingCanvas. The incorporation required a new parameter in some of the methods of the class AbstractFigure; these methods now compare the identities of the current session owner and the figure owner before making changes to the figures.

In the class SimpleDrawingCanvas, programmers modified the function cutSelections(...) to prevent figures not belonging to the current session owner from being cut from the canvas. Programmers also implemented several new methods to allow access to the current session owner information stored in class SimpleDrawingCanvas.

Change propagation parallels impact analysis, but it involves real code modifications. The classes SimpleDrawingCanvas and AbstractFigure are the starting points for the change propagation. The complete set of classes

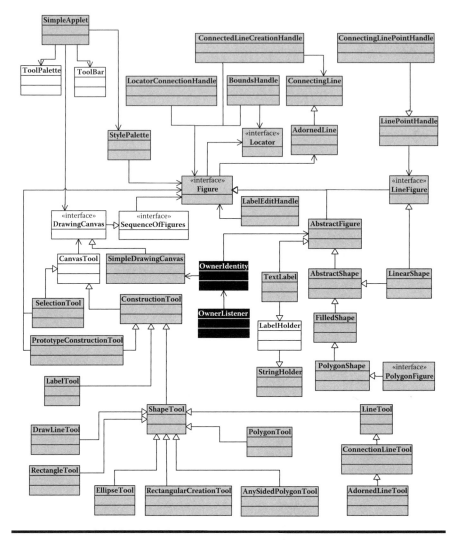

Figure 17.3 The estimated impact set. From Rajlich, V., & Gosavi, P. (2004). Incremental change in object-oriented programming. *IEEE Software, 21*, 62–69. Copyright 1998 Elsevier. Reprinted with permission.

changed during the change propagation is equivalent to the estimated impact set of Figure 17.3.

17.4 Testing

The system test for the original baseline contains unit tests and functional tests. The unit test harness consists of 385 unit tests, with 1,369 assertions and about 4,800 lines. The functional test consists of the basic functions that include Draw (a figure is drawn on the canvas), Select (a figure is selected), Move (a figure is moved to a different location), Resize (a figure is resized), and so forth. All together it consists of 141 test cases.

The phase of actualization added new test cases to both the unit test harness and the functional test. During the change propagation, the old tests that were impacted by the change were updated.

During the change, 91 lines of production code (0.5%) and 124 lines (2.5%) of the test code were modified; hence, for each modified production code line, there were approximately 1.4 modified lines of test code.

Prefactoring Can Shorten Change Propagation

The change presented in this chapter is not excessively complicated, but it propagates to a large number of classes. Change propagation is an error-prone activity, and each additional modified class requires a thorough validation and retesting and increases the risk that bugs will be introduced into the code. Therefore, it is important to find whether any prefactoring would shorten the change propagation. Here, we present two separate and mutually independent prefactoring techniques that shorten change propagation.

MOVING MISPLACED CODE TO BASE CLASS

During impact analysis, the programmers inspected the classes that are the change-propagation targets, and they found misplaced code that unnecessarily extends the impact set. Moving this misplaced code into its proper place shortens change propagation.

The classes that contain this misplaced code are classes that draw some figures, including rectangle and ellipse. Other classes that draw other figures, including line and polygon, are not impacted by the change. A closer inspection of these impacted classes reveals that the impacted classes contain the following algorithm:

- Draw the new figure in a default location.
- If the figure was drawn in a wrong location, move it by calling the method move(...).

However, this method has changed, and it is now protected against unauthorized use, and the classes that invoke it have to obtain the authorization, and therefore, they also have to change. The structure of the code can be improved by the following prefactoring:

- Create a new method move _ new _ figure(...) in the affected classes, and put the call of the method move(...) in it.
- Pull up move _ new _ figure(...) into the base class ConstructionTool.
- Merge method move _ new _ figure(...) into method ConstructionTool::new Figure(...).

This refactoring improves the code by removing redundancies and shortening the change propagation that now stops at class ConstructionTool, as the data in Table 17.2 show.

SPLITTING THE ROLES

A more radical prefactoring is *splitting the roles*. Splitting roles applies when the code uses the same class or same method in two slightly different roles. Because the roles are similar, the same code can handle both of them. The propagating change, however, can highlight the differences in these two roles. Only one of them might need updating, while the other one remains the same. Splitting the two roles and updating only one of them shortens the change propagation.

In our example, programmers observed that the method move(...) is used in Drawlets in two different ways: to move the figure as requested by the user, or to move it as part of

Table 17.2   The Three Strategies of Prefactoring

Technique Used in IC	Classes Modified
No prefactoring + incorporation + propagation	36
Moving code + incorporation + propagation	36
Moving code	12
Incorporation + propagation after moving code	25
Splitting + incorporation + propagation	24
Splitting	5
Incorporation + propagation after splitting	20

the algorithm for drawing new figures. The method's dual role partially causes the extended change propagation.

It is obvious that a user-initiated move must check the user identity, while the creation of new figures need not. Splitting these two roles into two separate functions—a new method `secure-Move(...)` and the old method `move(...)`—shortens the change propagation. The new method `secureMove(...)` first checks the user's identity and then invokes the old method `move(...)`.

Table 17.2 contains the data showing how the original change and the prefactoring variants compare. While the number of lines modified remains about the same, the prefactoring significantly improves the number of modified classes.

Summary

SimpleApplet is a drawing program, and the change in it followed the processes and the phases discussed in part 2 of this book. The change did not require any advanced knowledge of the program; the knowledge of the program domain was sufficient. Programmers learned additional necessary facts during the process.

Further Reading and Topics

Drawlets is available from RoleModel Software (2002). Additional information on this example may be found in a paper by Rajlich and Gosavi (2004). The testing before and after the change is described by Skoglund and Runeson (2004).

Exercises

17.1   Find a suitable application in http://sourceforge.net/ and a suitable change request for that application; make the corresponding change.

17.2   How much initial knowledge of Drawlets code do you have to have in order to make a change similar to the one presented in this example?

References

Rajlich, V., & Gosavi, P. (2004). Incremental change in object-oriented programming. *IEEE Software, 21*, 62–69.

RoleModel Software. (2002). *Drawlets*. Retrieved on July 5, 2011, from http://www.rolemodelsoft.com/drawlets/

Skoglund, M., & Runeson, P. (2004). A case study on regression test suite maintenance in system evolution. In *Proceedings of 20th IEEE International Conference on Software Maintenance*. Washington, DC: IEEE Computer Society Press.

Chapter 18

Example of Solo
Iterative Process (SIP)

Objectives

This chapter illustrates a development of a small point-of-sale application by a solo programmer. While reading this chapter, you will see an example of a software development that consists of the following:

- Initial development of a greatly simplified version
- Two iterations of SIP that expand this initial version and consist of a sequence of software changes

***

Point of Sale (PoS) is an application that supports a small store. It controls the cash registers, prints sales receipts, keeps data about the cashiers, and controls the inventory. It is developed in several steps, the first one being initial development, followed by evolution that consists of two iterations of SIP.

18.1 Initial Development

Because the application starts from scratch, the first stage is the initial development. The first phase of initial development, the software plan, is greatly reduced because the single programmer does not need to address the issues of management and collaboration. Nevertheless, the software plan addresses two issues: the selection of project technologies and the assessment of available resources.

18.1.1 Project Plan

The programmer chose the following *technologies* for the project:

- Java programming language and Eclipse software environment
- Swing framework for graphical user interface (GUI)
- JUnit framework for unit testing
- Abbot Java GUI Test Framework for functional testing
- Version control system "Subversion"

The rationale for the choice is the following: Java is one of the most common object-oriented languages, and it is the language the programmer is familiar with. The Eclipse software environment is a widely available and proven environment that supports development of Java applications. The Swing framework is a popular and proven toolkit for graphical user interfaces (GUI) for Java applications, and its wide availability guarantees that there will be no unpleasant surprises during the development.

For testing, JUnit is the standard tool for unit testing, and it is well integrated with Eclipse, so again it is a logical choice. Abbot is also a proven tool and supports functional testing of Swing GUIs. Subversion is one of the most widely used version control systems, and although other systems are available, Subversion is likely to support the project well.

As far as the *project resources* is concerned, the programmer's time is the most important resource; the time available is sufficient for the development of a small application. All necessary hardware and Internet connectivity are also available.

In conclusion, the planned technology is proven and the resources are adequate, and the project can go ahead.

18.1.2 Requirements

The following requirements were elicited:

- The program keeps track of an inventory of items by Universal Product Code (UPC), item name, price, tax, and current quantity available.
- It keeps track of the store's total cash balance.
- It allows cashiers to log in and keep track of sales made during a cashier session. A session involves the time between the cashier logging in and out, and the program keeps a record of sales made during this time.
- The sale price of an item overrides the regular price and can vary on specific dates and hours.

- A customer receipt contains one or more items, as well as data such as the date of sale and information on the processing cashier.
- Acceptable payments include cash, credit, and check.

The programmer first decomposed the requirements into tasks, and selected the following task as the only task in the initial backlog:

- Build a very simple version that keeps a constant price and tax of a single item.
- Keep the quantity of the item.
- Support a single cashier.
- Keep track of the store cash balance, and allow only the exact cash payment without supporting returning change.

The fledgling application described by the initial backlog is able to support a store that sells only one kind of item and uses only cash, which is common with street vendors. Nevertheless, this initial product backlog tests all project technologies. The implementation is fast, giving timely feedback to the programmer and other project stakeholders. The remaining features of the product backlog are postponed to the phase of evolution that follows initial development.

18.1.3 Initial Design

This initial product backlog leads to a design that consists of a single class. The class Store is able to handle all responsibilities requested in the initial backlog. The UML diagram of the class is in Figure 18.1.

Store
-balance : double
-inventory : int
-price : double
-tax : double
+getBalance() : double
+processSale() : double
+resetStore() : void
+calcSubTotal() : double
+calcTotal() : double
+getInventory() : int
+setInventory() : void
+addToInventory() : void
+removeFromInventory() : void
+getPrice() : double
+getTax() : double
+main() : void

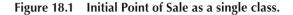

Figure 18.1   Initial Point of Sale as a single class.

18.1.4 Implementation

The programmer implemented code of class `Store` in Java together with the other code parts. The results of the implementation are:

- Java code for the class `Store`
- The unit test for the class `Store`, implemented as a class `StoreTest`; it contains 12 assertions
- GUI that allows the user to select the current features of the program and is supported by the Swing framework
- The functional test of all features of the GUI recorded by Abbot

This version can be presented to the stakeholders for evaluation and comments. Despite its primitive features, it uses all project technologies. These technologies are likely to accompany this project to the end of its life span, and the initial development is a tryout for these technologies. The longer the project uses these technologies, the harder it is to replace them.

18.2 Iteration 1

The additional requirements that are not a part of the initial backlog and have been deferred are implemented in the stage of evolution. The process of evolution is SIP, and two iterations are presented; they implement all remaining requirements.

First, the requirements are divided into tasks of manageable size. For example, there is the requirement "Program allows cashiers to log in, and keep track of sales made during a cashier session. A session involves the time between the cashier logging in and out, and the program keeps a record of sales made during this time." This requirement is divided into three tasks:

a. Support the log-in of a single cashier
b. Support multiple cashiers
c. Add cashier session that involves the time between the cashier logging in and out, and keeps a record of sales made during this time

Tasks are then prioritized. In this case, the most important prioritization criterion is the process needs. For example, the log-in of a single cashier precedes support for multiple cashiers, and this sequencing supports a gradual increase of the program complexity. The iteration backlog of Iteration 1 then consists of a sequence of the following tasks:

1. Expand inventory to support multiple items.
2. Attach multiple prices to a single item. Each price will have an effective date, so when the user sells an item, the software will calculate the correct total based on the most current pricing information.
3. Support the log-in of a single cashier.
4. Support multiple cashiers.

The remaining requirements are postponed to Iteration 2, which is described in the next section.

This section describes the selected tasks in more detail. Because the program under development is small, concept location is simple, and the programmer is able to identify the concept location immediately, after the significant concept is extracted from the change request.

18.2.1 Expand Inventory to Support Multiple Items

The initial development produced an application that is able to handle a store that sells a single item only. The change request for the first task is: "Expand inventory to support multiple items." The significant concepts are "inventory" and "item," and their original extensions are present in in class `Store`.

Two classes are extracted by prefactoring, one being a new class `Inventory` that includes the methods `setInventory`, `getInventory`, `addToInventory`, and `removeFromInventory`. A second class, `Item`, was then extracted from `Inventory`. It contains the variables `int inventory`, which contains the number of the items, `double price`, and `double tax`, and the methods `getPrice` and `getTax` (see Figure 18.2). In the figure, the methods moved out of a class are crossed out, and the methods moved into a class are in boldface.

During the next phase of actualization, new variables are added to the `Item` class for data such as the UPC, item name, and current quantity of the item. The `Inventory` class is enhanced with a new data structure to hold a collection of items. This new data structure is a `HashMap` from the Java framework, and it uses the UPC as a key. The function members of the class are updated so that they can handle this data structure. The class diagram of the resulting program is in Figure 18.3, with additional class members in boldface.

Inspection of the code reveals that the `calcTotal` and `calcSubTotal` methods deal with the class `Item` more than the class `Store` where they reside; they use the data from the class `Item`. As a postfactoring, they are moved to the class `Item`. The UML class diagram of the resulting program is in Figure 18.4. Two new test classes with 22 assertions were created in this task.

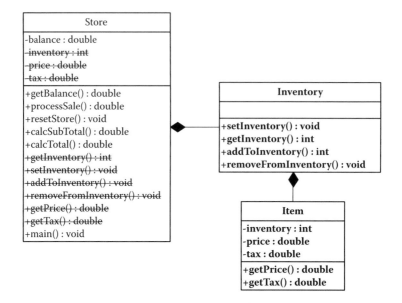

Figure 18.2 PoS after prefactoring.

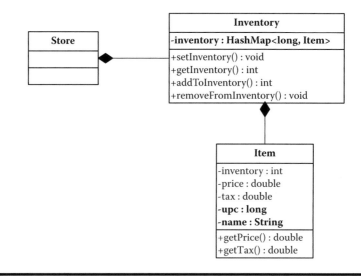

Figure 18.3 PoS after actualization.

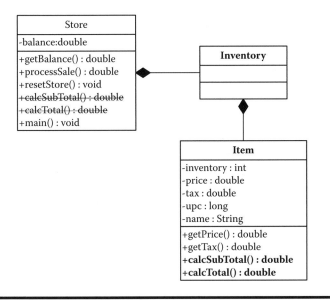

Figure 18.4   PoS supporting multiple items.

18.2.2 Support Multiple Prices with Effective Dates

The change request is the following: "Attach multiple prices to a single item. Each price will have an effective date, and the software will calculate the correct price based on the most current pricing information." The significant concept of this change request is "price," which is located in the class Item. A prefactoring "extract component class" creates a new class Price (see Figure 18.5).

In actualization, a list is added to the Price class that implements the effective date of a price, and get and set methods for this list are added as well. A test class with three assertions is created for unit testing.

18.2.3 Support the Log-In of a Single Cashier

The change request is the following: "Support log-in of a single cashier." The significant concept is "cashier." Currently there is no code that represents this concept, and the system assumes that anyone who runs the software is an authorized cashier.

Because the concept of "cashier" is implicit, the programmer located an area of the code that is somehow related to the cashier. The Store class has variables for the cash balance and, therefore, it is a logical location for the related cashier information as well.

The class Store will change, and the impact analysis inspects the class Inventory. Because it needs modification, it is added to the estimated impact set. After this, its neighbor class Item is visited, but will not change and does not propagate the change further.

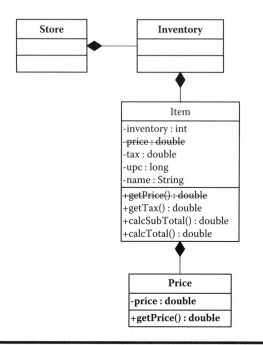

Figure 18.5   Extraction of the class `Price`.

The actualization then creates a new class `Cashier` as a new component of the class `Store` (see Figure 18.6). No postfactoring is needed after these modifications are completed. The programmer also created a new test class `CashierTest` with assertions that test the functionality of the new methods; 16 new assertions are made.

18.2.4 Support Multiple Cashiers

The significant concept is "cashier," and since there is a class that implements this concept, concept location is easy; the new concept will be implemented in the `Cashier` class. For impact analysis, the `Store` class contains an instance and calls the method contained in the `Cashier` class, so it is likely to require the change and is added to the estimated impact set. `Inventory` is the only other neighbor class to `Store` and `Cashier`, and it is likely to require modification, so it is also added to the estimated impact set.

As a prefactoring, a new `CashierRecord` component class is extracted from the `Cashier` class and contains the variables `cashierId`, `password`, `firstName`, and `lastName`. The `login` and `logout` methods are not specific to any individual cashier; this functionality is related to all cashiers, so it remains in the `Cashier` class.

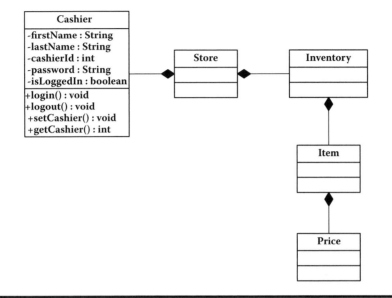

Figure 18.6 New class supporting single cashier incorporated into PoS.

As actualization, two new variables are added to the CashierRecord class, loginTime for storing the current login time, and lastLogin, which stores the last date and time the cashier logged into the point-of-sale system. Two new methods are created: initLogin, which sets the isLoggedIn Boolean value to true, and initLogout, which sets the isLoggedIn Boolean value to false, and sets the lastLogin variable to the current login date.

The Cashier class is visited first, and is modified to support multiple cashiers in the system. The cashier variable is replaced with an ArrayList of CashierRecord objects. The login method is updated to accept a cashierId, which is used to search the ArrayList, and a password that is used for authentication. The Store class is visited, but it is determined that no change is needed here. The Cashier class has no more neighboring classes, so the change propagation ends.

The "rename class" refactoring is used to rename the Cashier class to Cashiers. Although this is a small and simple refactoring, it leads to a more accurate description of the responsibility that the class now handles. Figure 18.7 contains the class diagram after this software change.

The iteration concludes with a thorough test and production of the next version. This new version of the program can handle multiple items in inventory and multiple cashiers; hence, it is more useful than the earlier version. However, some requirements are still deferred and, therefore, another iteration is required.

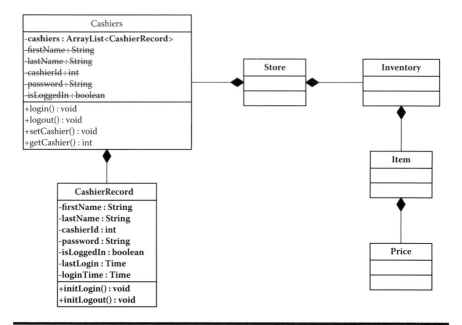

Figure 18.7   PoS with support for multiple cashiers.

18.3 Iteration 2

The iteration backlog for Iteration 2 consists of the tasks that have been deferred during initial development and during the first iteration. The tasks are ordered by process needs:

5. Add cashier session.
6. Implement promotional prices.
7. Keep detailed sales records, such as item sold and date/time of sale.
8. Support multiple items per transaction.
9. Expand concept of cash payment to include cash tendered and returned change.
10. Implement credit card payment.
11. Implement check payment.

They are implemented one by one in a similar fashion as the tasks of the first iteration. The growth of the program and the corresponding unit tests are summarized in Table 18.1.

When all these tasks are completed, the next version fulfills all originally elicited requirements. The resulting class diagram is in Figure 18.8.

Table 18.1   Growth of the Program

	Step	Classes	Unit Test Assertions
Initial development	0	1	12
Iteration 1	1	3	34
	2	4	37
	3	5	53
	4	6	55
Iteration 2	5	7	65
	6	8	40
	7	9	68
	8	10	71
	9	11	77
	10	13	89
	11	14	98

This second iteration completed the implementation of the product backlog that was created at the beginning of the project. However, in the meantime, new requirements may have arrived, and the next iteration selects its tasks from them. An example of such future requirement is support for a customer database that records past customers and their credit history, or a database of suppliers, or a record of holidays when the store is closed, or a feature that allows the user to declare sales to clear a part of inventory, or daily, weekly, monthly, or yearly reports from the store, and so forth. These future iterations will be handled by the same techniques that were explained in this book.

Summary

Point of Sale is a small application that controls the basic functions of a small store. This chapter presents a process that develops this application. The process consists of the initial development followed by two iterations of the solitary iterative process (SIP). The iterations consist of several tasks that add features to the application.

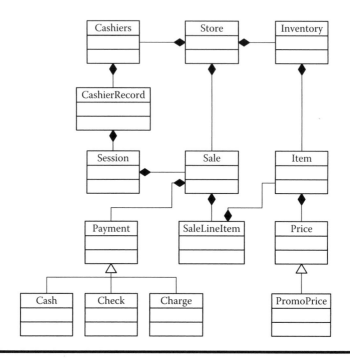

Figure 18.8   PoS after the second iteration.

Further Reading and Topics

Additional details of this example are available in works by Febbraro and Rajlich (2007) and Febbraro (2008). The same development accomplished in its entirety by the initial development is presented in a book by Coad, North, and Mayfield (1995). The results of these two development processes are compared in a paper by Febbraro and Rajlich (2007).

Exercises

18.1   Consider task 2: "Support multiple prices with effective dates." Describe all phases of this task that apply.

18.2   Suppose that you want to accomplish more during the initial development and want to merge the current initial product backlog with the first task of the evolution. What will be the process of the initial development?

18.3   Write a program that plays checkers, using SIP. For the initial development, implement a greatly simplified game with only one piece of each color on the board, without kings and without jumps. Define a product backlog and the first iteration. Then implement all tasks of this first iteration.

18.4   Create a product backlog and add one more iteration to the Point of Sale system of this chapter.

References

Coad, P., North, D., & Mayfield, M. (1995). *Object models: Strategies, patterns, applications.* Upper Saddle River, NJ: Yourdon Press.

Febbraro, N. (2008). *A case study on incremental change in agile software processes.* Master's thesis. Wayne State University, Detroit, MI.

Febbraro, N., & Rajlich, V. (2007). The role of incremental change in agile software processes. In *AGILE 2007* (92–103). Washington, DC: IEEE Computer Society Press.

Index